Strategies proven 2

Content instruction created just SSAT. Practice to reinforce learning.

✓ Strategies to use for each section of the Upper Level SSAT

✓ Content instruction specific to the test and age-appropriate

✓ Drills and practice sets to build skills and confidence

✓ Full-length practice tests to show students what to expect and avoid surprises on test day (*Success on the Upper Level SSAT* and *The Best Unofficial Practice Tests* only)

Complete selection of Upper Level SSAT titles now available from Test Prep Works LLC:

Success on the Upper Level SSAT: A Complete Course
- Strategies for each section of the test
- Reading and vocabulary drills
- In-depth math content instruction with practice sets
- 1 full-length practice test

30 Days to Acing the Upper Level SSAT
- Strategies for each section of the test
- Fifteen "workouts", each providing practice problems and detailed explanations for every section of the test
- Perfect for additional practice or homework

The Best Unofficial Practice Tests for the Upper Level SSAT
- 2 additional full-length practice tests

SUCCESS

ON THE **Upper Level SSAT**

A Complete Course

Christa Abbott, M.Ed.

Published by:
Test Prep Works, LLC
PO Box 100572
Arlington, VA 22210
www.TestPrepWorks.com

For information about buying this title in bulk, or for editions with customized covers or content, please contact the publisher at sales@testprepworks.com or (703) 944-6727.

ISBN: 978-1-68059-001-2

Contents

Notes for Parents

What is the SSAT?

The SSAT is a standardized admissions test. It is used by many of the top independent schools in the United States. You may have heard of another test, the ISEE (Independent School Entrance Exam). The schools that your student is applying to may accept either the SSAT or the ISEE, or they may exclusively use one test or the other. It can also depend upon what grade your child is applying for. Contact each school that your child will apply to in order to be sure that he or she is taking the correct test.

- Contact schools so that your child takes the correct test

What Level Should I Register My Child For?

This book is designed to help students who are taking the Upper Level SSAT. If students are currently in grades 8-11, applying for grades 9-12, then they should be taking the Upper Level SSAT.

- Upper Level is for students currently in grades 8-11, applying for grades 9-12

Just How Important is the SSAT to the Admissions Process?

Every school uses the test differently. In general, the more competitive the school, the more that test scores are going to matter, but there are certainly exceptions to that rule. Reading through a school's literature is a great way to figure out whether a school emphasizes or deemphasizes testing. Also, call the admissions office where your child will be applying. Admissions officers are often quite candid about what the testing profile of their admitted students tends to be.

- Talk to the schools that your child is applying to in order to get a sense of the scores they look for

How Can I Help My Student?

Keep your own cool. Never once has a student gotten a higher score because mom or dad freaked out. Approach this as a project. Good test taking skills can be learned and by working through the process with your child in a constructive manner, you are providing them with a roadmap for how to approach challenges in the future. We want them to be confident, but to earn that confidence through analysis, self-monitoring, and practice.

- Keep a positive attitude

What are the key elements of successful test preparation?

Analysis

It is important that students don't just do practice problem after practice problem without figuring out what they missed, and most importantly WHY they missed those problems. Is there a particular type of problem that they keep missing? One issue that many students have is categorizing problems. When you go through a problem that they are stuck on, be sure to point out the words in the problem that pointed you in the correct direction.

- Teach your child to analyze why he or she missed a question

Self-monitoring

Students should develop a sense of their strengths and weaknesses so that they can best focus preparation time. This book provides many practice opportunities for each section, but your child may not need that. For example, if they are acing the average problems, they shouldn't keep spending valuable time doing more of those problems. Maybe their time would be better spent on vocabulary. This is a great opportunity, and your student is at the perfect age, to be learning how to prioritize.

- Help your student prioritize material to work on

Practice

While it is important that a student understand WHY he is doing what he is doing, at a certain point it just needs to become automatic. This is a timed test and you want the strategies to spring to mind without having to reinvent the wheel every time. Practice will make this process fast and easy. On test day, all that practice will kick in to make this a positive and affirming experience for your student.

- Teach your child that he or she needs to practice what they have learned so that it is automatic on test day

What Do Parents Need to Know About Registration?

Registration is done through The Enrollment Management Association. Their website is www.ssat.org. When you register for the test, be sure to also order the official SSAT book, The Official Guide to the Upper Level SSAT. You can also sign up for their online practice portal for additional practice questions. Nothing can replace the practice tests in this book because they are written by the people who write the actual test that your student will be taking.

- Order the practice book from www.ssat.org and sign up for their online practice portal

There are a few other things you should know about registration options:

You can choose from either a national test date or a flex test date

On the national test dates, the SSAT is given in a group setting. It is a similar experience to what you might remember when you took the SAT or ACT. The flex test can be given in the office of an educational consultant in a small group, or even a one-on-one, setting.

There are many advantages of the flex testing

You can generally pick a day and time. If your child doesn't do well in the morning, schedule it for the afternoon. If you really want to get the test out of the way before the holidays and are away when the national test is given in December, then you can choose another day. Also, fewer students means fewer distractions. Flex testing is more expensive than national testing, but given the investment that you are making in independent school, it can be well worth it.

To find consultants in your area, visit www.ssat.org, go to the "About SSAT" link at the top of the page, and hover over "Registration" from the drop-down menu. From the sub-menu, choose "Find a Test Center." On that page, click on the "Flex Test w/ Consultant" tab and look for a consultant close to you. (This information is current as of August 2017 – if you cannot find this document then the SSAT website may have changed!)

One big disadvantage of the flex testing is that you can only do it once per testing (or academic) year

The SSATB only comes up with one form a year for the flex test, so a student can only do flex testing once each year. However, they can do flex testing and then one of the national dates if they want to retake the test (or vice versa).

The SSATB does offer score choice

What this means is that you can take the test as many times as you want and then choose the test date (or dates) that you wish to send. Don't make your student anxious by having him or her take the test a bunch of times, but for some students it reduces stress to know that they can have another shot at the test.

You must request accommodations if your child needs them

If your child has an IEP or receives accommodations in school, then start the paperwork with the SSATB promptly. Don't wait until the last minute, because accommodations must be approved before you register. Spots for students with accommodations may be limited at a testing site and fill early. If your child is going to get extended time, he or she should also know that as he or she works through practice tests.

Above all else, remember that your student will look to you to see how you approach this challenge. If you become anxious, they will too. If you are confident about developing a game plan and building confidence through practice, this experience will stay with them in a profoundly positive way.

How to Use This Book

This book is designed to teach you what you need to know in order to maximize your Upper Level SSAT performance.

There are strategies for each of the four multiple-choice sections as well as advice on the writing section. This book also includes a lot of content practice. There is a complete vocabulary section and detailed instruction for the math concepts that are tested on the SSAT.

You may find that you don't need to complete all of the content instruction. It is important to prioritize your time! If vocabulary is a weakness for you, then spend your time working through the vocabulary lessons. If some of the math concepts are challenging, then you should spend your study time working through the math sections.

There is one full-length practice test in this book. We have developed two additional practice tests, which are available in our publication titled *The Best Unofficial Practice Tests for the Upper Level SSAT*, available on www.TestPrepWorks.com and Amazon.com. If you have not already done so, be sure to order *The Official Guide to the Upper Level SSAT* from www.ssat.org, which contains two practice tests. Any time you are studying for a test, the best source for a full practice test is the people who write the test you will be taking!

I have spent years studying the test and analyzing the different question types, content, and the types of answers that the test writers prefer. Now you can benefit from my hard work! I will show how to approach questions so that you can raise your score significantly.

The Format of the Upper Level SSAT

You can expect to see four scored sections *plus* a writing sample *plus* an experimental section on the Upper Level SSAT.

The Four Scored Sections

- Quantitative (there will be two of these sections on your test)
    - ✓ A variety of math problems
    - ✓ Each section has 25 problems, for a total of 50 math problems
    - ✓ 30 minutes to complete each section, or a little more than a minute per problem

- Verbal
    - ✓ 30 synonym questions and 30 analogy questions
    - ✓ 30 minutes to complete the section, or about 30 seconds per question

- Reading Comprehension
    - ✓ Passages and questions
    - ✓ Passages can be fiction, nonfiction, and poetry
    - ✓ A total of 40 questions
    - ✓ Generally 7-9 passages with 4-6 questions each, but this is not carved in stone so you may see some variation
    - ✓ 40 minutes to complete the section, or a minute per problem

The four above sections are all multiple choice. Each question has five answer choices.

There are two other sections that you will see on the SSAT:

The Experimental Section

- 15 minutes to complete
- Will NOT contribute to your score – the SSAT is just trying out new problems for future tests
- You may not even see this section (if you have extended time, you probably will not)

The Writing Sample

- Will NOT be scored, but a copy will be sent to all of the schools that you apply to
- Choice of two writing prompts – one is the first sentence of a story that the student must finish and the other leads to a more traditional essay
- 25 minutes to write, and you will be given two pages to write on

Now, on to the strategies and content! The strategies covered in this book will focus on the multiple-choice sections since those are what is used to determine your percentile. Please also see the tips for the writing sample.

What Students Need to Know for the SSAT – Just the Basics

Here is what you really need to know to do well on the Upper Level SSAT:

How the Scoring Works

On the Upper Level SSAT, if you answer a question correctly, then you are given one point. If you answer a question incorrectly, then a quarter point is subtracted. If you don't answer a question at all, then nothing is added to or subtracted from your score.

- If you answer a question correctly, you get one point
- If you answer a question incorrectly, you lose $\frac{1}{4}$ of a point
- If you don't answer the question at all, you don't gain or lose any points

You might be asking why this crazy system is used. The thinking behind it is that on a regular test, you would get ahead by guessing. You would correctly answer some of the questions that you guessed on and therefore your score would be higher for blindly guessing. Chances are you would answer $\frac{1}{5}$ of the questions correctly if you blindly guessed because there are five answer choices for each question. By taking off a quarter point for the $\frac{4}{5}$ of the questions that you miss, the test writers are just making sure that you don't get ahead for guessing.

- Example: You guess on five questions.

$1 \ correct \ answer \times 1 = +1 \ point$

$4 \ incorrect \ answers \times -\frac{1}{4} = -1 \ point$

$0 \ points \ gained \ or \ lost$

When to Guess

You should only guess if you can rule out one or more answer choices.

The Percentile Score

You will get a raw score for the SSAT based upon how many questions you answer correctly or incorrectly. This raw score will then be converted into a scaled score. Neither of these scores is what schools are really evaluating. They are looking for your percentile scores that compare you to other students applying to independent schools.

- Percentile score is what schools are really looking at

The percentile score compares you to other students that are in your grade. For example, let's say that you are in eighth grade and you scored in the 70th percentile. What this means is that out of 100 students in your grade, you would have scored higher than 70 of them.

Many students applying to independent schools are used to answering almost every question correctly on a test. You will probably miss more questions on this test than you are used to missing, but because the percentile score is what schools are looking at, don't let it get to you. You may miss more questions than you are used to, but that is OK as long as other students your age also miss those questions.

The Mother of All Strategies

Use the Process of Elimination, or "Ruling Out"

If you remember nothing else on test day, remember to use process of elimination. This is a multiple-choice test, and there are often answers that don't even make sense.

When you read a question, you want to read all of the answer choices before selecting one. You need to keep in mind that the test will ask you to choose the answer choice that "best" answers the question. Best is a relative word, so how can you know which answer choice best answers the question if you don't read them all?

- After you read the question, read ALL of the answer choices
- Look for the "best" answer, which may just be the least wrong answer choice

After you have read all of the answer choices, rule them out in order from most wrong to least wrong. Sometimes the "best" answer choice is not a great fit, but it is better than the others. This process will also clarify your thinking so that by the time you get down to only two answer choices, you have a better idea of what makes choices right or wrong.

- Rule out in order from most wrong to least wrong

Above all else, remember that you are playing the odds on this test. To increase your score, you need to answer questions even when you are not positive of the answer.

Let's say that you rule out three answer choices on four questions. You then guess on those questions. If you get two of those questions correct (which is the most likely outcome), then the scoring would look like this:

$$2\ questions\ correct \times 1\ point\ each = +2\ points$$
$$2\ questions\ incorrect \times -\frac{1}{4}\ point\ each = -\frac{1}{2}\ point$$
$$total\ change\ to\ score = +1\frac{1}{2}\ points$$

Now let's say that you only answer 1 question correctly out of those 4 questions. The scoring would look like this:

$$1\ question\ correct \times 1\ point\ each = +1\ point$$
$$3\ questions\ incorrect \times -\frac{1}{4}\ point\ each = -\frac{3}{4}\ point$$
$$total\ change\ to\ score = +\frac{1}{4}\ point$$

As you can see, if you missed 3 questions and only answered 1 question correctly, you would still come out ahead.

- Ruling out allows you to play the odds – and that is how you will come out ahead of your peers

Verbal Section – Basic Strategies

In the verbal section, you will see two question types:

- Synonyms
- Analogies

On the synonyms questions, you will be given one question word and then you have to choose the answer choice that has the word that comes closest in meaning to the question word.

Synonyms questions look something like this:

1. JOYOUS:
   - (A) loud
   - (B) crying
   - (C) happy
   - (D) shy
   - (E) lame

Out of all the answer choice words, happy comes closest in meaning to joyous. Choice C is correct.

The synonyms questions probably won't be quite this easy, but you get the idea.

The analogies questions generally give you two words and you have to figure out the relationship between them and then choose the answer choice that has the same relationship.

The analogy questions usually look something like this:

2. Panther is to cat as

   (A)   lion is to jungle
   (B)   wolf is to dog
   (C)   chick is to blue jay
   (D)   mouse is to guinea pig
   (E)   horse is to cow

In this case, a panther is a wild cat. A wolf is a wild dog, so choice B is correct.

Sometimes, you will be given the first word in the answer relationship and you just have to choose the second word.

These questions look like this:

3. Tall is to short as narrow is to

   (A)   long
   (B)   square
   (C)   wide
   (D)   measured
   (E)   lax

Tall and short are opposites, so we are looking for the answer choice that is the opposite of narrow. Wide is the opposite of narrow, so choice C is correct.

Since synonym and analogy questions are very different, we use different strategies for them.

Synonyms Strategies

There are several strategies that we can use on the synonyms section. Which strategy you use for an individual question is highly variable. It depends on what roots you know, whether or not you have heard the word before, and your gut sense about a word.

Think of these strategies as being your toolbox. Several tools can get the job done.

One thing that you should note is that the synonyms questions tend to go in order from easiest to most difficult. The difficulty of the question will affect which strategy you use.

Here are the strategies:

- Come up with your own word
- Is it positive or negative?
- Can you think of a sentence or phrase in which you have heard the word?
- Are there any roots or word parts that you recognize?
- If you have to guess, see if there is an answer choice that has the same prefix, suffix or root as the question word

Strategy #1: Come up with your own word

Use this strategy when you read through a sentence and a word just pops into your head. Don't force yourself to come up with your own definition when you aren't sure what the word means.

- Use this strategy when a definition pops into your head

If you read a question word and a synonym pops into your head, go ahead and jot it down. It is important that you write down the word because otherwise you may try to talk yourself into an answer choice that "seems to come close". One of the biggest enemies on any standardized test is doubt. Doubt leads to talking yourself into the wrong answer, and physically writing down the word gives you the confidence you need when you go through the answer choices.

- Physically write down the definition – don't hold it in your head

After you write down the word, start by crossing out answer choices that are not synonyms for your word. By the time you get down to two choices, you will have a much better idea of what you are looking for.

- Cross out words that don't work

The following drill contains words that you may be able think of a definition for. These are the types of words that you are likely to see at the beginning of the synonym section. You should focus on creating good habits with these questions.

What are good habits?

- Jot down the definition – this will save time in the long run
- Use ruling out – physically cross out answer choices that you know are incorrect

Drill #1

1. RAPID:

   (A) marvelous
   (B) exhausted
   (C) swift
   (D) professional
   (E) icy

2. ABBREVIATE:

   (A) shorten
   (B) exhale
   (C) connect
   (D) secure
   (E) pace

3. DEBRIS:

   (A) whim
   (B) trash
   (C) core
   (D) knapsack
   (E) humor

4. AUTHORIZE:

   (A) eclipse
   (B) smite
   (C) oppose
   (D) permit
   (E) aggravate

5. SEQUENCE:

   (A) nation
   (B) resource
   (C) bid
   (D) farce
   (E) order

(Answers to this drill are found on p. 39)

Strategy #2: Use positive or negative

Sometimes you see a word, and you couldn't define that word, but you have a "gut feeling" that it is either something good or something bad. Maybe you don't know what that word means, but you know you would be mad if someone called you that!

- You have to have a gut feeling about a word to use this strategy

To use this strategy, when you get that feeling that a word is either positive or negative, then write in a "+" or a "−" sign next to the word. Then go to your answer choices and rule out anything that is opposite, i.e., positive when your question word is negative or negative when your question word is positive.

- Physically write a "+" or "−" sign after the question word

To really make this strategy work for you, you also need to rule out any words that are neutral, or neither positive nor negative. For example, let's say the question word is DISTRESS. Distress is clearly a negative word. So we could rule out a positive answer choice, such as friendly, but we can also rule out a neutral word, such as sleepy. At night, it is good to be sleepy, during the day it is not. Sleepy is not clearly a negative word, so it goes.

- Rule out words that are opposite from your question word
- Also rule out neutral words

To summarize, here are the basic steps to using this strategy:

1. If you have a gut negative or positive feeling about a word, write a "+" or "−" sign next to the question word
2. Rule out any words that are opposite
3. Also rule out any NEUTRAL words
4. Pick from what is left

Here is an example of a question where you may be able to use the positive/negative strategy:

1. CONDEMN:

   (A) arrive
   (B) blame
   (C) tint
   (D) favor
   (E) laugh

Let's say that you know that "condemn" is bad, but you can't think of a definition. We write a "–" sign next to it and then rule out anything that is positive. That means that choices D and E can go because they are both positive. Now we can also rule out neutral words because we know that "condemn" is negative. "Arrive" and "tint" are neither positive nor negative, so choices A and C are out. We are left with choice B, which is correct.

On the following drill, write a "+" or "–" sign next to each question word. Then rule out answer choices that are opposite or neutral. Pick from what is left. Even if you aren't sure if the question word is positive or negative, take a guess at it! You may get more correct answers than you would have imagined.

Drill #2

1. ALLURE:
   - (A) attraction
   - (B) color
   - (C) disgrace
   - (D) wilderness
   - (E) confidence

2. LAMENT:
   - (A) respect
   - (B) attack
   - (C) celebrate
   - (D) know
   - (E) mourn

3. HUMANE:
   - (A) invalid
   - (B) compassionate
   - (C) portable
   - (D) restricted
   - (E) bashful

4. DEJECTED:
   - (A) resourceful
   - (B) humid
   - (C) depressed
   - (D) proper
   - (E) cheery

5. REEK:
   - (A) express
   - (B) qualify
   - (C) thrill
   - (D) stink
   - (E) flavor

(Answers to this drill are found on p. 39)

Strategy #3: Use context – Think of where you have heard the word before

Use this strategy when you can't define a word, but you can think of a sentence or phrase where you have heard the word before.

- This strategy only works when you have heard the word before

To apply this strategy, think of a sentence or phrase where you have heard the question word before. Then try plugging the answer choices into your phrase to see which one has the same meaning within that sentence or phrase.

- Think of a sentence or phrase where you have heard the word before
- Plug question words into that sentence or phrase

Here is an example:

1. SHIRK:
   - (A) rush
   - (B) send
   - (C) learn
   - (D) avoid
   - (E) clutter

Now let's say you have heard the word "shirk" but can't define it. You remember your mom telling you "don't shirk your responsibilities" when you tried to watch TV before your chores were done. So we plug in the answer choices for the word shirk in your sentence. Does it make sense to say "don't rush your responsibilities?" It might make sense, but it wouldn't have the same meaning as your context. You weren't in trouble for rushing your chores, you were in trouble for not doing them at all so we can rule out choice A. Does it make sense to say "don't send your responsibilities?" Not at all. Choice B is out. Does "don't learn your responsibilities" work? Nope, choice C is out. Would your mom say "don't avoid your responsibilities?" You bet. Choice D is correct. We would also plug in choice E to make sure it wasn't a better fit, but in this case it is not, and choice D is correct.

Sometimes the only word or phrase that you can think of uses a different form of the word. That is OK as long as you change the answer choices when you plug them in.

- You can use a different form of the word, just change answer choices as well

Here is an example:

2. CHERISH:

    (A) treasure
    (B) enforce
    (C) utter
    (D) concern
    (E) calm

Maybe you have heard your English teacher talk about Little Women as "one of my most cherished books." We can use that context, we just have to add the "–ed" to the answer choices when we plug them in. Does it make sense to say "one of my most treasured books?" Yes, it does, so we will keep choice A. Would "one of my most enforced books" work? No, so we can rule out choice B. What about "one of my most uttered books" or "one of my most concerned books" or "one of my most calmed books?" No, no, and no, so we rule out choices C, D, and E. Choice A is correct.

In the following drill, if you have heard the word before, then come up with a sentence or phrase and practice our strategy. If you have not heard the word before, you can't use the strategy of thinking where you have heard the word before! Use another strategy and ruling out to answer the question. You may not answer every question correctly, but remember, nothing ventured, nothing gained.

Drill #3

1. WILY:

   (A) serious
   (B) flattering
   (C) tough
   (D) cunning
   (E) powerful

2. PROPHESY:

   (A) quiver
   (B) copy
   (C) mystify
   (D) predict
   (E) advance

3. ABOLISH:

   (A) end
   (B) salute
   (C) liberate
   (D) manage
   (E) baffle

4. APPALLING:

   (A) worthy
   (B) horrifying
   (C) available
   (D) omitted
   (E) various

5. CONSENT:

   (A) worry
   (B) knowledge
   (C) approval
   (D) draft
   (E) requirement

(Answers to this drill are found on p. 39)

Strategy #4: Look for roots or word parts that you know

This strategy works when you recognize that a word looks like another word that you know or when you recognize one of the roots that you have studied in school or in this book.

If you see something familiar in the question word, underline the roots or word parts that you recognize. If you can think of the meaning of the root, then look for answer choices that would go with that meaning. If you can't think of a specific meaning, think of other words that have that root and look for answer choices that are similar in meaning to those other words.

- Underline word parts that you recognize
- Think of the meaning of that word part
- If you can't think of a meaning, think of other words with that word part

Here is an example of a question that uses a word with recognizable word parts:

1. EXCLUDE:
   - (A) prohibit
   - (B) feel
   - (C) rest
   - (D) drift
   - (E) rejoice

There are two word parts in the word "exclude" that can help us out. First, we have the prefix "ex-", which means out (think of the word "exit"). Secondly, "clu" is a word root that means to shut (think of the word "include"). Using these word parts, we can see that "exclude" has something to do with shutting out. Choice A comes closest to this meaning, so it is correct.

For the following drill, try to use word parts to come up with the correct answer choice. If you can't think of what the word root, prefix, or suffix means, then think of other words that have the same root, prefix, or suffix.

Drill #4

1. MAGNANIMOUS:

    (A) possible
    (B) generous
    (C) cruel
    (D) restrained
    (E) barren

2. POSTPONE:

    (A) allow
    (B) recruit
    (C) delay
    (D) stifle
    (E) label

3. SUBTERRANEAN:

    (A) partial
    (B) tragic
    (C) appreciative
    (D) hectic
    (E) underground

4. MISCREANT:

    (A) degenerate
    (B) pious
    (C) variable
    (D) noteworthy
    (E) avid

5. CULPABLE:

    (A) phantom
    (B) secret
    (C) achievable
    (D) guilty
    (E) conventional

(Answers to this drill are found on p. 39)

Strategy #5: Guess an answer choice with the same prefix, suffix, or word root as the question word

If nothing else, if you have no idea what the word means but you see an answer choice that has the same root, prefix, or suffix, guess that answer choice! You would be amazed how many correct answers have the same root as the question word. What if there are two answer choices with the same root? Guess one of them. Remember, if we can rule out even one answer choice, we should guess.

Let's look at the following example:

1. PERMISSIBLE:

   (A) edible
   (B) crazy
   (C) strong
   (D) allowable
   (E) gentle

Even if you don't know what "permissible" means, the "-ible" ending tells us that it must mean able to do something. The "-ible" and "-able" suffixes have the same meaning, so we could guess between choices A and D. "Edible" means able to be eaten, but "allowable" is a synonym for "permissible", so choice D is correct.

Complete the following drill by looking for answer choices that repeat roots, prefixes, or suffixes.

1. CONGEAL:

   (A) bury
   (B) habituate
   (C) coagulate
   (D) reimburse
   (E) limit

2. DISPARAGE:

   (A) resurrect
   (B) discredit
   (C) deceive
   (D) praise
   (E) label

3. COMPREHENSIBLE:

   (A) laudable
   (B) independent
   (C) remorseful
   (D) authentic
   (E) understandable

(Answers to this drill are found on p. 39)

Now you have the strategies that you need to succeed on the synonyms section! To keep improving your score, keep studying that vocabulary.

Analogies Strategies

The analogies section tests not only your vocabulary, but also your ability to see how words are related.

We have three main strategies for the analogies section:

- If you know the question words, make a sentence
- If you don't know one of the question words, head to the answer choices
- On the last ten analogies, guess the weirdest answer choices

Strategy #1: Make a sentence from the question words

In order to use this strategy, you have to at least have a vague sense of what both question words mean. Basically, you make a sentence from the question words and then plug answer choices into that sentence to see which answer choice has the same relationship.

Here is an example of a question with words that we know and can make a sentence from:

1. Water is to ocean as
    (A) cloud is to sky
    (B) mountain is to hill
    (C) paint is to watercolor
    (D) ice is to glaciers
    (E) sneaker is to marathon

If we make a sentence from the question words, we might say "water fills the ocean". Now we plug in our answer choices, subbing in the answer words for the question words. Does it make sense to say "cloud fills the sky?" Sometimes that is true, but if we have to use the word sometimes, then it is not a strong relationship so we can rule out choice A. Does a "mountain fill a hill"? No, so choice B is gone. Does "paint fill a watercolor"? Not in the same way that water fills an ocean, so we can rule out choice C. Does "ice fill glaciers"? Yes. Choice D is correct. (We would keep going and plug in choice E just to make sure that it wasn't a better fit, but choice D is correct).

The general steps to use this strategy are:

1. Make a sentence with question words
2. Plug answers into that sentence
3. Do NOT use the words "could", "maybe", "can", "sometimes" – if you have to use those words the relationship is not strong enough

There are several relationships that show up frequently on the SSAT. If you become familiar with them, it makes it much easier to make up your own sentences quickly. Keep in mind that not every analogy on the SSAT will use one of these relationships, but most of them will.

They are:

1. Occupation – One word is the job of the other word
   Example: Architect is to building

2. Part of – One word is a part of the other word
   Example: Kitchen is to house

3. Type of – One word is a type of the other word, which is a broader category
   Example: Whale is to mammal

4. Used for – One word is used to do the other word
   Example: Shovel is to dig

5. Degree – The words have roughly the same meaning, only one is more extreme
   Example: Hungry is starving

6. Characteristic of – One word is a characteristic of the other
   Example: Massive is to elephant

7. Synonyms – The words have roughly the same meaning
   Example: Deceitful is to dishonest

8. Antonyms – The words are opposite in meaning
   Example: Friendly is to rude

9. Found in – One word is found in the other
   Example: Shark is to ocean

10. Grammatical – One word has a grammatical relationship to the other
    Example: Meet is to met

Note about the degree relationship: The degree relationship is very common on the SSAT. A potential trick with these questions is to have answer choices that are synonyms. It is very tempting to choose these answer choices – particularly if you don't know the meanings of the words in the correct answer choice. Just remember that we are looking for a pair where one word is more extreme, not one with words that have the same meaning. Rule out these synonyms if the question words have a degree relationship.

For the following drill, provide the number of the relationship from above that the words use.

Drill #6

1. Instruct is to teacher – uses relationship #_____

2. Sonnet is to poem – uses relationship #_____

3. Seahorse is to ocean – uses relationship #_____

4. Flat is to plains – uses relationship #_____

5. Wrench is to tightening – uses relationship #_____

6. Processor is to computer – uses relationship #_____

7. Bleak is to hopeful – uses relationship #_____

8. Audacious is to bold – uses relationship #_____

9. Radius is to radii – uses relationship #_____

10. Large is to humongous – uses relationship #_____

(Answers to this drill are found on p. 39)

Strategy #2: If you don't know one of the question words, head to the answer choices

If you read through the question words and don't know what one (or both) of the question words mean, all is not lost. Sometimes there are answer choices with words that are not even related. Rule these out. Then plug the question words into the sentences you made from the remaining answer choices and see if they could work. Rule out any that don't. Guess from what you have left.

Here are the steps to this strategy:

1. Rule out answer choices that have unrelated words
2. If two answer choices have the same relationship, rule them out (there can only be one right answer, so if two choices have the same relationship then they are both wrong)
3. Make a sentence with the remaining answer choices
4. Plug your question words into those sentences and see what could work
5. Remember to guess if you can rule out even one answer choice

Keep in mind that if you find yourself using "could", "maybe, "can", or "sometimes", it is not a strong relationship so you should rule it out. If you hear yourself using those words, you are talking yourself into a wrong answer choice!

- If you have to use "could", "maybe", "can", or "sometimes" it is not a strong relationship and you should rule out that answer choice

Here is an example:

1. (Weird word) is to ship as
   - (A) luck is to delay
   - (B) fun is to laughter
   - (C) helmet is to football
   - (D) mansion is to house
   - (E) first is to last

Since we don't know one question word, we go to the answers. If we try to make a sentence from choice A, we can see that luck and delay just don't have a strong relationship. You could say that if you are lucky, you might not have a delay. However, that would be talking yourself into a relationship that isn't strong at all (if you have to use "sometimes", "might", "may", or "could", it is not a good relationship). Choice A is out. For choice B, you could say that laughter is the result of fun. However, if we plug the question words back into that sentence, is there anything that ship is a result of? Not really, so we can rule out choice B. If we look at choice C, you could say that that a helmet is worn to play football. But if we plug our question words into that sentence, is there anything that worn to play ship? No. Choice C is out. On to choice D. A mansion is a type of house. Could something be a type of ship? Absolutely, so we keep choice D. Finally, choice E. First and last are opposites. But is there a word that means the opposite of ship? No, so choice E is out. We were able to narrow it down to one choice (choice D) without even knowing one of the question words.

For the following drill, you may not know one (or both!) of the question words. Rule out any answer choices that have words that are not related. Rule out any two answer choices that have the same relationship. From what is left, plug the question words into the sentences that you made from the answer choices. Rule out any answer choices that don't work. Remember, if you can rule out even one answer choice, then you should guess.

Drill #7

1. Assiduous is to tireless as

   (A) clever is to lazy
   (B) fast is to timid
   (C) questionable is to sound
   (D) resolute is to determined
   (E) funny is to crowded

2. Nefarious is to villain as

   (A) beneficent is to hero
   (B) crazy is to rock star
   (C) funny is to politician
   (D) loud is to nun
   (E) fast is to cast

3. Obliterate is to destroy as

   (A) leave is to go
   (B) build is to correct
   (C) horrify is to upset
   (D) ease is to worsen
   (E) encourage is to prohibit

4. Zealot is to extremist as

   (A) tiger is to lion
   (B) mansion is to shack
   (C) cuff is to shirt
   (D) criminal is to juvenile
   (E) car is to automobile

5. Raconteur is to storyteller as

   (A) novice is to beginner
   (B) virtuoso is to musician
   (C) rascal is to saint
   (D) comedian is to microphone
   (E) illness is to health

(Answers to this drill are found on p. 39)

Strategy #3: On the last ten analogies, guess the weirdest answer choices

You can use this strategy if you get to the last ten questions and you have no idea what the right answer is. If you know the question words, and you know that one answer choice works, then by all means choose that answer choice. We don't want you to second-guess yourself. This strategy comes into play when you would otherwise leave a question unanswered, or if you are running out of time and need to be able to guess quickly.

- Use this strategy when you have no other way to answer the question
- Also use this strategy if you are running out of time and need to guess quickly

The questions in the analogies section go from easy to most difficult. Most students miss the last questions. However, most students REFUSE to guess words that they don't know. You know what this means, right? It means that if you want to raise your percentile score, you have to guess the answer choice that most students aren't going to guess.

- Ask yourself what answer choice other students are LEAST likely to guess

Try to read through the answer choices in your head. The more difficulty you have pronouncing the words, the more likely it is to be the right answer choice on the last part of the analogies. This isn't an exact science, but it works often enough that you will come out ahead.

- Try pronouncing the answer choices – the harder it is to pronounce, the more likely it is to be the correct answer on the last ten

For example, let's say you guess the weirdest words on the last ten analogies and only answer half of these correctly. You get 5 points for the five that you answered correctly, and you only lose 1.25 points for the five that you missed. You come out ahead.

- Remember that we are trying to play the odds

On the following drill, try to guess the weirdest answer choice.

Drill #8

1. Cumbersome is to onerous as

   (A) loud is to alone
   (B) strong is to lazy
   (C) hapless is to piteous
   (D) sullen is to constructive
   (E) unique is to fearless

2. Infamous is to gangster as

   (A) treacherous is to turncoat
   (B) expert is to amateur
   (C) brief is to speech
   (D) splendid is to rain
   (E) fortunate is to fool

(Answers to this drill are found on p. 39)

Now you have the basic strategies for synonyms and analogies. The other important piece of improving your verbal score is studying vocabulary.

Be sure to check all of the answers to the drills, if you have not already. If you missed a question, think about WHY the correct answer was correct and how you could have thought about the question differently and chosen the correct answer.

Answers to Synonyms and Analogies Drills

Drill #1
1. C
2. A
3. B
4. D
5. E

Drill #2
1. A
2. E
3. B
4. C
5. D

Drill #3
1. D
2. D
3. A
4. B
5. C

Drill #4
1. B
2. C
3. E
4. A
5. D

Drill #5
1. C
2. B
3. E

Drill #6
1. #1
2. #3
3. #9
4. #6
5. #4
6. #2 or #4
7. #8
8. #7
9. #10
10. #5

Drill #7
1. D
2. A
3. C
4. E
5. B

Drill #8
1. C
2. A

Additional Analogies Practice

Many students find the analogies to be particularly challenging. The following are drills that will give you more practice with the skills that you learned in the strategy section. You may not need this extra practice, but many students find it very helpful.

Drills #1-5 (p. 42-46) give you practice with making sentences from two words or determining if two words are not related. You can use these skills for making sentences from question words/answer choices and ruling out answer choices that have unrelated words.

It is important that you do the drills one at a time and check your answers between drills. We want you to figure out WHY you missed questions so that you can apply that knowledge to the next drill. You won't learn as you go if you just do all the drills in a row without checking answers.

- Check your answers after each drill
- Figure out what to do differently before you move on to the next drill

Drills #6-8 (p. 51-53) give you practice with figuring out answer choices when you don't know the meaning of one of the question words. Again, check your answers and read the explanations before moving onto the next drill.

Now onto the drills!

Drills #1-5

For these drills, you will be given two words in the format of an analogies question or answer choice. On the blank next to each word, write a sentence that relates the two words. If the words are NOT related at all, write NR on the blank.

- Write a sentence relating the two words if they are related
- If the words are not related, write NR on the blank

Be sure to check your answers and read explanations for any questions that you missed before you move onto the next drill. Your sentences will not be exactly like the answers given, but they should get at the same meaning.

- Check your answers and read explanations before moving onto the next drill

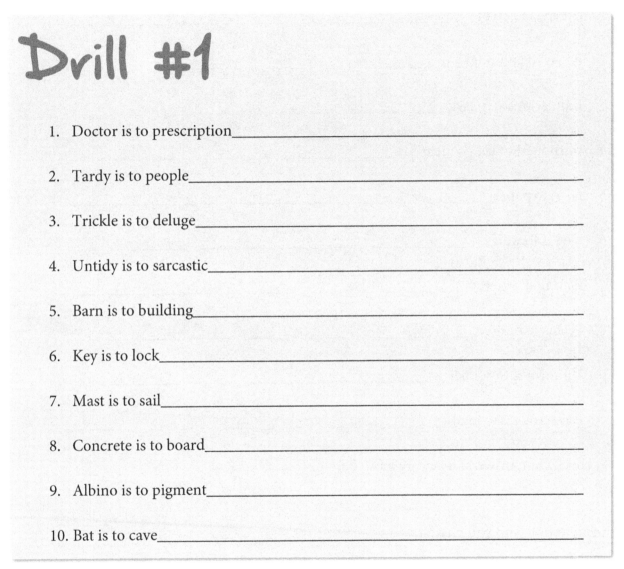

Drill #1

1. Doctor is to prescription_____

2. Tardy is to people_____

3. Trickle is to deluge_____

4. Untidy is to sarcastic_____

5. Barn is to building_____

6. Key is to lock_____

7. Mast is to sail_____

8. Concrete is to board_____

9. Albino is to pigment_____

10. Bat is to cave_____

Now, check your answers. They are located on p. 46.

Which questions did you miss?

What is one thing that you learned from the questions that you missed?

Drill #2

1. Creep is to crept_____

2. Pen is to painting_____

3. Industrious is to lazy_____

4. Introduction is to conclusion_____

5. Jar is to paper_____

6. Dog is to wolf_____

7. Placemat is to tray_____

8. Peel is to orange_____

9. Uniform is to soldier_____

10. Boisterous is to loud_____

Now, check your answers. They are located on p. 46.

Which questions did you miss?

What is one thing that you learned from the questions that you missed?

Drill #3

1. Possible is to definite_____

2. Regal is to queen_____

3. Pond is to mountain_____

4. Watercolor is to painting_____

5. Pole is to firehouse_____

6. Idea is to occupation_____

7. Foggy is to hot_____

8. Uniqueness is to conformity_____

9. Fertile is to flattering_____

10. Stethoscope is to doctor_____

Now, check your answers. They are located on p. 47.

Which questions did you miss?

What is one thing that you learned from the questions that you missed?

Drill #4

1. Mansion is to shack_____

2. Archipelago is to island_____

3. Meager is to overabundant_____

4. Request is to command_____

5. Lamp is to mirror_____

6. Cougar is to cat_____

7. Broom is to disinfect_____

8. Sill is to window_____

9. Satiated is to hungry_____

10. Violin is to piccolo_____

Now, check your answers. They are located on p. 47.

Which questions did you miss?

What is one thing that you learned from the questions that you missed?

Drill #5

1. Decibel is to volume_____

2. Electricity is to coal_____

3. Treaty is to countries_____

4. Chemistry is to physics_____

5. Monkey is to tundra_____

6. Steel is to girder_____

7. Sport is to soccer_____

8. Limber is to flexible_____

9. Orange is to grass_____

10. Lavish is to Spartan_____

Now, check your answers. They are located on p. 48.

Which questions did you miss?

What is one thing that you learned from the questions that you missed?

Answers to Drills #1-5

Drill #1

1. A doctor's job is to write prescriptions.
2. NR – A person could be tardy, but "could" tells us that it is not a strong relationship.
3. A deluge is a really big trickle. This is a degree relationship where one word is just more extreme than the other. It is OK to reverse the order of the words when we make a sentence as long as we then reverse the order of the answer choice words when we plug them into the sentence to see if the meaning is the same.
4. NR – These two words aren't related.
5. A barn is a type of building.
6. A key is used to open a lock.
7. A mast is used to hold up a sail.
8. NR – Concrete and board seem to go together because they are both used in construction, but there is not a strong relationship between the two words. Words that are part of the same larger category are not necessarily related to each other.
9. A characteristic of albino is a lack of pigment.
10. A bat is found in a cave, or a bat lives in a cave.

Drill #2

1. Crept is the past-tense form of creep. (Remember that we can reverse the order of the question words as long as we reverse the order in the answer choices as well.)
2. NR – even though these words "seem to go together", they are not related. A pen is used for writing and not for painting.
3. Industrious is the opposite of lazy.
4. An introduction comes before a conclusion or an introduction is the opposite of a conclusion.
5. NR – jar and paper are not related. Jars are not made of paper and do not hold paper. If you used one of these relationships, you were probably trying too hard. On this test, the relationships don't require stretching the meaning of the word.
6. A wolf is a wild dog. We can switch the order of the question words as long as we switch the order of the words when we plug answer choices into the same sentence.
7. NR – a tray could be placed on a placemat, but if we find ourselves using the word "could", we know that the relationship is not strong enough for this test.
8. A peel is found on the outside of an orange or a peel is used to protect an orange.
9. A uniform is worn by a soldier.
10. Boisterous is another word for loud (they are synonyms).

Drill #3

1. This is a degree relationship that is hard to make an exact sentence for. Possible is not the opposite of definite. Rather, if we think of a spectrum running from never happening to definite, possible would fall about in the middle. We would look for an answer choice with the same type of relationship.
2. Regal is a characteristic of a queen.
3. NR – A pond and a mountain are both land features, but remember that just because two words are part of the same larger category does not mean that they have a strong relationship with one another.
4. A watercolor is a type of painting.
5. A pole is used in a firehouse to go downstairs.
6. NR – Occupation is another word for job, which is not directly related to an idea.
7. NR – Foggy and hot are both types of weather, but they are not necessarily related to one another.
8. Uniqueness means without conformity or uniqueness is the opposite of conformity. Either sentence would get the job done.
9. NR – Fertile describes land that grows plants easily, which is not related to whether or not something is flattering.
10. A stethoscope is used by a doctor.

Drill #4

1. A mansion is a much nicer shack. This is a degree relationship. They are both houses, just at opposite ends of the spectrum of how nice a house can be.
2. An archipelago is a group of islands. We can change island to islands as long as we also make the second word in the answer choices plural when we plug them into our sentence.
3. Meager is the opposite of overabundant.
4. Request is to ask someone to do something nicely and command is to order someone to do something. This is a degree relationship.
5. NR – A lamp and a mirror might both be found in a home, but they are not related to one another directly.
6. A cougar is a type of cat.
7. NR – A broom is not used to disinfect.
8. A sill is the bottom part of a window (it is the piece of wood just under the window).
9. Satiated is the opposite of hungry.
10. NR – A violin and a piccolo are both types of instruments, but belonging to the same larger category is not a relationship on the SSAT.

Drill #5

1. A decibel is used to measure volume (how loud something is).
2. Electricity is made from coal.
3. A treaty is an agreement between countries.
4. NR – They are both sciences but that doesn't mean there is a strong relationship between the two.
5. NR – A monkey does not live in the tundra.
6. A girder is made from steel. A girder is one of those big beams that is used when large buildings are constructed.
7. Soccer is a type of sport. (We can change the order of the words as long as we change the order of the words in the answer choices when we plug into out sentence.)
8. Limber and flexible are synonyms.
9. NR – Orange is not the color of grass.
10. Lavish and Spartan are antonyms.

Drills #6-8

In these drills, you will be given a question with one word that is just ????????????s. This represents a word that you do not know the meaning of.

- The ??????????????s represent a word that you do not know

To answer these questions, first rule out answer choices that are not related. Then make sentences from the remaining answer choices. Plug the question word that you do know into each answer choice sentence and then rule out answer choices that wouldn't work given the question word that you do know. Finally, we can rule out answer choices that have the same relationship. For example, let's say choices A and D both have words that are synonyms. Since there can only be one right answer choice, we can rule out both choices A and D because otherwise there would be more than one correct answer. You may not be able to rule out down to one answer choice. In this case, on the real test you would guess from what you have left. The answers for this drill will let you know which answer choices are possibilities.

- First rule out answer choices that are not related
- Make sentences from remaining answer choices and rule out any that would not work with the word that you do know
- If there is more than one answer choice with the same relationship, rule out all the answer choices that have the same relationship
- If you have more than one answer choice left, you would just guess from what you have left

Be sure to check your answers and read explanations for any questions that you missed before you move on to the next drill.

- Check your answers and read explanations before moving onto the next drill
- Remember that you may wind up with more than one answer choice that works – the answer key will let you know all the answer choices that are possibilities

Drill #6

1. ??????????????? is to obese

   (A) fast is to loud
   (B) corrupted is to rejected
   (C) plain is to ornate
   (D) dreary is to tired
   (E) brave is to courageous

2. House is to ???????????????? as

   (A) fleet is to ship
   (B) boat is to raft
   (C) shovel is to digging
   (D) knee is to elbow
   (E) voter is to candidate

3. Confusing is to ????????? as mocking is to

   (A) poetry
   (B) prose
   (C) letters
   (D) satire
   (E) song

4. Villain is to ????????? as

   (A) guardian is to protective
   (B) principal is to stern
   (C) teacher is to punctual
   (D) nurse is to sleepy
   (E) architect is to eloquent

5. ?????????? is to leather as

   (A) neighborhood is to homes
   (B) blanket is to wool
   (C) barge is to canoe
   (D) sparkle is to downpour
   (E) chapter is to book

Now, check your answers. They are located on p. 53.

Which questions did you miss?

What is one thing that you learned from the questions that you missed?

Drill #7

1. ????????? is to somber

   (A) lazy is to smug
   (B) harmonious is to cacophonous
   (C) hasty is to patient
   (D) frank is to direct
   (E) lame is to green

2. Manageable is to ?????????? as obedient is to

   (A) unruly
   (B) kind
   (C) submissive
   (D) painful
   (E) ravenous

3. ???????? is to cutting

   (A) hammer is to sawing
   (B) leg is to table
   (C) dimmer is to brightness
   (D) whisk is to mixing
   (E) mourn is to funeral

4. ??????? is to adaptable as

   (A) indifferent is to zealous
   (B) vivid is to bright
   (C) startled is to humid
   (D) parched is to sated
   (E) wise is to visible

5. ????????? is to opinion as exhaustion is to

   (A) humor
   (B) youth
   (C) luck
   (D) comfort
   (E) energy

Now, check your answers. They are located on p. 54.

Which questions did you miss?

What is one thing that you learned from the questions that you missed?

Drill #8

1. ????????? is to limousine as

   (A) shack is to mansion
   (B) cab is to truck
   (C) bicycle is to tricycle
   (D) spaceship is to barge
   (E) airplane is to jet

2. ??????? is to knight as

   (A) top is to table
   (B) shell is to mussel
   (C) plow is to sheep
   (D) instrument is to musician
   (E) novice is to expert

3. ?????????? is to resist as push is to

   (A) crank
   (B) loosen
   (C) pull
   (D) deflate
   (E) curtail

4. ????????? is to possible as

   (A) grotesque is to beautiful
   (B) hardworking is to happy
   (C) revolutionary is to complacent
   (D) humane is to compassionate
   (E) hostile is to sincere

5. Mammal is to ?????????????? as

   (A) plant is to fish
   (B) carnivore is to cow
   (C) marsupial is to opossum
   (D) goldfish is to tadpole
   (E) canine is to horse

Now, check your answers. They are located on p. 55.

Which questions did you miss?

What is one thing that you learned from the questions that you missed?

Answers to Drills #6-8

Drill #6

1. C or E could be correct. Answer choices A and B have clearly unrelated words so we can rule them out. Answer choice D is a little trickier since the words "seem to go together". While dreary weather could make you feel tired, the word "could" means that it isn't a strong relationship. Answer choice D can be eliminated. We would then guess from what we have left. If the ?????? was a word that was opposite in meaning from obese, such as the word emaciated, then answer choice C would be correct. If the ??????? was a word that was similar to obese, such as the word corpulent, then answer choice E would be correct. Even if we can't rule out down to one choice, remember that if we can rule out even one answer choice, we should guess.

2. B is the correct answer. First, we can rule out answer choice D since knee and elbow are not directly related. Then we make sentences from the remaining answer choices. In choice A, a fleet is a group of ships that travel together. Is a house a group of objects that travels together? No, so we can rule out choice A. With choice B, a raft is a type of boat. Is there a word that could be a type of house? Absolutely, so we leave choice B. Now we look at choice C. A shovel is a tool used for digging. Is a house a tool used for something? No. We can rule out choice C. Now let's look at choice E. A voter chooses a candidate. Does a house choose something? No, so we can also eliminate choice E. We are left with only choice B.

3. D is the correct answer. For these types of questions, we have to find a word that is related to the last word in the question. Although we don't know what the ?????????s represent, it is a good guess that confusing is a characteristic of the ?????????s. We are looking for the answer choice that has mocking as a characteristic. Poetry, prose, letters, and songs all could be mocking in tone, but they don't have to be. Even if we don't know what "satire" means, we know that the others can be eliminated, so we choose answer choice D. A satire is a play whose purpose is to mock.

4. A is the correct answer. Our first step is to rule out any answer choices that are unrelated. If we look at answer choice A, it is a guardian's job to be protective, so those two words are related. If we look at answer choice B, a principal can be stern but the word "can" tells us that it is not a strong relationship. Answer choice B is eliminated. If we look at answer choice C, you would hope that a teacher is punctual (on time), but this is not true by definition, so we can rule out choice C. If we look at choice D, a lot of nurses are probably sleepy from working the night shift, but not all

nurses are sleepy and not all sleepy people are nurses. We can rule out choice D. Finally, we have choice E. Eloquent means well-spoken, which has nothing to do with designing buildings, so we can eliminate choice E. We are left with choice A.

5. B is the correct answer choice. First, we should rule out any answer choices that have unrelated words. Choice D can be eliminated because sparkle has nothing to do with downpour. Now we make sentences from the remaining answer choices. A neighborhood is a group of homes. Is there a word that means a group of leather? No, so answer choice A can be ruled out. For answer choice B, blankets are commonly made from wool. Could ?????? be something that is commonly made from leather? Sure, so we will leave choice B. If we look at choice C, a barge is a much larger form of a boat than a canoe. Is there a word that means a larger form of leather? That doesn't make sense so choice C is out. Finally, we have choice E. We divide a book into sections called chapters. Can we divide leather into sections called ??????? No, so answer choice E is eliminated. We are left with choice B.

Drill #7

1. D is the correct answer choice. First, we have to rule out answer choices that have unrelated words. Lazy is not related to smug and lame is not related to green, so we can eliminate choices A and E. Now we have to make sentences from the remaining answer choices. If we look at choice B, we can make the sentence that harmonious is the opposite of cacophonous. Could somber be the opposite of some word? Sure, so we keep answer choice B. Now we move on to answer choice C. We could make the sentence hasty is the opposite of patient. We know that somber could be the opposite of some word but the problem is that if the relationship being tested was antonyms there would be more than one correct answer. We can rule out both choices B and C since they have the same relationship. Now we have ruled out every choice except for choice D. Frank and direct are synonyms and there could very well be a word that is a synonym for somber (the word somber means serious).

2. A or C could both be correct. We know that we need to choose an answer that is related to the word obedient. We can rule out choices B, D, and E since those words are not related to being obedient (ravenous means really hungry, by the way). The word unruly is the opposite of obedient and the word submissive is a synonym for obedient. Since we don't know the second word in the question, we can't be sure what the correct answer is, but keep in mind that if we answer the question correctly we get plus one point and if we answer the question incorrectly we only lose a quarter point.

3. D is the correct answer. First, we rule out choice A because a hammer and sawing are unrelated. If we look at answer choice B, a leg is part of a table. Is something part of cutting? Not in the same way, so we can rule out choice B. Now we move on to choice C. A dimmer is used to lessen brightness. Is there a word that means something that lessens cutting? No, you can't really lessen cutting. You either cut or you don't. Answer choice C is out. Let's look at choice D. A whisk is used for mixing. Could ?????? be a word that means something used for cutting? Absolutely, so we leave choice D. Finally, we have choice E. Mourning is done at a funeral. Is something done at a cutting? No. Choice E is gone. We are left with choice D.

4. B is the correct answer choice. First, we have to rule out any answer choices with unrelated words. Startled is not related to humid and wise is not related to visible, so we can eliminate choices C and E. Now we make sentences from the remaining choices. In answer choice A, indifferent is the opposite of zealous (indifferent means to not care and zealous means to be fanatical). Since a word could be the opposite of adaptable, we keep answer choice A. In answer choice B, vivid is a synonym for bright. The ???????s could represent a word that is a synonym for adaptable, so we keep answer choice B. If we look at answer choice D, parched is the opposite of sated (parched means extremely thirsty). Now we can see that answer choices A and D have the same relationship, so we can rule out both of them. We are left with choice B as the correct answer.

5. E is the correct answer. For this question, we just have to find a word that is related to exhaustion. Of the answer choices, only the word energy has a relationship to exhaustion – exhaustion means without energy.

Drill #8

1. A or E could be correct. Let's start by ruling out any answer choices that have unrelated words. Spaceship and barge are unrelated (a barge is a really big boat), so answer choice D can be eliminated. Now we look at the remaining choices. In choice A, we have a degree relationship. The words shack and mansion are on opposite ends of the spectrum describing houses. Could the same relationship work with limousine? You bet, so we keep A. Now we look at B. A cab is the front part of the truck where the driver sits. Is there a word for the front part of the limousine where the driver sits? Not really. We can rule out B. With choice C, a tricycle is just a bicycle with one more wheel. Is there a vehicle that we add one wheel to in order to get a limousine? No, so we eliminate choice C. Now we look at choice E (we already ruled out D). A

jet is a type of airplane. Could a limousine be a type of something? Yes, it could. We are left with both choice A and choice E, so we would guess one of them and move on.

2. B is the correct answer. First, we rule out any answer choices that are not related. Plow and sheep are not related (sheep do not pull plows), so answer choice C is gone. Now we look at what we have left. In choice A, a top goes on top of a table. Is there something that goes on top of a knight? Not really in the same way, so choice A is ruled out. In choice B, a shell protects a mussel. Is there a word for something that protects a knight? Yes, so we keep choice B. If we look at choice D (we already eliminated C), an instrument is played by a musician. Is there anything that a knight plays? Not really. Choice D is eliminated. Finally, we have choice E. A novice is the opposite of an expert. Is there a word that could the opposite of a knight? Not really. We are left with just choice B.

3. C is the correct answer. To answer this question, we just have to find a word related to push. Push and pull are opposites, so choice C is correct.

4. D is the correct answer. First, we rule out any answer choices that do not have related words. Hardworking is not necessarily related to happy and hostile is not related to sincere, so we can eliminate choices B and E. Now we look at what we have left. In choice A, grotesque and beautiful are opposites. Could a word mean the opposite of possible? Yes, so we keep answer choice A. Now we look at choice C. Revolutionary and complacent are also opposites, so we can eliminate both choices A and C since there can't be two correct answer choices. We are left with choice D. Humane and compassionate are synonyms and there could be a word that means the same thing as possible.

5. C is the correct answer choice. First, we eliminate answer choices with unrelated words. Plant and fish are not related, so we can rule out choice A. If we look at choice B, a cow is not a carnivore, so we can rule out choice B. If we look at choice D, a goldfish does not develop from a tadpole, so we can eliminate choice D. Finally, a horse is not a canine, so we can rule out choice E. We have eliminated everything but choice C. An opossum is a type of marsupial, and there could definitely be something that is a type of mammal. By the way, you may not have known some of these relationships. That is OK. Just rule out what you can on the real test and then guess from what you have left.

Vocabulary Review

A key component of improving your verbal score is increasing your vocabulary. Following are ten lessons that will help you do just that.

Each lesson has twenty new words for you to learn. There are good words, there are bad words, and there are even words with roots. Exciting, eh?

After you learn the words, complete the activities for each lesson. The best way to learn new words is to think of them in categories and to evaluate how the words relate to one another. The activities will help you do this.

The activities also give you practice with synonyms and analogies. You will be working on strategy while you are learning new words – think of it as a two for one!

If there are words that you have trouble remembering as you work through the lessons, go ahead and make flashcards for them. Continue to review these flashcards until the words stick. There may also be words that you run across in the analogies or synonyms practice that you do not know the meaning of. Make flashcards for these words as well.

After each lesson are the answers. Be sure to check your work.

After the lessons, there are also three-word lists. These word lists are labelled "challenging", "more challenging", and "most challenging." The harder the words are, the less likely they are to show up on the test, but if you already know the easier words then you will need to study the harder words to make progress. These three-word lists include one-word synonyms, since that is what the SSAT generally provides. For further clarification, you can see example sentences using these words by visiting:

www.testprepworks.com/student/download

Lesson One

Words to Learn

Below are the twenty words used in Lesson One; refer back to this list as needed as you move through the lesson.

Marina: dock
Trivial: unimportant
Terrain: ground
Apathetic: disinterested
Calamity: disaster

Devastate: destroy
Sentient: aware
Mariner: sailor
Grapple: struggle
Inter: bury

Cognizant: informed
Ameliorate: improve
Prosperity: good fortune
Aloof: withdrawn
Perceptive: sensitive

Adversity: misfortune
Subterranean: underground
Crucial: important
Submarine: underwater
Oblivious: unaware

Word List Practice

Use the words from the list above to complete the following activities.

List three words that describe a person who doesn't know or doesn't care.

1.
2.
3.

List three words that could describe a person who knows what is going on.

1.
2.
3.

List three words that have a decidedly negative meaning.

1.
2.
3.

Analogies Practice

One of the common relationships used in the analogy part of the test is the antonym relationship. In this relationship, words are used that are opposite in meaning.

To complete the questions below, use the following word bank:

Sentient
Adversity
Trivial
Oblivious

Use the antonym relationship and the list of words above to complete the following questions.

1. Happy is to sad as prosperity is to_____.

2. Fearless is to scared as cognizant is to_____.

3. Good is to bad as crucial is to_____.

4. Joy is to pain as aloof is to_____.

Roots Practice

Below are three words. Write the definition for the words on the line provided. Based on their meanings, define the common root.

Marina_____

Mariner_____

Submarine_____

1. The root "mar" means:

Inter_____

Subterranean_____

Terrain_____

2. The root "terr/ter" means:

3. If "aqu/a" is the root meaning water, what do you think the word "aquamarine" means?

4. Based on the roots terr/ter and aqu/a, what do you think the word "terraqueous" means?

5. Based on the words submarine and subterranean, can you figure out the meaning of the root "sub?"

Synonyms Practice

1. CALAMITY:

   (A) laughter
   (B) disaster
   (C) heaven
   (D) species
   (E) morale

2. DEVASTATE:

   (A) help
   (B) forgive
   (C) glow
   (D) destroy
   (E) break

3. AMELIORATE:

   (A) improve
   (B) cook
   (C) construct
   (D) relax
   (E) defy

4. GRAPPLE:

   (A) release
   (B) remember
   (C) struggle
   (D) blend
   (E) incorporate

5. PERCEPTIVE:

   (A) ignorant
   (B) convivial
   (C) incompatible
   (D) dense
   (E) sensitive

6. APATHETIC:

   (A) enthusiastic
   (B) overjoyed
   (C) hyper
   (D) disinterested
   (E) tired

7. CRUCIAL:

   (A) loud
   (B) miniature
   (C) important
   (D) late
   (E) crunchy

Answers to Lesson One

Word list practice

1. apathetic
2. aloof
3. oblivious

1. sentient
2. cognizant
3. perceptive

1. calamity
2. devastate
3. adversity

Synonyms practice

1. B
2. D
3. A
4. C
5. E
6. D
7. C

Analogies practice

1. adversity
2. oblivious
3. trivial
4. sentient

Roots practice

1. sea
2. earth
3. color of sea water
4. formed of land and water
5. under/beneath

Lesson Two

Words to Learn

Below are the twenty words used in Lesson Two; refer back to this list as needed as you move through the lesson.

Enunciate: pronounce
Procrastinate: delay
Inscribe: write
Cleave: split
Magnitude: importance

Abashed: embarrassed
Indescribable: beyond words
Denigrate: criticize
Hew: cut
Figurative: symbolic

Grotesque: ugly
Proscribe: forbid
Corpulent: fat
Eminence: superiority
Incorporate: include

Metaphorical: figurative (not literal)
Repugnant: loathsome (nasty)
Exhilarated: elated (thrilled)
Manifest: demonstrate
Corporeal: bodily

Word List Practice

Use the words from the list above to complete the following activities.

List three words that describe something you could do to someone.

1.

2.

3.

4. If you called someone "corpulent," they might think that you are _____.

5. If you realized at school that your pants were cleaved in two, you would probably feel _____.

Analogies Practice

One of the common relationships used in the analogy part of the test is the synonym relationship. This relationship uses words that have the same meaning.

To complete the questions below, use the following word bank:

Metaphorical
Procrastinate
Hew
Repugnant

Use the synonym relationship and the list of words above to complete the following questions.

1. Mock is to tease as cleave is to _____.

2. Clear is to translucent as figurative is to _____.

3. Jump is to hop as delay is to _____.

4. Calm is to placid as grotesque is to _____.

Roots Practice

Below are three words. Write the definition for the words on the line provided. Based on their meanings, define the common root.

Inscribe _____

Proscribe _____

Indescribable _____

1. The root "scribe" means:

   Corpulent _____

   Incorporate _____

   Corporeal _____

2. The root "corp" means:

3. Based on the meaning of "corp," what popular term for business also means "body of men?" (This is not a word from our lesson, but rather one you might know from another place.) _____

4. A doctor has to _____ many drugs before you can take them (this word is similar to one of the words in this lesson, but it is NOT that word!).

5. Based on one of the roots above, can you think of a term meaning "one who writes?"

   _____

Synonyms Practice

Since you practiced with synonyms in the analogy section, use the crossword below to spend more time with the words from this lesson.

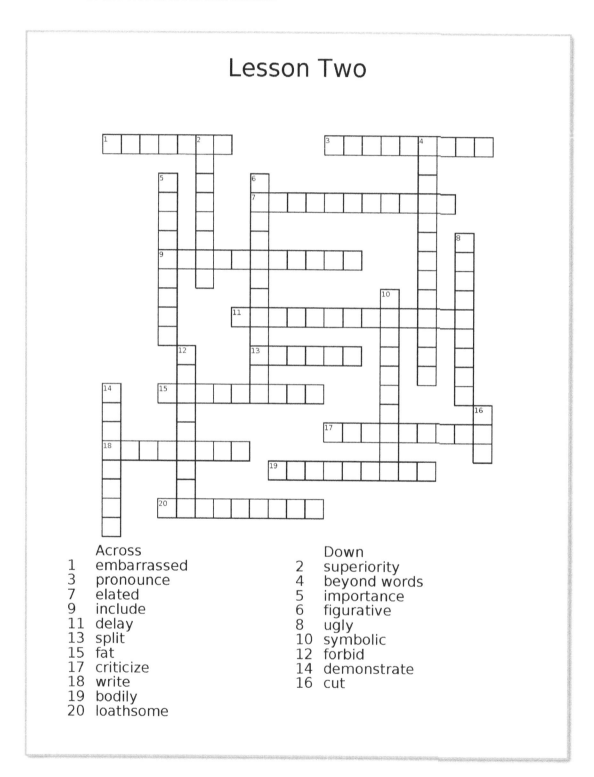

Lesson Two

Across
1. embarrassed
3. pronounce
7. elated
9. include
11. delay
13. split
15. fat
17. criticize
18. write
19. bodily
20. loathsome

Down
2. superiority
4. beyond words
5. importance
6. figurative
8. ugly
10. symbolic
12. forbid
14. demonstrate
16. cut

Answers to Lesson Two

Word list practice

1. proscribe
2. denigrate
3. incorporate
4. repugnant
5. abashed

Analogies practice

1. hew
2. metaphorical
3. procrastinate
4. repugnant

Roots practice

1. to write
2. body
3. corporation
4. prescribe
5. scribe

Synonyms practice

1. abashed
2. eminence
3. enunciate
4. indescribable
5. magnitude
6. metaphorical
7. exhilarated
8. grotesque
9. incorporate
10. figurative
11. procrastinate
12. proscribe
13. cleave
14. manifest
15. corpulent
16. hew
17. denigrate
18. inscribe
19. corporeal
20. repugnant

Lesson Three

Words to Learn

Below are the twenty words used in Lesson Three; refer back to this list as needed as you move through the lesson.

Animate: enliven (bring to life)
Boisterous: noisy
Paraphrase: summarize
Irate: angry
Rejuvenate: refresh

Surfeit: excess
Circumvent: go around
Magnanimous: generous
Vitality: energy
Fractious: bad-tempered

Ravenous: starving
Equanimity: composure (calmness)
Intimidate: frighten
Miscreant: villain
Satiated: satisfied

Vivacious: lively
Craving: hunger or desire
Incensed: enraged
Convivial: friendly
Culprit: wrongdoer

Word List Practice

Use the words from the list above to complete the following activities.

1. Would you rather spend time with someone who is fractious or convivial?

2. If you were rejuvenated, you would have more _____.

List three words that can be related to eating and/or being hungry:
   1.

   2.

   3.

Analogies Practice

One of the common relationships used in the analogy part of the test is the degree relationship. In this relationship, the words have roughly the same meaning, only one word is more extreme than the other word.

To complete the questions below, use the following word bank:

Miscreant
Incensed
Surfeit
Ravenous

Use the degree relationship and the list of words above to complete the following questions.

1. Happy is to exhilarated as craving is to _____.

2. Sadness is to depression as culprit is to _____.

3. Cold is to icy as irate is to _____.

4. Lack is to dearth as plenty is to _____.

Roots Practice

Below are three words. Write the definition for the words on the line provided. Based on their meanings, define the common root.

Animate _____

Equanimity _____

Magnanimous _____

1. The root "anim" means:

Vivacious _____

Vitality _____

Convivial _____

2. The root "vi/viv" means:

3. Based on the meaning of the root "anim," why do you think cartoons are called "animation?"

4. The root "magna" means large. What is an alternate definition of "magnanimous," using its two roots?

5. If "oviparous" means producing young in eggs, based on one of the roots above, what do you think the word "viviparous" means?

Synonyms Practice

1. BOISTEROUS:

    (A) happy
    (B) uncoordinated
    (C) noisy
    (D) silly
    (E) sad

2. PARAPHRASE:

    (A) forget
    (B) give away
    (C) release
    (D) summarize
    (E) take

3. CIRCUMVENT:

    (A) frighten
    (B) go around
    (C) jump
    (D) drive
    (E) cross

4. FRACTIOUS:

    (A) bad-tempered
    (B) overjoyed
    (C) despondent
    (D) crucial
    (E) hardworking

5. INTIMIDATE:

    (A) alleviate
    (B) resist
    (C) boil
    (D) conspire
    (E) frighten

6. REJUVENATE:

    (A) drain
    (B) refresh
    (C) assist
    (D) wash
    (E) create

Answers to Lesson Three

Word list practice

1. convivial
2. vitality

1. craving
2. ravenous
3. satiated

Analogies practice

1. ravenous
2. miscreant
3. incensed
4. surfeit

Roots practice

1. life, spirit
2. life
3. cartoons bring drawings or still images to life
4. large spirit
5. producing live young

Synonyms practice

1. C
2. D
3. B
4. A
5. E
6. B

Lesson Four

Words to Learn

Below are the twenty words used in Lesson Four; refer back to this list as needed as you move through the lesson.

Pandemonium: uproar
Hierarchy: ranked system
Subsist: exist (barely get by)
Eulogy: speech in praise
Unwittingly: unknowingly

Paraphernalia: belongings
Desist: cease (stop)
Cadaverous: ghastly (ghost-like)
Imminent: impending (about to happen)
Agitator: troublemaker

Wrangle: dispute
Deciduous: falling off
Prevalent: widespread
Stagnant: sluggish (not moving)
Decadence: decline

Epiphany: insight
Accolades: praise
Serf: slave
Pilgrimage: journey
Reimburse: pay back

Word List Practice

Use the words from the list above to complete the following activities.

1. Your parents probably give you this for bringing home good grades.

2. Trees with leaves that turn colors each fall are called deciduous. Why?

3. A speech written for a funeral is called a _____.

4. Though often used to describe rich desserts and other food or pleasure, this word actually means something negative:

Analogies Practice

One of the common relationships used in the analogy part of the SSAT is the "found in" relationship. In this relationship, one word is found in the other, such as "fish is to sea".

To complete the questions below, use the following word bank:

Serf
Paraphernalia
Eulogy
Pandemonium

Use the "found in" relationship and the list of words above to complete the following questions.

1. Animal is to zoo as agitator is to _____.

2. Beans is to burrito as accolades is to _____.

3. Jail is to prisoner as farm is to _____.

4. Suitcase is to clothes as a bag is to _____.

Roots Practice

Below are three words. Write the definition for the words on the line provided. Based on their meanings, define the common root.

Subsist _____

Desist _____

Stagnant _____

1. The root "sist/sta" means:

    Cadaverous _____

    Decadence _____

    Deciduous _____

2. The root "cad/cid" means:

3. Based on desist, decadence, and deciduous, what do you think the root "de" means?

4. Based on the meaning of "cadaverous," what does the word "cadaver" mean?

5. If the root "cad" means "to fall," what did a "cadaver" fall from?

6. What makes water "stagnant?"

Synonyms Practice

To spend some more time with the words from this lesson, complete the crossword below.

Lesson Four

Across

3. pay back
4. sluggish
5. ranked system
7. slave
8. cease
9. decline
11. belongings
14. journey
15. falling off
17. unknowing
19. exist
20. troublemaker

Down

1. widespread
2. dispute
6. ghastly
10. uproar
12. praise
13. insight
16. speech
18. impending

Answers to Lesson Four

Word list practice

1. accolades
2. because the leaves fall off
3. eulogy
4. decadence

Analogies practice

1. pandemonium
2. eulogy
3. serf
4. paraphernalia

Roots practice

1. stand
2. to fall
3. opposite or away from
4. corpse
5. life
6. If water is standing or not moving, it becomes stagnant.

Synonyms practice

1. prevalent
2. wrangle
3. reimburse
4. stagnant
5. hierarchy
6. cadaverous
7. serf
8. desist
9. decadence
10. pandemonium
11. paraphernalia
12. accolades
13. epiphany
14. pilgrimage
15. deciduous
16. eulogy
17. unwittingly
18. imminent
19. subsist
20. agitator

Lesson Five

Words to Learn

Below are the twenty words used in Lesson Five; refer back to this list as needed as you move through the lesson.

Pragmatic: sensible
Mercurial: temperamental (moody)
Morose: depressed
Frustrate: disappoint
Serene: calm

Carnivorous: meat-eating
Ostentatious: flashy
Insolent: disrespectful
Omniscient: all-knowing
Effervescent: bubbly

Stupendous: wonderful
Incarnation: embodiment (a spirit being born into a body)
Omnivorous: eats everything
Impetuous: impulsive
Mediocre: unexceptional

Grovel: beg
Reincarnation: rebirth
Omnipotent: all-powerful
Interminable: boring
Fraudulent: deceptive

Word List Practice

Use the words from the list above to complete the following activities.

1. Would you rather have a mediocre meal or a stupendous meal?

2. It would be _____ for the bank to tell you that your account had $100 in it, when you had actually deposited $500.

3. _____ people think through decisions. Those who are _____ often do not.

Analogies Practice

One of the common relationships used in the analogy part of the test is the "characteristic of" relationship. In this relationship, one word is a characteristic of the other word, such as "tiny is to ant".

To complete the questions below, use the following word bank:

Serene
Ostentatious
Interminable
Effervescent
Mercurial

Use the "characteristic of" relationship and the list of words above to complete the following questions.

1. Elephant is to massive as long lines is to _____.

2. Ice is to freezing as Las Vegas is to _____.

3. Silk is to smooth as pacifist is to _____.

4. Sugar is to sweet as carbonated beverages is to _____.

5. Hero is to brave as toddler is to _____.

Roots Practice

Below are three words. Write the definition for the words on the line provided. Based on their meanings, define the common root.

Carnivorous _____

Incarnation _____

Reincarnation _____

1. The root "carn" means:

   Omniscient _____

   Omnipotent _____

   Omnivorous _____

2. The root "omni" means:

3. If an "herbivore" eats plants, what does a "carnivore" eat?

4. What, then, does an "omnivore" eat?

5. Based on the meaning of the root, for whom does an "omnibus" provide transportation?

6. Based on the meanings of "incarnation" and "reincarnation," what do you think the root "re" means?

Synonyms Practice

1. INSOLENT:

   (A) happy
   (B) frightened
   (C) disrespectful
   (D) furious
   (E) timid

2. IMPETUOUS:

   (A) disillusioned
   (B) impulsive
   (C) curious
   (D) smooth
   (E) beautiful

3. MOROSE:

   (A) gleeful
   (B) conciliatory
   (C) jaded
   (D) depressed
   (E) sleepy

4. GROVEL:

   (A) beg
   (B) answer
   (C) touch
   (D) flee
   (E) forgive

5. FRUSTRATE:

   (A) assist
   (B) locate
   (C) endure
   (D) master
   (E) disappoint

6. MEDIOCRE:

   (A) grand
   (B) unexceptional
   (C) easy
   (D) constricted
   (E) forgotten

Answers to Lesson Five

Word list practice

1. stupendous
2. fraudulent
3. pragmatic; impetuous

Analogies practice

1. interminable
2. ostentatious
3. serene
4. effervescent
5. mercurial

Roots practice

1. flesh
2. all, every
3. flesh (meat)
4. everything
5. everyone (many people)
6. back, again

Synonyms practice

1. C
2. B
3. D
4. A
5. E
6. B

Lesson Six

Words to Learn

Below are the twenty words used in Lesson Six; refer back to this list as needed as you move through the lesson.

Disdain: scorn
Prognosis: forecast
Bias: prejudice
Lenient: permissive
Jaded: indifferent (not easily impressed)

Philanthropy: humanitarianism (giving to people in need)
Limpid: clear
Confound: confuse
Diagnose: identify (usually a problem)
Arrogant: proud

Arduous: difficult
Philosophy: beliefs
Bellicose: belligerent (looking for a fight)
Compassion: pity
Consensus: agreement

Bibliophile: booklover
Humility: modesty
Gnostic: wise
Distort: warp
Haphazard: disorganized

Word List Practice

Use the words from the list above to complete the following activities.

1. What word found in the word list is an antonym for humble (the adjective form of the word humility)?

2. Most people want their parents to be more _____ when it comes to curfews and house rules.

3. It can be hard for _____ people to reach a consensus with people that they disagree with.

4. It is easy to become confounded when instructions are _____.

5. Studying for exams like the SSAT is an _____ process.

Analogies Practice

One of the common relationships used in the analogy part of the test is the "means without" relationship. In this relationship, one word means without the other word, such as "prison is to freedom".

To complete the questions below, use the following word bank:

Disdain
Jaded
Arduousness
Bellicose
Arrogance

Use the "means without" relationship and the list of words above to complete the following.

1. Hearing is to deaf as naivety is to _____.
2. Food is to starving as peace is to _____.
3. Poor is to money as compassion is to _____.
4. Naked is to clothing as humble is to _____.
5. Blind is to sight as ease is to _____.

Roots Practice

Below are three words. Write the definition for the words on the line provided. Based on their meanings, define the common root.

Philanthropy _____

Philosophy _____

Bibliophile _____

1. The root "phil" means:

   Prognosis

   Diagnose

   Gnostic

2. The root "gnos" means:

3. If the root "soph" means "wise," what is a meaning of "philosophy" derived directly from its two roots?

4. Based on the meaning of "prognosis," what does someone who "prognosticates" do?

5. If the root "anthro" means "man," what is a meaning of "philanthropy" derived directly from its two roots?

Synonyms Practice

Use the crossword below to spend more time with the words in this lesson.

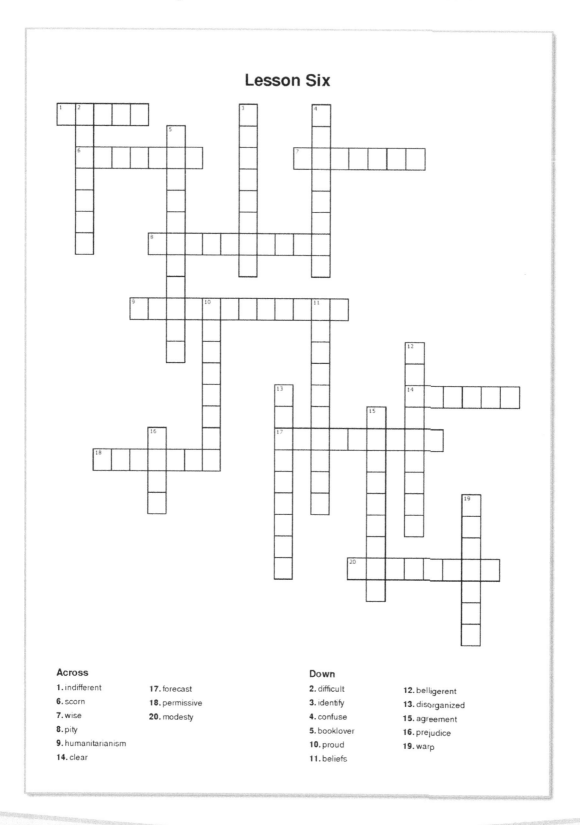

Lesson Six

Across

1. indifferent
6. scorn
7. wise
8. pity
9. humanitarianism
14. clear
17. forecast
18. permissive
20. modesty

Down

2. difficult
3. identify
4. confuse
5. booklover
10. proud
11. beliefs
12. belligerent
13. disorganized
15. agreement
16. prejudice
19. warp

Answers to Lesson Six

Word list practice

1. arrogant
2. lenient
3. bellicose
4. haphazard
5. arduous

Analogies practice

1. jaded
2. bellicose
3. disdain
4. arrogance
5. arduousness

Roots practice

1. love of
2. know
3. love of wisdom
4. make predictions
5. love of man(kind)

Synonyms practice

1. jaded
2. arduous
3. diagnose
4. confound
5. bibliophile
6. disdain
7. gnostic
8. compassion
9. philanthropy
10. arrogant
11. philosophy
12. bellicose
13. haphazard
14. limpid
15. consensus
16. bias
17. prognosis
18. lenient
19. distort
20. humility

Lesson Seven

Words to Learn

Below are the twenty words used in Lesson Seven; refer back to this list as needed as you move through the lesson.

Mediator: negotiator
Allege: claim
Deficient: lacking
Eloquent: expressive (good with words)
Exasperate: irritate

Facile: easy
Artifice: hoax (deceptive trick)
Frivolous: light-minded
Ecstasy: rapture (extreme happiness)
Proletariat: workers

Mortician: undertaker (funeral home worker)
Facilitate: help
Confection: candy
Notary: public official (who verifies signatures)
Dynamic: energetic

Facsimile: copy
Psychiatrist: therapist
Absolution: forgiveness
Cursory: brief
Lobbyist: advocate

Word List Practice

Use the words from the list above to complete the following activities.

List the five words that describe a job or occupation:
1.
2.
3.
4.
5.

6. It's best not to take a _____ look at these words, but rather to spend some time with them.

Analogies Practice

One of the common relationships used in the analogy section of the test is the "occupation" relationship. In this relationship, one word means the job of the other word, such as "architect is to building".

To complete the questions below, use the following word bank:

Notary
Mediator
Lobbyist
Proletariat
Psychiatrist

Use the "occupation" relationship and the list of words above to complete the following.

1. Legality is to lawyer as mental health is to _____.
2. Build is to contractor as advocate is to _____.
3. Article is to journalist as document is _____.
4. Ceramics is to potter as agreement is to _____.
5. Surgery is to doctors as manual labor is to _____.

Roots Practice

Below are three words. Write the definition for the words on the line provided. Based on their meanings, define the common root.

Facsimile _____

Facile _____

Facilitate _____

1. The root "fac" means:

   Artifice _____

   Deficient _____

   Confection _____

2. The root "fic/fect" means:

3. Give an alternate definition for "facilitate," using the root and the definition of "facile": to _____.

4. Based on one of the roots above, what do you think happens in a factory?

5. If the root "magni" means great, using one of the roots above, what could the definition of "magnificent" be?

6. If something is "artificial," do you think it is created by man or does it occur in nature?

Synonyms Practice

1. FRIVOLOUS:

   (A) serious
   (B) active
   (C) light-minded
   (D) bashful
   (E) ornery

2. ELOQUENT:

   (A) expressive
   (B) certain
   (C) terrified
   (D) rapacious
   (E) chatty

3. ALLEGE:

   (A) lie
   (B) frighten
   (C) leap
   (D) sigh
   (E) claim

4. DYNAMIC:

   (A) goofy
   (B) energetic
   (C) distinguished
   (D) hopeful
   (E) happy

5. ECSTASY:

   (A) rage
   (B) hope
   (C) truth
   (D) rapture
   (E) fear

6. CURSORY:

   (A) brief
   (B) easy
   (C) convoluted
   (D) shy
   (E) complicated

7. EXASPERATE:

   (A) subdue
   (B) irritate
   (C) trace
   (D) behave
   (E) despise

8. ABSOLUTION:

   (A) dinner
   (B) honesty
   (C) scent
   (D) pile
   (E) forgiveness

Answers to Lesson Seven

Word list practice

1. psychiatrist
2. mortician
3. mediator
4. lobbyist
5. notary
6. cursory

Roots practice

1. to make, to do
2. to make
3. make easy
4. things are *made*
5. made greatly
6. made by man

Analogies practice

1. psychiatrist
2. lobbyist
3. notary
4. mediator
5. proletariat

Synonyms practice

1. C
2. A
3. E
4. B
5. D
6. A
7. B
8. E

Lesson Eight

Words to Learn

Below are the twenty words used in Lesson Eight; refer back to this list as needed as you move through the lesson.

Nostalgia: longing
Precocious: advanced
Elegy: funeral song
Recuperate: recover
Enhance: increase

Posterity: descendants
Excavate: dig
Precaution: carefulness
Futile: useless
Undaunted: unafraid

Litigation: legal proceeding
Prelude: introduction
Instigate: provoke (start a fight)
Curriculum: studies
Fluctuate: waver

Demoralize: depress
Posthumous: after death
Deteriorate: worsen
Posterior: rear
Curvature: arc

Word List Practice

Use the words from the list above to complete the following activities.

1. If a book was published posthumously, would the author be able to read the finished edition? Why or why not?

2. Would a superhero more likely be described as demoralized or undaunted?

3. If something doesn't get better, it either stays the same or it _____.

4. It takes a long time to _____ after an illness like whooping cough.

Analogies Practice

One of the common relationships used in the analogy part of the SSAT is the "used for" relationship. In this relationship, one word is used for the other word, such as "voice is to sing".

To complete the questions below, use the following word bank:

Excavate
Litigation
Elegy
Curriculum

Use the "used for" relationship and the list of words above to complete the following questions.

1. Car is to transportation as jazz procession is to _____.

2. Recipe is to meal as lesson plan is to _____.

3. Pen is to writing as legal maneuver is to _____.

4. Broom is to sweep as shovel is to _____.

Roots Practice

Below are three words. Write the definition for the words on the line provided. Based on their meanings, define the common root.

Posterior _____

Posterity _____

Posthumous _____

1. The root "post" means:

Prelude _____

Precocious _____

Precaution _____

2. The root "pre" means:

3. How does the meaning of the root "pre" factor into the meaning of "precocious?" If someone is "precocious," they are "advanced before" what?

4. There is another word meaning "after death" that uses the root words "post" and "mort." Can you guess what it is?

5. If the root word "inter" means "between," and a prelude is an introduction, when do you think an "interlude" happens?

6. If "posterior" means at the end (or rear), what very similar word means "at the beginning?" (Hint: "ante" means before)

Synonyms Practice

To spend more time with the words in this lesson, complete the crossword puzzle below.

Lesson Eight

Across

2. longing   8. after death   13. recover   18. increase
3. depress   10. carefulness   15. provoke   19. useless
5. worsen   11. introduction   17. unafraid

Down

1. legal proceeding   7. descendants   14. dig
4. advanced   9. studies   16. arc
6. waver   12. rear   20. funeral song

Answers to Lesson Eight

Word list practice

1. no, because the author would be dead
2. undaunted
3. deteriorates
4. recuperate

Analogies practice

1. elegy
2. curriculum
3. litigation
4. excavate

Roots practice

1. after, behind
2. before
3. what is normal for his or her age
4. postmortem
5. in the middle
6. anterior

Synonyms practice

1. litigation
2. nostalgia
3. demoralize
4. precocious
5. deteriorate
6. fluctuate
7. posterity
8. posthumous
9. curriculum
10. precaution
11. prelude
12. posterior
13. recuperate
14. excavate
15. instigate
16. curvature
17. undaunted
18. enhance
19. futile
20. elegy

Lesson Nine

Words to Learn

Below are the twenty words used in Lesson Nine; refer back to this list as needed as you move through the lesson.

Potent: powerful
Collaborate: cooperate
Retribution: punishment
Burnish: polish
Convergence: union

Stalwart: robust (strong and dependable)
Coincide: correspond (happen at the same time)
Gusto: enjoyment
Spontaneous: impulsive
Zealous: fervent (passionate)

Deflect: divert (turn away)
Fortuitous: lucky
Succinct: brief
Genuflect: kneel
Deliberate: intentional

Premeditated: planned
Voluble: talkative
Inflection: tone (of voice)
Hybrid: mixed
Resolute: determined

Word List Practice

Use the words from the list above to complete the following activities.

When we are electing the next president, we hope that he or she is what three things from the list above?

    1.

    2.

    3.

4. If we have to watch her give a speech, however, we hope that she is not _____.

5. What is "mixed" about a hybrid car?

6. Is winning the lottery "fortuitous" or "deliberate?"

Analogies Practice

This lesson will give you more practice with the antonym relationship. Remember, antonyms are words with opposite meanings.

To complete the questions below, use the following word bank:

    Potent
    Deliberate
    Spontaneous
    Voluble

Use the antonym relationship and the list of words above to complete the following questions.

1. Up is to down as fortuitous is to _____.

2. In is to out as succinct is to _____.

3. Hard is to soft as powerless is to _____.

4. Wet is to dry as premeditated is to _____.

Roots Practice

Below are three words. Write the definition for the words on the line provided. Based on their meanings, define the common root.

Deflect _____

Genuflect _____

Inflection _____

1. The root "flect" means:

   Convergence _____

   Coincide _____

   Collaborate _____

2. The root "co/con" means:

3. What "bends" when it comes to inflection?

4. What "bends" when someone genuflects?

5. If an "incident" is an event or occurrence, what happens in a "coincidence?"

6. Using the meaning of the root "di" (apart) and the word convergence, what is a word meaning "to go in different directions from a common point?"

Synonyms Practice

1. BURNISH:

   (A) reduce
   (B) roll
   (C) light
   (D) polish
   (E) strike

2. ZEALOUS:

   (A) hyper
   (B) peaceful
   (C) ragged
   (D) slow
   (E) fervent

3. STALWART:

   (A) weak
   (B) shy
   (C) unavailable
   (D) robust
   (E) tired

4. GUSTO:

   (A) hope
   (B) fear
   (C) enjoyment
   (D) certitude
   (E) flight

5. RETRIBUTION:

   (A) punishment
   (B) glee
   (C) enjoyment
   (D) happiness
   (E) planning

6. HYBRID:

   (A) sore
   (B) mixed
   (C) clean
   (D) spinning
   (E) clear

Answers to Lesson Nine

Word list practice

1. potent
2. stalwart
3. resolute
4. voluble
5. power sources for the engine: gasoline and electric
6. fortuitous

Analogies practice

1. deliberate
2. voluble
3. potent
4. spontaneous

Roots practice

1. to bend
2. with, together
3. a voice, or the tone of a voice
4. knees
5. two events come together
6. diverge

Synonyms practice

1. D
2. E
3. D
4. C
5. A
6. B

Lesson Ten

Words to Learn

Below are the twenty words used in Lesson Ten; refer back to this list as needed as you move through the lesson.

Sustenance: nourishment
Lackluster: dull
Trajectory: path
Insurgent: rebel
Genesis: origin

Antagonistic: hostile
Illustrious: celebrated
Unkempt: messy
Trite: overused
Insurrection: revolt

Contemplate: ponder (think about)
Vogue: popularity
Lustrous: shining
Resurrect: bring back
Excruciating: agonizing

Subsistence: survival
Provenance: birthplace
Duplicity: deceptiveness
Ruminate: reflect
Averse: opposing

Word List Practice

Use the words from the list above to complete the following activities.

List three words from above that you would like to have associated with you:
1.
2.
3.

List three words from above that you would NOT like to have associated with you:
4.
5.
6.

7. If a definition of "subsist" is "keep going," do you think subsistence living includes luxuries? Why or why not?

Analogies Practice

This lesson will give you more practice with the synonym relationship. Remember, synonyms are words with the same meaning.

To complete the questions below, use the following word bank:

Genesis
Antagonistic
Ruminate
Unkempt

Use the synonym relationship and the list of words above to complete the following questions.

1. Plush is to comfortable as averse is to _____.

2. Seek is to search as contemplate is to _____.

3. Illustrious is to celebrated as messy is to _____.

4. Provenance is to birthplace as creation is to _____.

Roots Practice

Below are three words. Write the definition for the words on the line provided. Based on their meanings, define the common root.

Insurgent _____

Resurrect _____

Insurrection _____

1. The root "surg/surr" means:

   Lackluster _____

   Lustrous _____

   Illustrious _____

2. The root "lust" means:

3. Do you think supermodels prefer their hair to be "lackluster" or "lustrous?"

4. Based on the meaning of "resurrect," what do you think "resurrection" means?

5. Based on the meaning of one of the roots above, what do you think it means when the tide "surges?"

Synonyms Practice

Use the crossword puzzle below to spend more time with the words in this lesson.

Lesson Ten

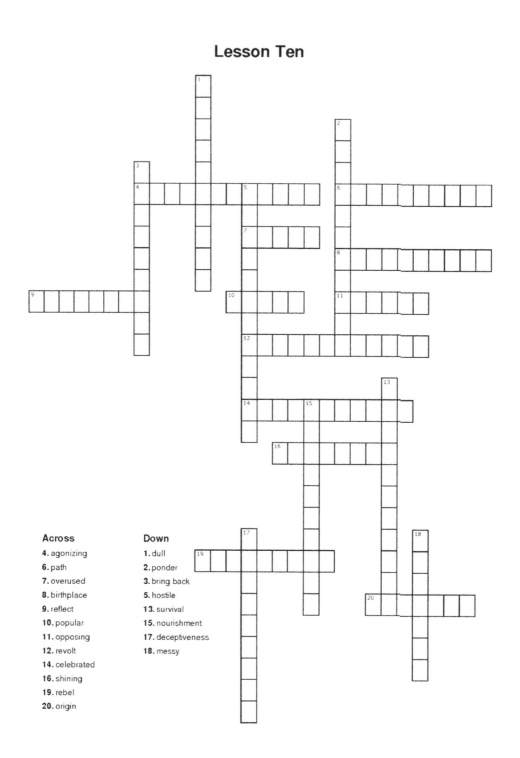

Across

4. agonizing
6. path
7. overused
8. birthplace
9. reflect
10. popular
11. opposing
12. revolt
14. celebrated
16. shining
19. rebel
20. origin

Down

1. dull
2. ponder
3. bring back
5. hostile
13. survival
15. nourishment
17. deceptiveness
18. messy

Answers to Lesson Ten

Word list practice

1. vogue
2. illustrious
3. lustrous
4. lackluster
5. unkempt
6. antagonistic
7. No – because you are living with just enough to keep going or just enough for existence.

Analogies practice

1. antagonistic
2. ruminate
3. unkempt
4. genesis

Roots practice

1. rise
2. shine
3. lustrous
4. the act of being brought back to life
5. the tides rise

Synonyms practice

1. lackluster
2. contemplate
3. resurrect
4. excruciating
5. antagonistic
6. trajectory
7. trite
8. provenance
9. ruminate
10. vogue
11. averse
12. insurrection
13. subsistence
14. illustrious
15. sustenance
16. lustrous
17. duplicity
18. unkempt
19. insurgent
20. genesis

Additional Word Lists

Challenging Vocabulary Word List

Visit www.testprepworks.com/student/download to see sample sentences with these words.

Words that make something better

allay	*soothe*
bolster	*support*
buttress	*support*
embellish	*to beautify*
rectify	*to correct*
ratify	*approve*
subside	*lessen*

Words with a positive meaning

benevolent	*kind*
deft	*nimble*
diligent	*persevering*
dogged	*persistent*
exuberant	*enthusiastic*
invincible	*undefeatable*
prudent	*wise*
reputable	*respectable*
ardor	*passion*
allure	*attract*
unerring	*perfect*
impartial	*unprejudiced*
proficient	*experienced*
timely	*well-timed*

Words that make something worse

affront	*offend*
depreciate	*lose value*
defile	*pollute*
taint	*pollute*
rend	*divide*

Words with a negative meaning

callous	*insensitive*
hapless	*unlucky*
cynical	*pessimistic*
humdrum	*boring*
laborious	*arduous*
qualm	*apprehension*
quandary	*predicament*
somber	*gloomy*
rue	*regret*
skeptical	*doubtful*

Words with a very negative meaning

appalling	*horrific*
atrocious	*dreadful*
bane	*curse*
bedlam	*chaos*
ire	*anger*
chagrin	*disappointment*
contemptible	*despicable*
despondent	*hopeless*
disreputable	*dishonorable*
havoc	*devastation*
morbid	*gruesome*
impertinent	*insulting*

Words that refer to a gathering

bevy	*group*
consolidate	*to unite*
glean	*infer or gather*
compile	*gather*
medley	*mixture*
tabulate	*to group*

Words that bring about an ending

curtail	*cut back*
dispel	*scatter*
eradicate	*exterminate*
evasion	*avoidance*
quell	*extinguish*
revoke	*take back*
revert	*regress*

Words related to being polite

demure	*reserved*
genteel	*polite*
discretion	*judgment*

Words used for name-calling

glutton	*one who overindulges*
hovel	*shack*
parochial	*insular*
naïve	*unsophisticated*
nonchalant	*unconcerned*
portly	*stout*
provincial	*unsophisticated*
putrid	*decaying*
tawdry	*cheap*
uncouth	*awkward*

Words related to happiness

enrapture	*enchant*
enthrall	*captivate*
revel	*merriment*
superlative	*outstanding*
incandescent	*glowing*

Words related to something not real

cryptic	*mysterious*
dupe	*to trick*
fallacy	*misconception*
feign	*pretend*
furtive	*stealthy*
hoax	*fraud*
bogus	*counterfeit*

Synonyms for confusing

mystical	*mysterious*
opaque	*murky*
disconcert	*perplex*

Words related to activity

inert	*unmoving*
invigorating	*energizing*
dormant	*inactive*
listless	*spiritless*
slothful	*lazy*
wan	*feeble*

Fighting words

brandish	*wield*
incite	*encourage*
incriminate	*accuse*
parry	*to deflect*
radical	*extreme*
rebuff	*reject*
rift	*disagreement*
skirmish	*conflict*
tumult	*riot*

Words related to height

apex	*peak*
dominant	*most important*
pinnacle	*peak*
ultimate	*highest*

Words related to humor

droll	*witty*
satire	*parody*
banter	*joke*

Additional words

auditory	*related to hearing*
axiom	*a truth*
befall	*happen*
belie	*contradict*
conclusive	*definitive*
delve	*research*
dilate	*expand*
dirge	*funeral song*
duct	*channel*
emancipate	*to free*
enumerate	*list*
feasible	*possible*
flaunt	*show off*
foible	*weakness*
germinate	*to grow*
idiom	*an expression*
imperative	*required*
inclination	*preference*
induce	*to cause*
inevitable	*unavoidable*
pensive	*reflective*
pertinent	*relevant*
plausible	*believable*
pliable	*flexible*
stolid	*unemotional*
sundry	*diverse*
tangent	*touching*
temperance	*moderation*
vigilant	*watchful*
wend	*to journey*
whet	*sharpen*

More Challenging Vocabulary Word List

Visit www.testprepworks.com/student/download to see sample sentences with these words.

Fighting words

accost	*attack*
assail	*attack*
contend	*compete*
pugnacious	*quarrelsome*
incendiary	*inflammatory*
renegade	*dissenter*
tirade	*diatribe*
transgress	*violate*

Words related to being a good person

affable	*friendly*
judicious	*responsible*
congenial	*friendly*
scruple	*moral*
adage	*proverb*
mien	*demeanor*
mettle	*courage*

Words that describe size and length

abridge	*shorten*
amplitude	*magnitude*
brevity	*shortness*
terse	*concise*

Words related to wanting something

acquisition	*possession*
bequeath	*grant*
covet	*desire*
procure	*obtain*
pillage	*plunder*
forbearance	*self-control*

Words that mean to approve

condone	*approve*
consecrate	*sanctify*
sanction	*approve*

Words that mean to disapprove

indict	*accuse*
refute	*disprove*
unfounded	*unjustified*

Words that make something worse

adulterated	*cheapened*
alienate	*estrange*
discredit	*tarnish*
deplete	*reduce*
relinquish	*give up*
detriment	*disadvantage*
fetter	*restrain*
impediment	*obstacle*

Words related to dislike

aversion	*disliking*
odious	*offensive*
revulsion	*dislike*

Words related to being unpleasant

condescending	*patronizing*
contemptuous	*disdainful*
disdain	*disapproval*
reproof	*criticism*
extortion	*blackmail*
ominous	*threatening*
overbearing	*domineering*
affectation	*pretension*

Words related to time

defer	*delay*
impending	*imminent*
impromptu	*unplanned*
ensuing	*following*
antiquated	*outdated*

Words indicating a lack of truth

dubious	*doubtful*
erroneous	*wrong*
fabricate	*invent*
concoct	*make up*
devious	*crafty*
ruse	*trick*
incredulous	*skeptical*
awry	*wrong*

Words indicating clarity (or a lack thereof)

ambiguous	*unclear*
contort	*twist*
precarious	*insecure*
tentative	*uncertain*
erratic	*unpredictable*
translucent	*clear*

Words related to staying calm

pacifist	*peaceful*
placid	*calm*
sedate	*relaxed*
tranquil	*restful*
repose	*relaxation*

Words to make a dramatic point

celestial	*heavenly*
eminent	*distinguished*
emphatic	*definite*
fervent	*enthusiastic*
fervor	*enthusiasm*
immaculate	*spotless*
nullify	*invalidate*
obliterate	*destroy*
rampant	*widespread*
resplendent	*gleaming*
scourge	*plague*
vehement	*insistent*
zenith	*peak*
rabid	*extreme*

Words related to memory

commemorate	*remember*
momentous	*important*
reminiscent	*suggestive of*
memento	*souvenir*

Celebratory words

carouse	*celebrate*
exultation	*rejoicing*
jocular	*joking*
raucous	*rowdy*

Words describing physical qualities

emaciated	*scrawny*
glower	*glare*
slovenly	*unclean*
supple	*flexible*
tepid	*lukewarm*
vibrant	*energetic*
disheveled	*untidy*
derelict	*abandoned*
fallow	*inactive*
inanimate	*lifeless*
decrepit	*weakened*
dilapidated	*crumbling*

Desirable qualities

candid	*honest*
debonair	*elegant*
peerless	*unrivaled*
virtuoso	*genius*

Undesirable qualities

monotone	*droning*
complacent	*unconcerned*
deranged	*insane*
inane	*insignificant*
infamous	*notorious*
fastidious	*demanding*
pompous	*arrogant*
inept	*unskilled*
gullible	*naïve*

Words describing quantity or amount

devoid	*without*
influx	*inpouring*
myriad	*many*
negligible	*paltry*
permeate	*saturate*
glut	*overfill*

Words related to putting things together

affix	*attach*
assimilate	*conform*
composite	*combined*
converse	*discuss*
discourse	*conversation*
kindred	*related*
liaison	*contact*

Words related to sadness

doleful	*sorrowful*
encumbered	*burdened*

Words that describe going off course

diffuse	*spread*
disperse	*spread*
meander	*wander*
vagrant	*wandering*

Additional words

abdicate	*resign*	lineage	*genealogy*
abrasion	*scrape*	palatable	*tasty*
abstain	*refrain*	pathos	*pity*
align	*straighten*	recourse	*reaction*
ascribe	*credit*	redundant	*repetitious*
audit	*inspect*	renaissance	*rebirth*
bulwark	*protection*	replenish	*refill*
cessation	*stopping*	rigorous	*strict*
deviate	*stray*	saunter	*stroll*
discern	*recognize*	secede	*break away*
engross	*immerse*	servitude	*slavery*
evoke	*to summon*	solace	*comfort*
fissure	*opening*	squander	*waste*
flagrant	*obvious*	stark	*bare*
habitable	*livable*	subsequent	*following*
incongruous	*incompatible*	surmount	*overcome*
infringe	*violate*	taut	*tense*
insinuate	*imply*	traverse	*cross*
invaluable	*precious*	whimsical	*fanciful*
kinetic	*moving*		

Most Challenging Vocabulary Word List

Visit www.testprepworks.com/student/download to see sample sentences with these words.

Words describing highly capable people

adroit	*skillful*
astute	*perceptive (smart, but not necessarily book smart)*
preeminent	*superior (better than anyone else)*

Words describing kind and pleasant people

altruistic	*generous*
amicable	*friendly*
credulous	*trusting*
amenable	*willing*
deference	*respect*
laudable	*praiseworthy*

Synonyms for boring or uninteresting

banal	*unoriginal*
insipid	*bland*
mundane	*ordinary*
prosaic	*dull*
vapid	*uninteresting*

Words related to a lack of progress

debase	*devalue (to reduce the value of)*
relegate	*demote (to put in a lesser position)*
impasse	*deadlock*
impede	*obstruct*

Words describing poor treatment of others

beguile	*trick*
crass	*gross*
coerce	*to force*
connive	*conspire*
flippant	*disrespectful*
animosity	*hatred*
caustic	*bitter*
deride	*mock*
disparage	*belittle (to put down)*
harangue	*scold*

Punishment or condemnation

censure	*criticize*
chastise	*discipline*
decry	*condemn*

Words related to an ending

culminate	*to complete*
definitive	*ultimate (final answer)*
incessant	*unending*

Words related to being broken

defunct	*nonfunctioning*
erode	*deteriorate*
fiasco	*failure*

Words related to enthusiasm

avid	*enthusiastic*
effervescence	*enthusiasm*
vociferous	*noisy*

Desirable qualities

discreet	*prudent (respectful of privacy)*
ingenuous	*honest*
intrepid	*fearless*
paragon	*a model (a perfect example)*
solicitous	*attentive*

Undesirable qualities

pungent	*strong smelling*
fetid	*smelly*
hackneyed	*stale (or overdone)*
ignominious	*disgraceful*
indolent	*lazy*
pariah	*outcast*
supercilious	*haughty (or snobby)*
petulant	*irritable*
taciturn	*uncommunicative*
volatile	*mercurial (changing frequently)*

Words related to truth and clarity

candor	*honesty*
guile	*deception*
conjecture	*speculate (make an assumption without the facts)*
incognito	*disguised*
indeterminate	*vague*
inexplicable	*mystifying*
nebulous	*vague*
overt	*obvious*
innuendo	*insinuation*

Words indicating a lack of energy

languid	*inactive*
lethargy	*laziness*
staid	*sedated*

Words indicating absolute or unchangeable

adamant	*uncompromising*
inalienable	*absolute*
incorrigible	*unchangeable*
indomitable	*unconquerable*

Words related to size or quantity

augment	*enlarge (make bigger)*
infinitesimal	*miniscule (tiny)*
prolific	*abundant*

Words describing an extravagant lifestyle

garish	*showy*
infamy	*disrepute (fame in a bad way)*
notoriety	*fame (for all the wrong reasons)*
opulent	*luxurious*
pretentious	*showy*

Words describing physical characteristics

lithe	*flexible*
pallid	*pale*
sedentary	*sitting*
stature	*height*

Words related to the spread of something

imbue	*permeate*
pervasive	*spread throughout*
inundate	*overwhelm*

Words with very negative meanings

ludicrous	*absurd*
lurid	*gruesome*
scathing	*severe*
squalid	*repulsive*
travesty	*mockery*

Words related to religion

sacrilege	*blasphemy (defying religion)*
sagacity	*wisdom*
hallowed	*holy*
heretic	*dissenter (vocal nonbeliever)*

Additional words

facetious	*not serious*
emanate	*originate (start from)*
abduct	*kidnap*
affinity	*attraction*
digression	*deviation (to go off course)*
entreat	*beg*
ethereal	*light*
exhort	*to caution*
extol	*to praise*
extricate	*liberate*
foray	*raid*
garner	*gather*
penitent	*remorseful*
prerogative	*a right*
remiss	*careless*
reticence	*reluctance*
vacillate	*to waver*
felicity	*happiness*
levity	*lightness*

Reading Strategies

In the SSAT reading section, you are given passages and then asked questions about these passages. In general, there tends to be about seven to nine passages in this section, but there can be slightly more or slightly less. There also tends to be four to six questions per passage, but again this is only a general guideline. For the entire section, there will be a total of forty questions. You will have forty minutes to complete the section. There will be only one reading section on your test.

- About 7-9 passages (can be more or less, though)
- Roughly 4-6 questions for each passage
- 40 total questions
- 40 minutes to complete the section
- Only one reading section

You may be thinking, "I know how to read, I am good on this section." However, most people applying to independent school know how to read. In order to get the median 50th percentile score for eighth graders on the reading section, you need to answer a little more than half of the questions correctly (and not answer the others). This means that half of the eighth graders taking this test are getting less than that.

- To get the median score for 8th grade, you need to get a little more than half of the questions correct (and not answer the others)

The issue is that not every student can get a perfect score on the reading section, so the test writers have to create a test where some students who know how to read are going to miss several questions.

So how do the test writers get you to answer so many questions incorrectly? First of all, the questions can be very detail-oriented. Think of this not as a reading test, but as looking for a needle in a haystack – with very little time to find it. Secondly, they include answer choices that take the words from the passage and switch them around so that all the same words are there… but the combination suddenly means something else. Lastly, they use your own brain against you! How do they do this?? As we read, we automatically fill in details to create a bigger picture. On this test, however, these details are often the wrong answer choices.

- Very detail-oriented questions
- Test writers rearrange words from passage to mean something else in an answer choice
- We fill in details as we read, but they aren't always correct

By making a plan and sticking to it, however, you can overcome these obstacles and beat the average score – by a lot!

In this section, first we will cover the general plan of attack and then we will get into the details that make the difference.

Reading Section Plan of Attack

Students can significantly improve their reading scores by following an easy plan:

Step 1: Plan your time
Know how many passages there are and how much time you have for each passage.

Step 2: Prioritize passages
Play to your strengths. Don't just answer the passages in the order that they appear.

Step 3: Go to the questions first
Mark questions as either specific or general. You want to know what to look for as you read.

Step 4: Read the passage
If you run across the answer to a specific question as you are reading, go ahead and answer that. But do not worry if you miss an answer.

Step 5: Answer specific questions
If there are any specific questions that you did not answer yet, go back and find the answers.

Step 6: Answer general questions
Answer any questions that ask about the passage as a whole.

Step 7: Repeat steps 3-6 with next passage
You've got it under control. Just keep cranking through the section until you are done.

Keep in mind that this section is not a test of how well you read. It is a test of how well you test. You need to manage your time and think about the process rather than the actual reading.

Step #1 – Plan Your Time

Before you do anything, take thirty seconds to plan how much time you have for each passage. To do this, count the total number of passages and then divide 40 by this number. If it doesn't come out evenly, round down so you won't run out of time.

- If there are 6 passages, you have about 6 minutes per passage
- If there are 7 passages, you have about 5 minutes per passage
- If there are 8 passages, you have 5 minutes per passage
- If there are 9 passages, you have about 4 minutes per passage

Now, look at the starting time and make a quick chart of when you should finish each passage at the top of your first page. For example, let's say there are seven passages and you start at 9:23, then your chart should look like this

Start – 9:23
1 – 9:28
2 – 9:33
3 – 9:38
4 – 9:43
5 – 9:48
6 – 9:53
7 – 9:58
End – 10:03

Note that there are an extra five minutes between when you end the 7th passage and the actual end of the section. This is because 40 minutes is not evenly divisible by 7 passages. However, you saved the hardest passages for last (you did save the hardest passages for last, right?), so you will appreciate having a few extra minutes for these.

- You may have a little extra time at the end, but you saved your hardest passages for last so you can use the extra time on those questions

Drill #1

Let's say you start a reading section and there are 8 passages.
The start time is 9:32. Fill in the chart below:

Start –

1 –

2 –

3 –

4 –

5 –

6 –

7 –

8 –

End –

(Answers to this drill are found on p. 157)

These times will give you rough milestones as you move through the test. Not every section will take you exactly the same amount of time, so don't stress if a long passage with six questions takes you a little longer. The point of planning your time is that you will know if you are taking way too long on each passage – or if you are unnecessarily rushing.

- Make a chart timing each passage before you begin
- This chart is a rough guideline – not an absolute schedule

Step #2 — Prioritize Passages

Take a quick look at your passages. In general, do your non-fiction first, then your fiction, then poetry last (if there is any poetry). If there are any passages that stick out as being really long, save those for last as well. As long as you stay on track with the timing of other passages, you can use your extra time at the end to finish these passages.

- Save really long passages for last
- Save poetry passage for the end

The following are some of the types of passages that you may see:

- *Arts* – These passages may give you a brief biography of an artist or talk about the development of a certain type of art. These tend to be straightforward, so look for them to answer early in the section.

    ✓ Answer arts passages toward the beginning of the section

- *Science* – These passages describe some scientific phenomenon or advancement in the medical field. No need to worry about deep implying or inferring questions here – we won't be asked what the stethoscope was feeling! These are good passages to answer early on.

    ✓ Answer science passages toward the beginning of the section

- *Native culture* – These passages describe some aspect or ritual of a native culture, whether it be Native American, Australian Aboriginal, or some other group. Because they are also non-fiction, they tend to be more straightforward, so prioritize these passages.

    ✓ Answer native cultures passages toward the beginning of the section

- *History* – These non-fiction passages tell about a particular era in history. Like our other non-fiction passages, these are good to answer early.

    ✓ Answer history passages toward the beginning

- *Primary Document* – These passages provide part of a document that was written during a different period in history. Generally, they come from American history, so you may see part of a speech by Abraham Lincoln, or a newspaper account from the First World War. These are a little less straightforward. Technically, no knowledge of the time period is necessary. However, if you know about the background of what the passage addresses, the odds increase of answering the inferring and implying questions correctly. With these passages, look for the ones that you know something about but save the others for later.

  ✓ If you are familiar with the topic, answer primary document passages earlier in the section. If you are not familiar with the topic, save these passages for near the end

- *Essay* – These passages consist of an author writing eloquently about a particular topic or idea. The problem with essays is that they tend to use a lot of metaphors or analogies. This makes them more fun to read, but less fun to try to translate into multiple-choice questions. Save these for toward the end.

  ✓ Save essays for near the end

- *Fiction or Folktale* – A lot of the fiction passages that you see will be folktales. These are generally stories from other cultures that have a moral or lesson as the punch line. Fiction questions tend to be very picky and the correct answer may be found in just a word or two. Fiction passages don't have the same strict organization as other passages, so trying to find the answer can be like looking for a needle in a haystack – while someone times you. Save these for the end.

  ✓ Save fiction or folktale passages for near the end
  ✓ Questions tend to be pickier and organization makes it harder to find the right answer easily

- *Poetry* – If you get a poetry passage, it should be the absolute last passage that you answer. Poetry doesn't exactly lend itself to one size fits all interpretation, but this is a multiple-choice test. Don't be surprised if you find yourself disagreeing with the test writers about the correct answers on these passages. The kicker is that their vote counts and yours does not.

  ✓ If you get a poetry passage, answer it last
  ✓ It is hard to turn a poem into good multiple-choice questions

Do you see the trend here? Straightforward nonfiction passages make it easy to pick out the right multiple-choice answer. Fiction is a little trickier. And poetry as a multiple-choice endeavor? Never a good idea.

- Nonfiction = good
- Fiction = less good
- Poetry = iffy at best

In general, you also want to answer passages that interest you most first. You don't want to wear yourself out by dragging your way through a dreadfully boring passage and then be mentally exhausted out for a passage that you do like. For example, if you have more than one nonfiction passage, then you would first answer the one(s) that you find more interesting.

Drill #2

You start the reading section. After a quick scan of each passage, you have to prioritize the order of answering the passages. Quickly number the passages below in the order that you would answer them.

Number passages 1-7 with 1 being the first passage you would answer and 7 being the last passage you would answer.

Passage topics:

Native American folktale about how people got fire: #_____

Poem: #_____

Passage about the invention of the unicycle: #_____

News article from World War I: #_____

Traditional tale from China: #_____

Passage about why we have Leap Day: #_____

Passage from a novel: #_____

(Answers to this drill are found on p. 157)

Step #3 – When You Start a Passage, Go to Questions First

It is important that you identify specific (S) and general (G) questions before you begin to read. You may come across the answer to a specific question as you read, so you also want to underline what the question is asking about for specific questions.

- Mark questions "S" or "G"
- For specific questions, underline the key word that it is asking about (if there is one)

So how do you know if it is specific or general? Here are some examples of the form that specific questions often take:

- In the first paragraph, the word _____ means
- In line 5, _____ means
- In line 7, _____ most likely refers to

If there is a line reference or the question has a lot of details in it, then it is probably a specific question.

If there is a line reference, go ahead and put a mark next to that line in the passage. That way you will know to go answer that question when you are reading. If the question asks about a specific detail, underline what it asks about so that you know what to look for when you read.

- If there is a line reference, mark that line reference in the passage
- If the question asks about a specific detail, underline that detail in the question so that you know what to look for when you read

For example, let's say our question was:

1. How many years did it take Johnny Appleseed to plant his trees?

We would underline the word "years" since that is the detail we are looking for. Presumably, the whole passage would be about him planting trees so that would not be a helpful detail to look for.

Some questions may look general, but on the SSAT they are looking for a specific example.

Here is how these questions may look:

- The author would most likely agree
- According to the passage/author
- It can be inferred from the passage
- This passage infers/implies which of the following

The reason that these questions are specific is that on the SSAT the answers to these question types will be found in a single sentence or two. In real life, that may not be true, but on this test, it is. We can't underline anything for these questions, however, since the details we are looking for are in the answer choices.

- In real life, "according to the passage" or inferring/implying questions might not be specific, but on the SSAT they are
- Nothing to underline since it is the answer choices that give details and not the questions

General questions ask about the passage as a whole.

They might look like:

- This passage primarily deals with
- This passage is mainly about
- What is the best title of this passage?
- The author's tone is

If you see the words "main" or "primary", you have a general question on your hands and should mark it with a "G".

Please keep in mind that you do not have to be correct every time when you mark "S" or "G". Do not obsess over whether a question is specific or general. The point of this strategy is to save you time and it just isn't that big of a deal if you mark one question incorrectly.

- Mark "S" or "G" quickly – not a big deal if you get it wrong

Following are some practice drills for identifying specific and general questions. Mark each question as specific or general. If the question is specific, then underline the key word or phrase that you would look for in the passage.

Time yourself on each drill so that you can see your improvement – and how easy it is to do this quickly! And remember, absolute accuracy is not a must. If we obsess over correctly labeling the questions "S" or "G", then we won't save ourselves any time.

For the following drills:

- Mark "S" or "G"
- Underline what the question is looking for if it is specific

Drill #3

1. This passage is primarily about

2. As used in line 7, "graciously" most nearly means

3. It can be inferred from the passage that all of the following statements about types of grasses are correct EXCEPT

4. According to the passage, how long did it take to travel across the country on the first transcontinental railway?

5. The author's style is best described as

Time:

(Answers to this drill are found on p. 157)

Drill #4

1. The door to the barn was probably made from

2. The sounds referred to in the passage were

3. According to the author, the musicians stopped playing because

4. An "emu" is probably a type of

5. The mood of this passage can best be described as

Time:

Drill #5

1. The sound that came from the floorboards can best be described as

2. It can be inferred that from the passage that earlier settlers did not have windows in their homes because

3. What made the citizens call a town meeting?

4. As it is used in line 15, the word "substantial" most nearly means

5. Which of the following questions is answered by information in the passage?

Time:

Drill #6

1. Which of the following best states the main idea of the passage?

2. In line 4, John Adams' use of the word "furious" is ironic for which of the following reasons?

3. How does Adams' speech reflect the idea that government is "for the people, by the people"?

4. The purpose of Adams' speech was to

5. Why does Adams use the word "mocking" in line 13?

Time:

(Answers to Drills 4-6 are found on p. 157)

Step #4 – Read the Passage

Now, you can go ahead and read the passage. If you happen to run across the answer to one of your specific questions, go ahead and answer it. If not, don't worry about it.

You have to be a little Zen about looking for the answers while you read. You can spend five minutes obsessing over finding the answer for on particular question, but if you just move on, you are likely to come across the answer later.

*   It's a little like love, sometimes you just have to let it go and trust that it will come back to you

Step #5 – Answer Specific Questions

After you finish reading, answer any specific questions that you have not yet answered. For these questions, think of it as a treasure hunt. The right answer is there, you just have to find it. Generally, you should be able to underline the exact answer paraphrased in the passage. If you can't do that, you just haven't found it yet. Keep looking. You should also think about whether or not the question fits into a particular category (we will work on those in just a minute).

When you are looking for the answer to a specific question, skim! Don't read every word, you have already done that. Look quickly for the words that you underlined in the question. Also, remember our old friend ruling out.

- Skim when looking for the answers for specific questions
- Use ruling out
- For specific questions, you should underline the correct answer restated in the passage
- Look for questions that fit into a particular category of questions

Here are five categories of specific questions that you may see on the SSAT:

- Meaning
- Questions that look general but are really specific
- Inferred/implied
- EXCEPT
- Tone or attitude about a specific topic

There are many more specific questions that do not fall into a particular category. Just keep in mind that you want to underline the correct answer in the passage for any specific questions.

Meaning questions

These questions ask you to identify the meaning of a word or statement. There are several different ways that the test writers might phrase this kind of question.

How they might look:

- In the first paragraph, the word _____ means
- Which word is closest in meaning to _____?
- Which word could be substituted for _____ without changing the meaning?

These questions aren't hard if you use our approach! Here is what you do:

- First locate the reference in the passage
- Then cross out the reference in the passage
- Plug in answer choices and see what makes the most sense

The trick for meaning questions is to not be afraid of words that you don't know.

Rule out what you know doesn't work, and if you have to guess, don't shy away from a word just because you aren't sure what it means. Remember how test writers have to make sure that not everyone is getting a perfect score? Well, students HATE to guess words that they are unsure of the meaning of. So the correct answer on these types of questions is often a word that you do not know.

- Don't shy away from a word that you do not know – it could very well be the right answer

Following is a sample passage. Use this passage to answer all of the drills for the specific question types. This book is designed so that you can tear out the passage instead of flipping back and forth. Be sure to do this so that you can develop good habits such as:

- Underlining correct answers in the passage for specific questions
- Using ruling out – physically cross out answer choices that do not work

Use the Persephone passage on the following page to answer the questions.

This page left intentionally blank so that passage can be removed from book to use for drills.

Passage for Specific Questions Drills:

The Ancient Greeks used the adventures of gods and goddesses to help them understand complex events. They used myths to try to understand things like changes in the seasons. The story of Demeter, Persephone, and Hades tells the story of what the ancient Greeks believed caused the changes in the seasons.

Line 5

The Greeks believed that the goddess, Demeter, was responsible for the growth of their crops. She was the goddess of the harvest, food, and grain. She had a daughter named Persephone who was very beautiful. One day, Persephone was kidnapped by the god of the underworld, Hades. Demeter did not know what happened to her daughter, so she looked everywhere for her.

10

While Demeter searched for her daughter, all of the crops stopped growing all over the world. She was so sad to lose her daughter that she forgot to care for the grain and harvests. The growing season stopped, living things died, and the world was facing extinction. Zeus, the king of the gods, needed to do something.

15

Zeus sent Hermes, the messenger god, to talk to Hades about returning Persephone. Hades was a tricky god and he told Hermes that he would only return Persephone if she had not eaten anything during her time in the underworld. Much to Zeus' dismay, Persephone had eaten a few pomegranate seeds, so she was forced to stay in the realm of Hades.

20

But, with much begging and pleading, Zeus and Demeter were able to strike a deal with the ruler of the underworld. Hades allowed Persephone to return to her mother for half of the year with the understanding that she had to return to the underworld for the other half of the year.

The Ancient Greeks believed when Persephone was in the underworld, it

25

was the dry time when nothing would grow. But, when Persephone returned to her mother, Demeter made sure that the land was prosperous and food and crops were plentiful.

This page left intentionally blank so that passage can be removed from book to use for drills.

Drill #7

1. In line 26, the word "prosperous" most nearly means

   (A) dark
   (B) round
   (C) light
   (D) thriving
   (E) loud

2. From the passage, it can be inferred that the word "realm" (line 19) refers to

   (A) the sky
   (B) an area ruled by a leader
   (C) a god
   (D) Hades
   (E) flowers

(Answers to this drill is found on p. 158)

Questions that look general but are really specific

On the SSAT, there will be questions that if you saw them outside of this test, you would think they were asking about the passage in general. Because we are experts on the SSAT, however, we know that these questions are really looking for a detail.

The answer can generally be found in a single sentence.

These questions might look like:

- The author would most likely agree
- According to the passage/author
- The setting of the story is

Our approach to these questions is just like any other specific question. The trick to these questions is not in how to answer them, but rather in recognizing them in the first place. You may be asking why a question about setting would be specific. The reason is that the answer is often given in just a sentence or small phrase.

- You should be able to underline the correct answer in the passage
- Skim, skim, skim until you find the answer – it is often only one word
- Use ruling out – a lot

Tricks for questions that look general but are specific:

- The test writers often take a sentence from the passage and twist it around to mean something different – just make sure you can underline the answer in the passage
- You might think they are looking for a general theme, but they are usually looking for just one or two words

The following drill includes a couple of sample questions. They refer back to the passage about Persephone.

Drill #8

1. Which of the following statements would the author most likely agree with?

   (A) Zeus had no business interfering with the fight between Demeter and Hades.
   (B) When the Greeks experienced a drought, they blamed Hades.
   (C) Demeter was not distraught when Persephone was kidnapped.
   (D) Eating pomegranates is a mistake.
   (E) The Greeks used a myth to explain why there are different seasons.

2. Which of the following questions is answered by the passage?

   (A) Who is Hermes?
   (B) Does Hades like pomegranate seeds?
   (C) What causes night and day?
   (D) What was Persephone the goddess of?
   (E) How old was Persephone?

(Answers to this drill are found on p. 158)

Inferred / implied questions

These questions make you think that you should be reading deeply into the passage. This is not the case, however.

Perhaps the passage says:

"The boy hung his head and held back the tears as he brushed the sand from his feet."

The question then asks:

Which of the following was implied by the passage?
- (A) The boy was sad and upset that his friends did not include him.
- (B) completely unrelated answer
- (C) The boy had just returned from the beach.
- (D) completely unrelated answer
- (E) completely unrelated answer

You have ruled out three answer choices and are down to choices A and C. In school, you are expected to read into passages and look for emotions when there is an implied question, so it is tempting to select choice A. However, this is the SSAT and there is no evidence that he was sad BECAUSE his friends did not include him. However, he is brushing sand off his feet, so we can assume that he was in a sandy place such as the beach. The context of the rest of the passage would matter, but the general idea is that we are not looking for deep emotions, but rather more literal answers.

- When debating between two answer choices, look for the more literal answer choice

These questions can look like:

- It can be inferred from the passage
- This passage infers/implies which of the following

To approach these questions:

- Don't do too much thinking of your own. While the words *infer* and *imply* suggest that you should be making your own leaps of thought and conclusions, they are just looking for something paraphrased from the passage.
- These are still specific questions so we are looking to underline an answer in the passage.

Tricks for implying or inferring questions:

- The answer can often be found in just a few words and is not a main idea

Complete the following drill. The question refers back to the passage about Persephone.

Drill #9

1. Which of the following can be inferred from the passage?

   (A) Zeus and Hades were longtime enemies.
   (B) Persephone got hungry while she was in the underworld.
   (C) Demeter was angry when Hermes told her that Persephone had been kidnapped.
   (D) Greece does not have real seasons like colder climates do.
   (E) Every spring a festival is held in Greece when Persephone returns from the underworld.

(The answer to this drill is found on p. 158)

EXCEPT / NOT questions

How they might look:

- All of the following are mentioned EXCEPT
- All of the following questions are answered EXCEPT
- Which of the following is NOT true?

How to approach:

- Circle the word EXCEPT or NOT – even though they put them in all caps, it is easy to forget once you start looking for an answer
- For these questions, you should be able to underline four of the answers in the passage – it is the answer that you cannot underline that is the correct one
- After you underline an answer in the passage, cross out that answer choice so that you don't choose it by mistake!

Tricks for EXCEPT questions:

- Students tend to forget the EXCEPT or NOT!

The following drill refers back to the Persephone passage.

Drill #10

1. All of the following are mentioned in the passage EXCEPT

    (A) what Hermes job was
    (B) how Demeter and Persephone were related
    (C) where Zeus lived
    (D) what Demeter was the goddess of
    (E) what kind of personality Hades had

(The answer to this drill is found on p. 158)

Tone or attitude about a specific topic questions

There are two types of tone and attitude questions. One type asks you about the author's tone or attitude in general, and one type asks what the author feels about a particular subject. It is that second type that we will focus on here.

These questions may look like:

- The author's tone regarding _____ is
- The author's attitude about _____ is

Here is our approach for these tone and attitude questions that ask about only a small part of the passage:

- Locate the part of the passage that discusses this topic
- Stick to this area while you rule out answer choices

Tricks to look out for with tone or attitude questions:

- Rule out answers that are too extreme, in a positive or negative way
- Don't be afraid of words you don't know

Please complete the drill below. The question refers back to the Persephone passage.

Drill #11

1. Which of the following best describes the author's attitude about Hades?

   (A) that he is very cunning
   (B) that he is evil
   (C) he should not have taken Persephone
   (D) that he is ultimately harmless
   (E) he likes pomegranates

(The answer to this drill is found on p. 158)

Step #6 – Answer General Questions

After answering the specific questions, you have probably reread the passage multiple times. The trick for the general questions is not to get bogged down by the details, however. How do we do this? By rereading the last sentence of the entire passage before we answer general questions. This will clarify the main idea.

- Reread last sentence of passage before answering general questions

General questions are those that are about the passage as a whole and not just a specific part of the passage.

There are 4 main types:

- Main idea
- Tone or attitude
- Organization
- Style

Main idea questions

Main idea questions are looking for you to identify what the passage is about. You can identify them because they often use the words "main" or "primarily".

- Often have the words "main" or "primarily" in them

Here is what they may look like:

- This passage primarily deals with
- The main purpose of this passage is to
- Which of the following best expresses the author's main point?
- What is the best title of this passage?

How to approach main idea questions:

- Reread the last sentence of the entire passage and look for the answer that comes closest to this sentence

Tricks to look out for with main idea questions:

- Answers that give details from the passage but are not the main idea

Usually, the wrong answers are mentioned in the passage, but they are incorrect because they are not the main idea.

Following is a passage to be used for all the general question practice drills. This book is designed so that you can tear out the page instead of flipping pages while trying to answer questions.

Please complete the following drill using the Hantavirus passage on the following page.

Passage for General Questions Drills

Many recent visitors to Yosemite National Park have been diagnosed with Hantavirus Pulmonary Syndrome. The disease is caused by infected mice, and in particular, deer mice. Exposure to the mouse feces or urine could result in human infection.

Line 5   Park officials narrowed down the problem to just a few cabins in the area of the park known as Curry Village.

California Department of Public Health and Yosemite National Park Public Health Service officers conduct routine inspections and monitor rodent activity and mouse populations. Park officials also actively perform rodent proofing inspections of all facilities and buildings throughout the park.

The CDPH recommended the park increase rodent control measures to reduce the risk of exposing visitors to the Hantavirus. Extra inspections, more thorough cleaning of the cabins, and increased overall sanitation measures have been implemented to discourage mouse infestations.

Not every deer mouse carries the hantavirus, but this is not the first time deer mice with the disease have been found in various locations throughout the United States. The first instances of Hantavirus Pulmonary Syndrome were discovered in 1993, and since then there have been more than sixty cases reported in California and another 587 cases in other states. Approximately one third of HPS cases in humans are fatal, however, the animals that carry the virus do not become ill or show any symptoms.

Symptoms of the disease usually appear between one and six weeks after exposure and are similar to those of influenza, including fever, headaches, and muscle aches. The infection progresses rapidly into severe breathing problems and sometimes death. Because of these severe consequences, the park rangers at Yosemite have taken the current outbreak of Hantavirus very seriously and are working to let visitors know who might have been affected.

This page left intentionally blank so that passage can be removed from book to use for drills.

Drill #12

1. What is the main idea of this passage?

   (A) the symptoms of the hantavirus
   (B) the history of the hantavirus
   (C) the history of Yosemite Park
   (D) a recent outbreak of the hantavirus at Yosemite
   (E) how the hantavirus is spread

2. Which of the following would be the best title for this passage?

   (A) Terror at Yosemite Park
   (B) An outbreak of a virus at Yosemite
   (C) A brief history of the hantavirus
   (D) Summertime blues
   (E) The dangers of hiking in national parks

(Answers to this drill are found on p. 158)

Tone or attitude questions

Previously, we worked on tone and attitude questions that were about a particular topic. These tone and attitude questions refer to the entire passage.

They might look like this:

- The author's tone is
- The author's attitude is

If the question does not refer to a specific part of the passage, you can assume that it applies to the passage as a whole.

How to approach:

- Reread the last sentence of the passage
- Use ruling out

Tricks to look out for with tone or attitude questions:

- Rule out answers that are too extreme, in a positive or negative way
- Don't be afraid of words you don't know
- Think about the type of passage that you are reading (fiction or non-fiction)
- Non-fiction passages tend to have correct answers that are like the words objective, informative, interested, etc.
- Fiction passages tend to have more emotional answers such as nervous, excited, determined, etc.

The following drill refers back to the passage about Hantavirus at Yosemite.

Drill #13

1. The author's tone can best be described as

    (A) disappointed
    (B) ambivalent
    (C) jealous
    (D) outraged
    (E) informative

(The answer to this drill is found on p. 158)

Organization questions

Some questions require you to think about the organization of the passage a whole.

They might look something like this:

- Which of the following will the author discuss next?
- What will (name of a character) do next?

To approach these questions:

- Next to each paragraph, label in a word or two what it is talking about
- Use these labels to look for a natural flow in what would come next

Tricks to look out for on organization questions:

- Answers that repeat the main idea of another paragraph – the author is not likely to repeat themselves
- Answers that relate to the main idea but are pretty far removed or are a much broader topic than the passage

The following drill refers back to the passage about Hantavirus at Yosemite.

Drill #14

1. Which of the following is the author most likely to discuss next?

   (A) where the hantavirus was first discovered
   (B) the history of outbreaks at other parks
   (C) what park rangers at Yosemite have learned from this outbreak
   (D) how viruses change over time
   (E) the future of vaccines

(The answer to this drill is found on p. 158)

Style questions

These questions ask you to identify where you might find a passage.

They might look like:

- What is the style of the passage?
- This passage can best be described as
- The answer choices will give different types of writing such as a newspaper article, propaganda, a manual, etc.

How to approach:

- First, ask yourself if it is fiction or non-fiction. If it is fiction, rule out any non-fiction forms. If it is non-fiction, then rule out any fiction forms.

- If it is more scholarly non-fiction (i.e. dry and boring), then the correct answer is likely to be something like a textbook or encyclopedia entry.
- If it is non-fiction but still telling a story, it might be an account of an event, a news article or item, or found in a newspaper.
- If they are trying to persuade the reader, then it could be propaganda (selling an idea) or an advertisement (selling a product).
- Fiction passages tend to be found either in a novel or in some sort of anthology.

Tricks for style questions:

- Any form of writing that is too technical won't show up on this test (medical journals, manuals, etc.)

The following drill refers back to the passage about Hantavirus.

Drill #15

1. Where would this passage most likely be found?
   (A) a personal diary
   (B) a newspaper
   (C) a diagnosis manual
   (D) correspondence between two physicians
   (E) a novel

(The answer to this drill is found on p. 158)

Step #7 – Move on to Your Next Passage and Repeat!

When you complete a passage, check your time against the chart you created before starting the section and then move on to the next passage.

- Keep track of time
- Just keep on truckin'

Secrets for Choosing the Type of Answer that Test Writers Prefer

Ruling out is particularly important on the reading section. Often, you will read through the answer choices and right away you can rule out two or three answer choices.

The art of answering reading questions correctly comes down to three things:

- Look for answer choices that are harder to argue with
- Watch out for answer choices that take words from the passage and move them around so that the meaning is different
- Be careful not to let your brain fill in details that are not there

Secret #1: Look for answer choices that are harder to argue with

The people who write the SSAT have to make sure that there is no dispute over what the correct answer is to a question.

How do they do this? When they write a question, they come up with five answer choices. Then they go back and make sure that four of those answer choices have something in them that makes them wrong. Those are the details that we want to look for!

Basically, when you are debating between two answer choices, ask yourself which one is easiest to make a case against. Rule that one out.

- Four answer choices for every question have something that makes them wrong
- Wrong answer choices are easier to argue with
- Rule out the answer choices that are easier to argue with

So what is it that makes an answer choice easy to argue with?

1. Extreme words
2. Words that leave no room for negotiation (always, never, all, etc.)

What are extreme words?

Think of words existing on a spectrum. Words in the middle are pretty neutral, but words on either end are extreme.

Here is an example:

Let's say you were looking for a word to describe your experience with the latest phone app. Here is one possible range of the words that you might use:

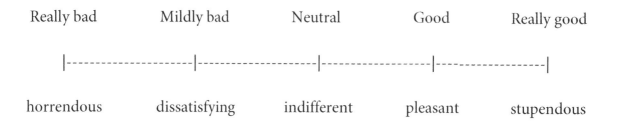

Horrendous and *stupendous* are extreme words, so they would not likely be the right answer choice on the SSAT. They are too easy to argue with. The words dissatisfying, indifferent, and pleasant, however, are more in the middle. It is harder to argue with them, so they are more likely to be correct on the SSAT.

- When you are trying to decide whether a word is extreme, think of where it would fall on a spectrum compared to other words with a similar meaning

To complete the following drill, rule out answer choices that are too extreme and choose from what is left. Yes, there is no passage! The point here is to use your knowledge of the type of answer choices that are preferred in order to answer the question.

Answer the following drill using just what you know about what types of answers tend to be right on the SSAT.

Drill #16

1. The author's attitude toward juvenile imprisonment can be described best as one of

    (A) hostile attack
    (B) enthusiastic support
    (C) sarcastic criticism
    (D) jubilant support
    (E) cautious optimism

2. Which of the following phrases would the author use to describe George Washington?

    (A) triumphant warrior
    (B) vile wretch
    (C) committed patriot
    (D) untalented ruler
    (E) tyrant

(Answers to this drill are found on p. 158)

Which words leave no room for negotiation?

Words such as always, never, and all are too easy to argue with. Let's say that I tell you that the bus is always late. That would be a really easy statement to argue with. If the bus was on time even once, then I would be wrong because I used the word always. Let's say that I tell you Abraham Lincoln never thought that the union would actually break apart. How could I possibly know that? A correct answer would say something like "there is no evidence that Abraham Lincoln thought that the union might break apart" rather than "Abraham Lincoln never thought the union would break apart."

- Words such as all, none, entirely, always, never, and all are too easy to argue with

For the following drill, pretend that you are down to two answer choices. You have ruled out the other three as definitely incorrect and now you have to choose the answer choice that is hardest to argue with. Circle the one that you would choose on the actual test.

Drill #17

1. Choice 1: Asteroids never hit the Earth.
   Choice 2: Scientists have not observed an asteroid colliding with the earth.

2. Choice 1: The facts of the story all point to the same conclusion.
   Choice 2: The story is described in a way that suggests one conclusion.

3. Choice 1: No sailors were found on the decks of the ship.
   Choice 2: None of the sailors survived the storm.

4. Choice 1: The basketball players were disappointed by the loss.
   Choice 2: All of the basketball players left the game upset because of the loss.

(Answers to this drill are found on p. 158)

Secret #2: Watch out for answer choices that take words from the passage and move them around so that the meaning is different

On the SSAT, answer choices often have words from the passage. More often than not, however, these words are twisted around so that the meaning is different. Usually the right answer choice has synonyms for words in the passage. That doesn't mean you should rule out all choices that repeat words from the passage, it just means that you should be careful when words are repeated from the passage.

- Be cautious when choosing an answer that repeats words from the passage

For example, let's say that the passage states:

John was upset when Sam got into the car with Trish.

The question may look something like:

1. Which of the following is implied by the author?
   (A) John was upset with Trish when Sam got into the car
   (B) John was upset with Trish when he got into the car
   (C) Sam and Trish were upset when John got into the car
   (D) John and Sam were cousins
   (E) John was not happy because Sam rode with Trish

Answer choices A, B, and C all use words from the passage, but do not have the same meaning as what the passage says. Choice D is just unrelated – which happens on the SSAT! Choice E restates the passage without using exact words from the passage.

In the following drill, there is a sentence from a passage. There is then a list of answer choices. You have to decide whether the answer choice has the same meaning as the passage, or whether the words have been twisted around to mean something else.

Drill #18

Passage 1: After being persuaded by the pleading of Father Thomas O'Reilly, when Sherman ordered the city of Atlanta burned, he spared the city's hospitals and churches.

Answer states:	Same meaning	Twisted meaning
1. When Sherman burned the city of Atlanta, only Father Thomas O'Reilly's church was spared.		
2. Atlanta's hospitals and churches were not ordered to be burned by Sherman.		
3. When Atlanta was burned, due to the influence of Father Thomas O'Reilly the city's churches and hospitals remained standing.		
4. Sherman ordered that Atlanta's hospitals and churches not be spared, despite the pleadings of Father Thomas O'Reilly.		

Passage 2: When the morning sun rose high above the horizon, a small boy could be spotted as he carried a bucket along the ridge of a hill in the distance.

Answer states:	Same meaning	Twisted meaning
5. A small boy was spotted along the horizon, looking almost like a bucket on the hill.		
6. Along the ridge, a child was carrying a pail in the morning.		
7. The small boy spotted the sun rising over a ridge as he carried a bucket.		
8. Far away, it was possible to see a boy carrying a bucket as he walked along the top of a hill in the morning sun.		

(Answers to this drill are found on p. 158)

Secret #3: Be careful not to let your brain fill in details that are not there

As we read, we automatically fill in details. However, the writers of the test know this and use this against you! Remember, the average student is missing a whole lot of reading comprehension questions, despite the fact that he or she probably knows how to read.

For example, let's say that the passage says:

"Samuel came from a family of enormous height – it was said that even his mother was six feet four inches tall."

Look at the following question and decide what answer choice would be a trap (we don't have enough information to pick out the right answer, we are just trying to identify the trick answer).

1. Which of the following about Samuel can be inferred from the passage?
   (A) He is well educated.
   (B) He is very tall.
   (C) His favorite past time is basketball.
   (D) He left school at an early age.
   (E) He was the first astronaut to be a pet owner.

As we read, our mind probably filled in that Samuel is tall since the passage says that his family is tall. However, the passage does NOT say that Samuel is tall. However, odds are good that our mind has already filled in the blank. The test writers know this and throw in choice B as a trick. This is exactly how they get strong readers to miss so many questions!

So how do we overcome this trick? By underlining the evidence in the passage for each answer choice for specific questions. Do not go on what you remember – if you can't underline it, it isn't the right answer choice.

- Underlining the evidence for the correct answer choice will keep you from choosing an answer where your brain has drawn its own conclusions

Also watch out for assigning emotions to other people. Let's say a story tells us that a little boy lost his dog. You might assume that he would be sad and choose an answer choice that indicates that. But maybe he always hated that dog! Unless there is evidence of a particular emotion, don't assume that the character would think or feel what you would think or feel.

- Don't assume what a character would feel, there has to be concrete evidence of that emotion

For the following drill, read the passage and then answer the question that follows. Remember to look out for our tricks!

Drill #19

> On a dark night, when there was no moon in the sky, a peddler pulled into an inn. He had come from very far away with wares to sell. When the peddler told the innkeeper why he was travelling, the innkeeper was distrustful. He had heard of peddlers and the tricks they liked to play. He said to the peddler, "I will
>
> Line 5 give you a room tonight, but in the morning I want you to show me one of your tricks for which you are so famous." The peddler wearily agreed. He stowed his nag for the night and barely made it to his room upstairs before falling asleep. In the morning, the peddler was feeling much better. As the innkeeper walked through the breakfast room, he saw the peddler talking with the innkeeper's wife
>
> 10 and showing her a quilt that matched one that the inn already had. The wife was quite excited as she was in need of another quilt. She counted out the coins for the quilt and the peddler was soon on his way once more. As he drove away, the innkeeper yelled after him, "Hey! I thought you were going to show me one of your famous tricks!" The peddler replied, "I just did. I just sold your wife the
>
> 15 quilt off of your own bed."

1. From the passage, which of the following can be inferred?

   (A) The innkeeper was furious at the peddler.
   (B) The peddler was tired after his long journey.
   (C) The innkeeper's wife was in charge off all the money in the inn.
   (D) The quilt on the innkeeper's bed was worn out.
   (E) There were no other guests at the inn that night.

(The answer to this drill is found on p. 158)

Now you know what you need to in order to excel on the reading section!

Answers to Drills

Drill #1

Start – 9:32
1 – 9:37
2 – 9:42
3 – 9:47
4 – 9:52
5 – 9:57
6 – 10:02
7 – 10:07
8 – 10:12
End – 10:12

Note that in this case the time for finishing the eighth passage was the same as the end time. This is because the forty minutes can evenly be divided among 8 passages. If there was a different number of passages, the end time wouldn't necessarily match the time to finish the last passage. You would use that extra time to go back to check your work or to work on the last passage. You did save the hardest passage for last, right?

Drill #2

There is not an absolute right order to answer these passages. The passage about the invention of the unicycle, the news article from WWI, and the passage about why we have Leap Day are all non-fiction, so they should have been in your top 3. Your order will vary depending upon what you find interesting! The Native American folktale, the traditional tale from China, and the novel passage should have been #4-6. Again, their exact order will depend on what looked good to you. The poem should be answered last. Always.

Drill #3

1. G
2. S
3. S
4. S
5. G

Drill #4

1. S
2. S
3. S
4. S
5. G

Drill #5

1. S
2. S
3. S
4. S
5. S

You might be asking yourself, would there really be a passage with all specific questions? There could be!

Drill #6

1. G
2. S
3. S or G – it depends on what the whole passage is about. Remember, we have to stay flexible when we do this.
4. G
5. S

Drill #7
1. D
2. B

Drill #8
1. E
2. A

Drill #9
1. B

Drill #10
1. C

Drill #11
1. A

Drill #12
1. D
2. B

Drill #13
1. E

Drill #14
1. C

Drill #15
1. B

Drill #16
1. E
2. C

Drill #17
1. Choice 2
2. Choice 2
3. Choice 1
4. Choice 1

Drill #18
Passage 1:
1. twisted meaning
2. same meaning
3. same meaning
4. twisted meaning

Passage 2:
5. twisted meaning
6. same meaning
7. twisted meaning
8. same meaning

Drill #19
1. B

Additional Reading Practice

The following are some passages and questions for you to practice your skills. You will see that after each passage and set of questions, there are additional questions about the process. Be sure to answer these. It is important that you don't just whip through the passages, but rather that you think about what you are doing as you go.

- Be sure to answer process questions after the questions that go with the passage

Each passage has a time recommended. You will notice that the times vary. This is because not every passage should take the same amount of time. On the real test, you will always be given the same number of minutes to complete each reading section, but the number of passages will vary so the minutes per passage will also be different. Don't think of the times given as a strict cut-off. Just know that if you take a lot longer than recommended, you need to work on speeding up the process. Alternately, if you are answering the passages a lot more quickly than recommended, you need to slow it down. Note that the process questions should NOT be included in the time given.

- Recommended times vary by passage
- Recommended times are not strict cut-offs but rather a guideline
- Process questions should NOT be done within the recommended time

Here is a general process for completing each passage:

1. Circle recommended time for each passage.
2. Start timer.
3. Mark questions "S" or "G".
4. Read, answering specific questions as you go if you can.
5. Answer any specific questions that you have not already answered.
6. Answer general questions.
7. STOP TIMER.
8. Answer process questions.
9. Check your answers – and think about WHY you missed any questions.

159

Passage 1

Recommended time: 6 minutes

When America engaged in the Civil War, men on both sides left their domestic posts and set off to meet their fates upon the battlefield. Very likely, there were many tearful farewells as husbands parted from wives and sons from mothers. Yet, in the wake of these departed warriors, most women did not sit idly *Line 5* by or wallow in their sorrow. Rather, they took hold of the swords passed on to them and led the charge of their households.

Both within and beyond their homes, many women employed their talents to contribute to the war efforts. Their passionate spirits were set ablaze with the desire for victory. Like the gallant soldiers sacrificing their lives for their 10 beliefs, women were also motivated by their views in support of or opposition to abolition, secession, and the goal of a united America.

Some, like Clara Barton, became "angels of the battlefield," nursing the wounded and providing them comfort. Some, like Rose O'Neal Greenhow, worked as spies, secretly collecting and sharing intelligence. And others, like 15 Jennie Hodgers, disguised their feminine attributes, adopted alter egos, and enlisted as soldiers. Whatever their role, these contributors displayed bravery, courage, and often, a blatant disregard for the expectations of female behavior that most people held at the time.

Passage questions

1. According to the passage, during the American Civil War women

   (A) learned to sword fight
   (B) sat idly and waited for their husbands to return
   (C) sometimes acted as spies and soldiers
   (D) were united in support of abolition
   (E) did not have an opinion on the war

2. It can be inferred that the women mentioned in the passage were greatly concerned with

   (A) what other people thought of them
   (B) defining the role of the American president
   (C) rebuilding the United States
   (D) creating nursing societies
   (E) supporting the work of male soldiers

3. This passage was probably written in order to

    (A) correct a misunderstanding about soldiers during the Civil War
    (B) explain the contribution of a particular group during the Civil War
    (C) describe the contributions of Clara Barton
    (D) prove that the Civil War would not have ended without the contribution of women
    (E) provide evidence that spies played an important role in the Civil War

4. All of the following are mentioned in the passage EXCEPT

    (A) how nurses were viewed during the Civil War
    (B) how women felt when their male relatives went off to battle
    (C) the contribution of Jennie Hodgers
    (D) causes of the Civil War
    (E) how females were expected to behave during the time of the American Civil War

5. The author's attitude toward women who lived during the American Civil War is one of

    (A) admiration
    (B) skepticism
    (C) nostalgia
    (D) amazement
    (E) indifference

6. The passage implies that an "alter ego" (line 15) is

    (A) a nurse
    (B) a soldier
    (C) a disguise
    (D) a battle
    (E) a period in American history

Process questions

Answer these questions AFTER you have stopped the timer.

1. How long did it take you to complete the passage and questions? Do you need to work more quickly next time or slow down?

2. Did you remember to mark questions as S or G before answering them? Which questions were specific? Which questions were general?

3. In question #1, some of the answer choices are traps. Which answer choices are traps and how are they trying to trick you?

4. Question #3 is a general question. One of the tricks on general questions is that answer choices provide details instead of the main idea. Which answer choices provide details from the passage but are wrong because it is a general question?

5. On tone and attitude questions, answers that are too extreme are generally wrong. Which answer choices in question #5 are too extreme?

Answers to Passage 1

Passage questions

1. C is the correct answer. The passage gives the examples of Rose O'Neal Greenhow, who became a spy, and Jennie Hodgers, who became a soldier, so we know that some women must have become soldiers or spies.

2. E is the correct answer. Choices A and D are mentioned in passage. The passage says the opposite of choice A, so we can eliminate that. Choice D is tempting because the passage says that Clara Barton was a nurse. The passage does not specifically mention nursing societies, however, so choice D is out. Choices B and C give issues that women could have been concerned about, but they aren't mentioned in the passage, so we can eliminate those. We are left with choice E.

3. B is the correct answer choice. Answer choice B is very vague – it mentions a "particular group" instead of using the word "women". If the answer choice used the word "women" instead of "a particular group", then too many students would answer the question correctly. Look for these kind of vague answers as they are often the correct answer choice.

4. D is the correct answer choice. In order to answer this question, we need to use process of elimination. Answer choices A, B, C, and E are mentioned, so we have to rule them out. We are left with answer choice D.

5. A is correct. The author's attitude about women in the Civil War is definitely positive, so we can rule out choices B and E. Choices C and D are also positive, but they are more extreme than choice A, so choice A is correct.

6. C is correct. The passage tells us that Jennie Hodgers and other women "disguised their feminine attributes, adopted alter egos".

Process questions

1. Answers will vary for this question.

2. Questions #1, #2, #4, and #6 are all specific questions. Questions #3 and #5 are general questions.

3. Answer choices A, B, and D are all traps. Answer choice A is a trap because the passage says that women "took hold of the swords" but the passage means this metaphorically and not that women were literally learning to sword fight. Answer choice B is a trap because it repeats the concept of sitting idly from the passage but the passage says that women did NOT sit by idly, so answer choice B is not correct. It would be tempting to pick B because it repeats words from the passage, however. Answer choice D also repeats words from the passage. The passage says that, "women were also motivated by their views in support of or opposition to abolition". There are a lot of tricky words there, so it can be hard to see that some women were in support of abolition and some women were against abolition. Answer choice D says that ALL of the women supported abolition, so answer choice D is also wrong.

4. Answer choices C and E both discuss details but are NOT main ideas. A common trick on general questions is answer choices that are mentioned but are NOT the main idea and therefore not the correct answer.

5. Answer choices C and D are too positive. The author definitely takes a positive attitude about the contribution of women, but answer choice A (admiration) is positive without being over the top.

Passage 2

Recommended time: 5 minutes

Have you ever wondered what happens to a plastic bottle after you deposit it in a recycling bin? Each empty vessel placed in a recycling container takes a multi-step journey of reincarnation.

Line 5   This journey begins when a recycling company collects the bottle and transports it to the local recycling plant. Since there are many types of plastic that must be processed separately, recycling facilities have workers or special equipment to sort the bottles. Then, after the bottles are sorted, food particles or other contaminants are removed. The plastic is cut into small pieces and melted down. Once this process is complete, the newly formed material is sold to other

10   companies.

What happens next is more open-ended. Depending on the type of plastic and the company that buys it, there are many possibilities for what the plastic might become. Did you ever imagine while drinking from a plastic bottle that it could one day be used to make a piece of furniture, a road, or a T-shirt?

15   Even uniforms worn by some athletes during the 2010 World Cup and 2012 Olympics were made partly from recycled plastic. Consider that the next time you finish a bottle and have to decide whether to trash it or recycle it. Why doom a bottle to endless years in a crowded landfill when it has the potential for a much more meaningful existence?

Passage questions

1. The passage implies that an important step in the recycling process is

   (A) buying the right type of plastic container
   (B) sorting different types of plastics
   (C) promoting recycled products
   (D) passing laws that encourage recycling
   (E) distributing recycling bins

2. This primary purpose of this passage is to

   (A) convince readers of the importance of a certain action
   (B) explain the different types of plastic
   (C) provide instructions for someone wanting to operate a recycling facility
   (D) describe how uniforms were made for the 2012 Olympics
   (E) create a sense of suspense about what happens to recycled bottles

3. From the passage, it can be inferred that

   (A) recycling rates are falling
   (B) more people are recycling
   (C) containers must be cleaned before they can be recycled
   (D) recycling trucks should be outfitted with automatic sorters
   (E) the same company collects used containers and produces recycled products

4. The passage mentions that all of the following products can be made from recycled plastic bottles EXCEPT

   (A) roads
   (B) uniforms
   (C) furniture
   (D) t-shirts
   (E) plastic bottles

5. The passages states that the type of product that is made from recycled plastic depends upon

   (A) the company that picks up the plastic containers from the recycling bin
   (B) how many containers are being recycled
   (C) the distance that the recycled plastic must be shipped
   (D) the type of plastic
   (E) incentives offered by the local government

Process questions

Answer these questions AFTER you have stopped the timer.

1. How long did it take you to complete the passage and questions? Do you need to work more quickly next time or slow down?

2. Did you remember to mark questions as S or G before answering them? Which questions were specific? Which questions were general?

3. Did you remember to use ruling out to answer #4? How did you know to use ruling out for this question?

4. Questions #1, #3, and #5 are all straightforward specific questions. Did you underline the answers to these questions in the passage?

Answers to Passage 2

Passage questions

1. B is the correct answer. The best way to answer this question is using process of elimination. There is simply not evidence for choices A, C, D, and E, so we can rule those out. This is a specific question and we can underline evidence for choice B, so that is the correct answer.

2. A is the correct answer choice. This is definitely a persuasive passage. The last line even asks the reader, "Why doom a bottle to endless years in a crowded landfill when it has the potential for a much more meaningful existence?" Don't be thrown by the fact that answer choice A does not mention the word "recycling". The words "a certain action" refer to recycling.

3. C is the correct answer. Remember that on the SSAT, we have to be able to underline evidence for the correct answer choice. The passage states that "after the bottles are sorted, food particles or other contaminants are removed", which is evidence that answer choice C is the right answer.

4. E is the correct answer. Although the passage talks about plastic bottles being recycled, it does not mention that new plastic bottles can be made from recycled plastic bottles. There is evidence for answer choices A-D, but since this an EXCEPT question we can rule out those answer choices.

5. D is the correct answer. In the third paragraph, the passage states "depending on the type of plastic and the company that buys it, there are many possibilities for what the plastic might become". This is the evidence that we can underline for choice D. The other answer choices certainly might affect the type of product that is made, but they are not mentioned in the passage, so they are not the correct answers.

Process questions

1. Answers will vary for this question.
2. Questions #1, #3, #4, and #5 are specific questions. Question #2 is general.
3. Any time we have an "EXCEPT" question, we have to use ruling out in order to find the answer choice that is NOT mentioned.
4. It is very important to underline the exact answer restated in the passage. These questions all have answer choices that could make sense but are wrong because they are not mentioned in the passage.

Passage 3

Recommended time: 4 minutes

Over the course of several years, all the residents of Everwood Drive had transformed from mere acquaintances to the closest of friends, with the exception, that is, of Ms. Harrington. While everyone else greeted each other with a polite smile and friendly wave, Ms. Harrington's countenance had only two
Line 5 states: grimace and scowl. The two masks looked quite similar; sharp lines cut into the forehead, furrowed brow, and downturned lips, all highlighted by a look of scorn projecting from the dark spheres set deep in their sockets. The sole difference between the two expressions was that while the grimace suggested a strong dislike, the scowl reflected an absolute hatred for whatever was within its
10 line of sight.

In fact, the only thing that Ms. Harrington didn't seem to have an intense disdain for was her flowers. The passing of months could be marked by the changing blooms that punctuated her lawn: tulips in April; rhododendrons in May; lilies in June; hydrangea in July. Despite the dark shadow that the gardener
15 cast over the street, her charges were a bright presence that imbued cheer and a joy for life. The other neighbors repeatedly marveled at the irony of it all. How could the one solitary weed within their garden of a community also be the most gifted green thumb any of them had ever seen?

Passage questions

1. The primary purpose of this passage is to

   (A) inform the reader about different types of plants
   (B) build to an exciting climax
   (C) describe a character
   (D) describe the residents of Everwood Drive
   (E) instruct readers on how to make a garden thrive

2. The passage implies that

   (A) the only time Ms. Harrington spoke with her neighbors was when they asked about her flowers
   (B) Ms. Harrington smiled when talking about her flowers
   (C) Ms. Harrington's house was not well cared for
   (D) Ms. Harrington grew different flowers in different months
   (E) Ms. Harrington lived alone

3. Ms. Harrington's countenance can best be described as

   (A) friendly
   (B) threatening
   (C) ambivalent
   (D) disinterested
   (E) calm

4. According to the passage, what leaves the residents of Everwood Drive puzzled?

   (A) how Ms. Harrington could be so mean and yet grow cheerful flowers
   (B) why Ms. Harrington is so unfriendly
   (C) how Ms. Harrington grows such a lovely lawn
   (D) why their yards look so bleak
   (E) how Ms. Harrington knows what to grow during each month

Process questions

Answer these questions AFTER you have stopped the timer.

1. How long did it take you to complete the passage and questions? Do you need to work more quickly next time or slow down?

2. Did you remember to mark questions as S or G before answering them? Which questions were specific? Which questions were general?

3. On question #1, why is answer choice D so appealing?

4. On question #2, why is answer choice E so appealing?

Answers to Passage 3

Passage questions

1. C is the correct answer choice. This passage is primarily a description of Ms. Harrington. Other answer choices are mentioned, but are details and not the main idea.

2. D is the correct answer. The passage states, "The passing of months could be marked by the changing blooms that punctuated her lawn". This is our evidence for choice D.

3. B is the correct answer choice. The word countenance is another way to say facial expression. Since she alternates between a grimace and a scowl, threatening is the best description of her expression. It isn't a perfect fit, but on this test, remember that we are looking for the "best" answer choice and since choice D is better than the other choices, it is the best answer choice.

4. A is the correct answer choice. The very last sentence of the passage tells us "How could the one solitary weed within their garden of a community also be the most gifted green thumb any of them had ever seen?" Answer choice A restates this question, so it is the correct answer.

Process questions

1. Answers will vary for this question.

2. Questions #2, #3, and #4 are all specific questions. Question #1 is general.

3. Answer choice D is mentioned in the very first sentence of the passage. It is tempting to think that the first sentence introduces the main idea, but on this test, it is actually the LAST sentence that we want to look at for general questions. Answer choices that repeat the idea from the first sentence are generally a trap.

4. As a good reader, you could easily infer that Ms. Harrington lived alone. She was cranky, had no friends, and had a lot of time on her hands for gardening. However, because there is no evidence that we could underline in the passage that she lived alone, answer choice E is not correct. This is an example of why it is so important to underline answers to specific questions because wrong answers are often logical conclusions from the passage and unless we go back and look for evidence, we don't realize that our brain has filled in that detail.

Passage 4

Recommended time: 5 minutes

> I had for my winter evening walk—
> No one at all with whom to talk,
> But I had the cottages in a row
> Up to their shining eyes in snow.
>
> *Line 5* And I thought I had the folk within:
> I had the sound of a violin;
> I had a glimpse through curtain laces
> Of youthful forms and youthful faces.
>
> I had such company outward bound.
> *10* I went till there were no cottages found.
> I turned and repented, but coming back
> I saw no window but that was black.
>
> Over the snow my creaking feet
> Disturbed the slumbering village street
> *15* Like profanation, by your leave,
> At ten o'clock of a winter eve.

Passage questions

1. Which word best describes the speaker of this poem?

    (A) lonesome
    (B) optimistic
    (C) tired
    (D) friendly
    (E) thankful

2. Why does the speaker of the poem "repent" in the middle of the poem?

    (A) He has not lived a good life.
    (B) He was mean to people who passed by.
    (C) He walked by the houses and did not choose to spend time with the
         people inside the cottages.
    (D) He disturbed the parties in the cottages.
    (E) He had not exercised enough.

3. The poem suggests that the "shining eyes" (line 4) are most likely

    (A) musical instruments
    (B) neighbors
    (C) a snow fort
    (D) cottage windows
    (E) a winter night

4. Which statement best summarizes the main lesson of this poem?

    (A) Always bundle up when you go for a walk on a winter night.
    (B) Music is important for happiness.
    (C) Walking can be lonely.
    (D) Enjoy yourself when you are young.
    (E) Do not pass up a chance to spend time with other people because you
         may not be given that chance again.

5. What do the black windows at the end of the poem represent?

    (A) nighttime
    (B) loneliness
    (C) death
    (D) triumph
    (E) winter

Process questions

Answer these questions AFTER you have stopped the timer.

1. How long did it take you to complete the passage and questions? Do you need to work more quickly next time or slow down?

2. Did you remember to mark questions as "S" or "G" before answering them? Which questions were specific? Which questions were general?

3. What do you notice about the questions for a poem passage?

4. Are poems a strength for you or are they better to answer last?

Answers to Passage 4

Passage questions

1. A is the correct answer choice. The poem describes a person walking who is looking in on other people but is not a part of the socializing. The poem also states that the speaker had "No one at all with whom to talk". This is evidence that the speaker was lonesome.

2. C is the correct answer. With poem questions, we want to stick to the words of the poem as closely as possible. To repent is to try to make up for something, so we need to look at the poem to see what the speaker might be trying to make up for. He has walked past houses without stopping in the first part of the poem and answer choice C best restates this idea.

3. D is the correct answer. Lines 3-4 state "But I had the cottages in a row/ Up to their shining eyes in snow". The speaker then goes on to describe how he can see the people who are in the cottages. This implies that the lights are on in the cottages, causing the windows to look like shining eyes.

4. E is the correct answer choice. This is a general question, so we want to be sure that we pick an answer choice that summarizes the main idea and not a detail from the passage.

5. B is the correct answer choice. At the beginning of the poem, the "shining eyes" or windows allow the speaker to feel like he is present in what is going on in the cottages. When he walks back though the village, there are no lights on, so he does not feel that he has a connection to the people in the cottages.

Process questions

1. Answers will vary for this question.

2. Questions #2, #3, and #5 are all specific questions. Questions #1 and #4 are general questions.

3. Poems have questions that require a better understanding of metaphorical (or not literal) language.

4. Answers will vary for this question. If you were very comfortable with reading into the poem then by all means answer poem passages earlier in the section. For most students, however, trying to translate a poem into multiple-choice answers is difficult and poem passages should be answered last.

Passage 5

Recommended time: 3 minutes

To the casual observer, that luminous ball of fire above us may appear to move across the heavens. It may even deceive witnesses into believing that it takes a daily journey along a path from east to west.

However, such perceived motion is merely an illusion. That magnificent
Line 5   star is static; frozen in its designated position at the heart of our solar system. The object which is actually moving is the massive globe upon which we stand. At breakneck speeds it spins us round its axis, each and every day. And year after year, it propels us in a ceaseless orbit around that central star.

Passage Questions

1. The star referred to in the passage is most likely

    (A)   the moon
    (B)   the sun
    (C)   the North star
    (D)   Earth
    (E)   Venus

2. The passage implies that some people who view the sun may believe

    (A)   the distance from the Earth to the sun changes
    (B)   the Earth is not round
    (C)   the solar system spins
    (D)   the sun moves from east to west
    (E)   we do not actually know whether it is the sun or the Earth that moves

3. What object is actually moving in the passage?

    (A)   the sun
    (B)   the moon
    (C)   the Earth
    (D)   the witnesses
    (E)   no objects are actually moving

4. According to the passage, which of the following best describes the motion of the Earth?

(A) it spins slowly
(B) it is static
(C) it is frozen in position
(D) it rotates very quickly
(E) it moves from east to west

Process questions

Answer these questions AFTER you have stopped the timer.

1. How long did it take you to complete the passage and questions? Do you need to work more quickly next time or slow down?

2. Did you remember to mark questions as S or G before answering them? Which questions were specific? Which questions were general?

3. In question #4, why are answer choices B, C, and E traps?

Answers to Passage 5

Passage questions

1. B is the correct answer choice. At the beginning of the passage, it refers to a "luminous ball of fire above us". Later, the passage refers to the same object as "that magnificent star". The star is the luminous ball of fire above us, or the sun.

2. D is the correct answer choice. In the first paragraph, the passage states that the sun may "deceive witnesses into believing that it takes a daily journey along a path from east to west". While it is not correct that the sun is moving, the passage does provide evidence that some people believe that.

3. C is the correct answer choice. The passage tells us that the "magnificent star", i.e. the sun, is static, or not moving. The object that actually is moving is the "the massive globe upon which we stand". Don't be confused by choice D. The witnesses standing on the Earth would be moving, but they are not an "object".

4. D is the correct answer choice. The passage states that the "globe upon which we stand…. at breakneck speeds it spins us round its axis". This is the evidence you should have underlined to support answer choice D.

Process questions

1. Answers will vary.

2. All of the questions for this passage were specific. Could this happen on the real SSAT? Absolutely.

3. Answer choices B, C, and E all contain words that show up somewhere in the passage, they just aren't describing the motion of the Earth.

Passage 6

Recommended time: 4 minutes

Edward sat next to his mother, analyzing the grass beneath his feet. The blades glistened with tiny dew drops, smaller than the occasional tears that slid down his mother's cheek. Every few minutes, he glanced up at the box in front of them. Behind the box stood a large portrait of his grandfather, and as long as
Line 5 Edward kept this picture from his view, he could pretend that it was a stranger in the casket.

He flipped through the memories of his grandfather arranged in his mind like files in a drawer, and one-by-one, he pulled out each memory and recalled its contents. He saw pastel colors painting the sky as the sun rose over the shore
10 where they fished together. His nostrils filled with the smell of burnt firewood from the fires they built while camping. He heard his grandfather's voice echo through his ears like rolling thunder. Often the stories told by that resounding voice were ones of far-off places full of fantastic creatures. Yet the tales Edward held dearest were the ones about a young soldier who developed his sense of
15 moral fortitude amidst the horrors of war.

So absorbed was Edward in his memories that he didn't even notice that the service had ended or that an elderly mourner stood stooped over in front of him.

"I'm sure you are going to miss your grandfather a great deal." Edward
20 startled to attention.

"Did you know my grandfather well?" he asked.

"Very well, indeed. I wouldn't even be standing here if it weren't for him saving my hide back in Normandy. Fifty years of my life are owed to him."

"Wow, sir. I didn't know my grandfather saved anyone. He told me
25 stories but never that one."

"I'm not surprised, young man. I'm not surprised at all…"

Passage questions

1. Which of the following best describes the relationship between Edward and his grandfather?

   (A) Edward resented his grandfather's success.
   (B) Edward did not know his grandfather well.
   (C) Edward and his mother lived with Edward's grandfather.
   (D) Edward was bored by his grandfather's stories.
   (E) Edward and his grandfather had a close relationship.

2. The passage suggests which of the following about Edward's grandfather?

   (A) He died too young.
   (B) He had very white hair.
   (C) His voice was deep.
   (D) He often retold the same stories.
   (E) He was gloomy by nature.

3. Why was the elderly mourner not surprised that Edward had not heard the story of his grandfather saving the elderly mourner's life?

   (A) Edward's grandfather had a strong character and would not boast.
   (B) Edward did not listen closely to his grandfather's stories.
   (C) Edward's grandfather was not actually responsible for saving the man's life.
   (D) Edward's grandfather did not like to share stories from war.
   (E) Edward did not often remember the stories that his grandfather told.

4. It can be inferred from the passage that the funeral was held

   (A) at a funeral home
   (B) outside
   (C) in a church
   (D) at Edward's house
   (E) at Edward's grandfather's house

Process questions

Answer these questions AFTER you have stopped the timer.

1. How long did it take you to complete the passage and questions? Do you need to work more quickly next time or slow down?

2. Did you remember to mark questions as "S" or "G" before answering them? Which questions were specific? Which questions were general?

3. In question #2, what words in the question let us know that this question is specific and looking for a little detail?

Answers to Passage 6

Passage questions

1. E is the correct answer. The passage tells us that Edward is quite upset by his grandfather's passing and gives examples of all the activities that the two did together. This is evidence that Edward and his grandfather had a close relationship.

2. C is the correct answer choice. The passage mentions "the stories told by that resounding voice". This question is looking for a detail and not the main idea, so we are expecting to find the answer in just a sentence or two.

3. A is the correct answer choice. This question is best answered by ruling out. Answer choice A uses the word "boast", which is kind of a strong word for the SSAT. Answer choices B-E are clearly wrong, however.

4. B is the correct answer choice. The passage states that Edward was "analyzing the grass beneath his feet". Since grass is found outside, answer choice B is correct.

Process questions

1. Answers will vary.

2. Questions #2, #3, and #4 are specific. Question #1 is general. You may not have marked question #1 as general to begin with because you may not have realized that the whole passage was about the relationship between Edward and his grandfather. Don't worry if you marked question #1 as specific. The point of this strategy is to save time and we don't want to obsess over getting the specific or general categorizations right every time. We need to stay flexible and adjust as we go.

3. The words "the passage suggests" indicate that we are looking for some picky detail. The question could also be phrased as "the passage implies which of the following" or "which of the following could be inferred from the passage". Since these questions do not give a key word to skim for, it would be tempting to think that they are general questions. Because we are experts on the SSAT, however, we know that these questions are specific and we should be able to underline the correct answer in the passage.

Passage 7

Recommended time: 5 minutes

In 1909, The New York Times declared that Robert Peary had discovered the North Pole. He was hailed as a hero after finally making it to the North Pole on his eighth attempt in 23 years. There was only one problem with this story, however. A mere week earlier, the New York Herald had declared that Frederick

Line 5   Cook had discovered the North Pole a full year earlier.

One problem with determining who first discovered the North Pole lies with the geography of the North Pole itself. Unlike the South Pole, which is located on a fixed landmass, the North Pole is set atop floating sea ice.

Generally, modern archaeologists can put together the observations of

10   many explorers from the same era and current land features to determine exactly where an explorer travelled. In the case of the North Pole, however, the sea ice could have drifted so that land features that were once over the North Pole could now be located a hundred miles from the North Pole.

Another complicating factor was that Frederick Cook wandered through

15   the wilderness for several months before being able to return to civilization again. Therefore, he was unable to report his discovery in a timely manner.

Passage questions

1. This passage is primarily about

    (A)   the geography of the North Pole
    (B)   Robert Peary's greatest achievement
    (C)   conflicting reports about a discovery
    (D)   the friendship between Robert Peary and Frederick Cook
    (E)   how Frederick Cook got lost

2. According to the passage, the South Pole

    (A)   is on solid ground
    (B)   is covered with floating sea ice
    (C)   was discovered by Robert Peary
    (D)   was discovered by Frederick Cook
    (E)   is a diverse ecosystem

3. The passage implies that Frederick Cook

   (A) was a friend of Robert Peary's
   (B) was the real discoverer of the North Pole
   (C) got lost in the South Pole
   (D) did not immediately tell other people that he had discovered the North Pole
   (E) was not a very good navigator

4. It can be inferred from the passage that modern archaeologists

   (A) think that Robert Peary first discovered the North Pole
   (B) do not find reports from other explorers of the North Pole to be helpful
   (C) consider Frederick Cook to be the real discoverer of the North Pole
   (D) credit native tribes as the first people to set foot on the North Pole
   (E) resist taking sides in the debate

5. This passage would most likely be found in

   (A) a novel
   (B) a scientific journal
   (C) an almanac
   (D) an autobiography
   (E) a history magazine

Process questions

Answer these questions AFTER you have stopped the timer.

1. How long did it take you to complete the passage and questions? Do you need to work more quickly next time or slow down?

2. Did you remember to mark questions as S or G before answering them? Which questions were specific? Which questions were general?

3. In question #3, why is answer choice D a better answer choice than answer choice E?

4. In question #1, what makes answer choice B wrong?

Answers to Passage 7

Passage questions

1. C is the correct answer. Other answer choices provide details, but not what the passage is "primarily" about.

2. A is the correct answer. This question is easy to miss because most of the passage is about the North Pole so it is easy to answer the question as if it asked about the North Pole. The only thing that the passage says about the South Pole, however, is that it is "located on a fixed landmass".

3. D is the correct answer choice. The very last sentence of the passage tells us "he was unable to report his discovery in a timely manner". Answer choice D restates this. Answer choice C is tempting because it seems as though Frederick Cook did get lost. He would have gotten lost around the North Pole, however, and choice C says he got lost in the South Pole.

4. B is the correct answer choice. The passage describes how sea ice could have drifted since Peary and Cook explored the North Pole so historical accounts would not be as helpful.

5. E is the correct answer choice. The best way to answer this question is to use process of elimination. It is a non-fiction passage, so we can rule out choice A. It is not a technical piece, however, so choice B can be ruled out. An almanac has maps in it but not historical descriptions therefore choice C can be eliminated. An autobiography is written in first person so we can rule out choice D. We are left with choice E.

Process questions

1. Answers will vary.

2. Questions #2, #3, and #4 are specific questions. Questions #1 and #5 are general.

3. It would be easy to infer that Frederick Cook was not a good navigator since he wandered in the wilderness for months. However, the passage does not give us evidence that he was lost because he was not a good navigator. On this test, the answer with the most evidence wins. Answer choice D is restated in the passage. The main lesson here is that even though the question uses the word "inferred", the better answer choice is the one that is restated in the passage.

4. The word "greatest" makes answer choice B wrong. Can you see how that word makes the answer choice easy to argue with? If the test writers had written "a great accomplishment of Robert Peary", then it would be much harder to argue with. But by saying that it was his "greatest" accomplishment, that is much more subjective to personal opinion and therefore a deal breaker on the SSAT.

Passage 8

Recommended time: 4 minutes

Men who write journals are usually men of certain marked traits—they are idealists, they love solitude rather than society, they are self-conscious, and they love to write. At least this seems to be true of the men of the past century who left journals of permanent literary worth—Amiel, Emerson, and Thoreau. Amiel's journal has more the character of a diary than has Emerson's or Thoreau's, though it is also a record of thoughts as well as of days. Emerson left more unprinted matter than he chose to publish during his lifetime.

Line 5

The journals of Emerson and Thoreau are largely made up of left-overs from their published works, and hence as literary material, when compared with their other volumes, are of secondary importance. You could not make another "Walden" out of Thoreau's journals, nor build up another chapter on "Self-Reliance," or on "Character," or on the "Over-Soul," from Emerson's, though there are fragments here and there in both that are on a level with their best work.

10

Passage questions

1. In line 2, the author states that men who write journals "love solitude rather than society". What does this imply about men who keep journals?

   (A) They enjoy writing.
   (B) They would prefer to be alone rather than in a group.
   (C) They have high ideals.
   (D) They are all exactly alike.
   (E) Their journals are very literary in nature.

2. What does the author mean when he writes that "Amiel's journal has more the character of a diary" (line 5)?

   (A) Amiel's journal shares just his personal thoughts.
   (B) Amiel's journal is more self-conscious.
   (C) Amiel's journal records more daily happenings.
   (D) Much of Amiel's journal is published in other places.
   (E) Amiel's journal has not been found in modern times.

3. Which of the following best describes the author's tone in this passage?

    (A) dismissive
    (B) amused
    (C) indifferent
    (D) excited
    (E) informative

4. Why does the author say that the journals of Emerson and Thoreau are of "secondary importance" (line 10)?

    (A) The author does not like to read those journals.
    (B) Amiel's journal has more description of daily life.
    (C) Much of the material in Emerson and Thoreau's journals was what remained from their published works.
    (D) The journals are not their best works.
    (E) They lack character.

Process questions

Answer these questions AFTER you have stopped the timer.

1. How long did it take you to complete the passage and questions? Do you need to work more quickly next time or slow down?

2. Did you remember to mark questions as S or G before answering them? Which questions were specific? Which questions were general?

3. In question #1, why are answer choices A and C both traps?

4. In question #2, why are answer choices B and D traps?

Answers to Passage 8

Passage questions

1. B is the correct answer choice. Solitude refers to being alone and society refers to being in a group. Answer choice B best restates the phrase that is referenced in the question.

2. C is the correct answer choice. We can use process of elimination for this question. We can easily rule out answer choices B, D, and E as being unrelated. Now we have to debate between choices A and C. The passage tells us that Amiel's journal is a record of daily happenings in addition to thoughts, and choice A says it "shares just his personal thoughts." We can rule out choice A. Answer choice C is the correct answer.

3. E is the correct answer choice. The passage is very dry and lacks emotion. We can rule out choices A, B, and D because they are too emotional. We can also rule out indifferent (choice C) because people do not choose to write about a subject that they are indifferent about. Informative is a great description of this passage, so choice E is the correct answer.

4. C is the correct answer. The author states that the "journals of Emerson and Thoreau are largely made up of left-overs from their published works". This implies that the journals are not as important because the best material from them is already published. Answer choice C best restates this idea.

Process questions

1. Answers will vary.
2. Questions #1, #2, and #4 are all specific questions. Question #3 is general.
3. Answer choices A and C are both restated in the same sentence as the phrase that the question references, so they are very tempting. However, the question does not ask about the whole sentence, it asks only about the meaning of a small part of the sentence.
4. Answer choices B and D repeat ideas that are found elsewhere in the passage. You could underline evidence for these answer choices, but the problem is that they do not answer the question that is asked.

Quantitative Sections – Basic Strategies

On the quantitative sections, there are problems from arithmetic, algebra, and geometry. The math is really not that hard. The SSAT is more about figuring out what concepts they are testing than remembering complicated equations.

- SSAT is more about figuring out what they are testing than hard math

You will NOT be allowed to use a calculator on the SSAT. Yes, you read that correctly. By using strategies, however, we can get to the right answers, often without using complicated calculations.

- No calculator

The goal here is for you to get a general understanding of the key strategies for the math section. Following the basic strategies are content lessons where you will get to apply these new strategies.

Drumroll, please! The strategies are:

- Use estimating – this is a multiple-choice test!
- If there are variables in the answer choices, try plugging in your own numbers
- If the question asks for the value of a variable, plug in answer choices
- If you can, find a range that the answer should fall within

Strategy #1: Use Estimating

You can spend a lot of time finding the exact right answer on this test, or you can spend time figuring out what answers couldn't possibly work and then choose from what is left.

For example, let's say the question is:

$$\frac{72,341}{2,281} =$$

1. The answer to above equation is closest to which of the following?

    (A) 72,000
    (B) 70,000
    (C) 36,000
    (D) 360
    (E) 36

If you were to do out the whole problem, that would take a long time without a calculator. However, if we look at our answer choices, we can see that most of them are pretty spread out. We just need to know roughly what the answer would be, so we can do 72,000 ÷ 2,000, which gives us 36, or answer choice E.

You can use estimating on many of the problems, but it is particularly important to estimate when the question uses the words "closest to" or "approximately".

- If you see the words "closest to" or "approximately", definitely use estimating

You can also estimate when they don't use these words. Remember that this is a multiple-choice test, so you don't have to be exact, you just have to be close enough.

In the following drill, use estimating to solve. Do not calculate an exact answer!

Drill #1

1. When 6,093 is divided by 193, which of the following is closest to the result?

   (A) 10
   (B) 20
   (C) 30
   (D) 200
   (E) 300

2. $\dfrac{49,825}{2,132}$ is closest to which of the following?

   (A) 50,000
   (B) 25,000
   (C) 2,500
   (D) 25
   (E) 2,200

(Answers to this drill are found on p. 206)

Strategy #2: Plug in Your Own Numbers if there are Variables in the Answer Choices

What do I mean by variables in the answer choices? If you look at the answer choices and some or all of them have letters in addition to numbers, then you have variables in your answer choices.

- Look for letters in the answer choices

Here is how this strategy works:

1. Make up your own numbers for the variables

   Just make sure they work within the problem. If they say that x is less than 1, do not make x equal to 2! If they say $x + y = 1$, then for heavens sake, don't make x equal to 2 and y equal to 3. Also, make sure that you write down what you are plugging in for your variables. EVERY TIME. You think you will remember that x was 4, but then you go to try out answer choices and it gets all confused. Just write it down the first time. Also, try to avoid using -1, 1, and 0 because they have funky properties and you might get more than one answer that works. The exception to this rule is when the question asks you what must be true. In that case, you want to use the funky numbers to try to rule out answer choices.

- Write down what number you are plugging in for the variable
- Avoid -1, 0, and 1 unless it is a "must be true" question

2. Solve the problem using your numbers

Write down the number that you get and circle it. This is the number you are trying to get with your answer choices when you plug in your value for the variable.

- Circle your target number

3. Plug the numbers that you assigned to the variables in step 1 into the answer choices and see which answer choice matches the number that you circled.

Below is an example. We know that this question is easy and you might not need the strategy to answer it. However, we are starting easy so you can see how the strategy works without being confused by a more difficult question.

1. Suzy has q more pencils than Jim. If Jim has 23 pencils, then how many pencils does Suzy have?

 (A) $\dfrac{q}{23}$

 (B) $q - 23$

 (C) $q + 23$

 (D) $23 - q$

 (E) $\dfrac{23}{q}$

Step 1: Plug in our own number

Let's make q equal to 4. Suzy now has 4 more pencils than Jim.

Step 2: Solve using our own numbers

If Jim has 23 pencils, and Suzy has four more than Jim, then Suzy must have 27 pencils. This is our target. Circle it. 27 is the number that we want to get when we plug in 4 for q in our answer choices.

Step 3: Plug into answer choices

We are looking for the answer choice that would be equal to 27.

(A) $\dfrac{q}{23} = \dfrac{4}{23}$

(B) $q - 23 = 4 - 23 = -19$

(C) $q + 23 = 4 + 23 = 27$

(D) $23 - q = 23 - 4 = 19$

(E) $\dfrac{23}{q} = \dfrac{23}{4}$

Choice C gives us 27, which is what we were looking for, so we choose C and answer the question correctly.

If the question asks you which answer choice is greatest or least, then you won't come up with a target number to circle. Rather, you will plug your values into the answer choices and see which one is greatest or least, depending on what the question asked for.

- If a question asks which answer choice is greatest or least, you won't come up with a target, you will just plug into answer choices

Here is an example:

2. If $m > 1$, which of the following is least?

(A) $\dfrac{m+1}{m}$

(B) $m - 1$

(C) $m + 1$

(D) $2m$

(E) $\dfrac{m}{m} - 1$

Step 1: Choose our own numbers

Let's make m equal to 2. This is a nice round number and works with the limits given by the problem (it is greater than one).

Step 2: Solve using our own numbers

For this kind of problem, we skip step 2. There is no target since we are looking to compare answer choices.

Step 3: Plug into answer choices and see what gives us the LEAST number

(A) $\dfrac{m+1}{m} = \dfrac{2+1}{2} = \dfrac{3}{2}$

(B) $m - 1 = 2 - 1 = 1$

(C) $m + 1 = 2 + 1 = 3$

(D) $2m = 2(2) = 4$

(E) $\dfrac{m}{m} - 1 = \dfrac{2}{2} - 1 = 1 - 1 = 0$

By plugging in our own numbers, we can clearly see that choice E gives us the LEAST number, so we choose choice E and get it right!

Another problem type may ask you to find an expression that gives the value of different numbers of coins. These problems have variables in the answer choices, so we can still plug in our own numbers.

- On coin problems, plug in your own numbers

The tricky thing about these problems is that they often don't put the coins in order of their value, so it is easy to mix them up. We get around that by plugging in our own numbers.

- Don't get tripped up by coins that are not in order of their value

The other trick with these questions is that they often give you a set number for one type of coin. For example, they might say that there is w quarters and r nickels, and 3 dimes. It is really easy to forget that you have to add in the actual value of the dimes, which is 30 cents, rather than just three. Plugging in your own values makes it much easier to get around this trick.

- On coin problems, be sure to plug in your own numbers so that you don't get tricked by the one coin that you know how many there are

Here is an example:

1. Which of the following gives the number of cents in b dimes, k quarters, and 3 pennies?

    (A) $\dfrac{b}{10} + \dfrac{k}{25} + 3$

    (B) $\dfrac{10}{b} + \dfrac{25}{k} + 3$

    (C) $10b + 25k + 1$

    (D) $10b + 25k + 3$

    (E) $10b + 25k + 300$

Step 1: Plug in our own number

Let's make b equal to 2 and k equal to 3.

Step 2: Solve using our own numbers

If we have 2 dimes, then the value of our dimes is 20 cents. If we have 3 quarters, then the value of our quarters is 75 cents. The problem tells us that we have 3 pennies, so the value of our pennies is 3 cents. If we add all of this together, we get 98 cents. That is our target – or the number we are looking for when we plug into answer choices.

Step 3: Plug into answer choices

We are looking for the answer choice that would be equal to 98.

(A) $\dfrac{b}{10} + \dfrac{k}{25} + 3 = \dfrac{2}{10} + \dfrac{3}{25} + 3$ (even without doing the math, we can see that this would not be even close to 98, so choice A is out)

(B) $\dfrac{10}{b} + \dfrac{25}{k} + 3 = \dfrac{10}{2} + \dfrac{25}{3} + 3$ (even without doing the math, we can see that this would not be even close to 98, so choice B is out)

(C) $10b + 25k + 1 = 10(2) + 25(3) + 1 = 96$

(D) $10b + 25k + 3 = 10(2) + 25(3) + 3 = 98$

(E) $10b + 25k + 300 = 10(2) + 25(3) + 300 = 395$

Since our target was 98 and choice D gave us 98 when we plugged in our values for the variables, we know that choice D is correct.

For the following drill, plug in your own numbers to find the correct answers. Even if you know another method of solving the problem, try to practice the strategy so you can see how it works.

Drill #2

1. Kevin has w more notebooks than Sarah. Sarah has 7 notebooks. How many notebooks does Kevin have?

   (A) $w - 7$

   (B) $7 - w$

   (C) $\dfrac{w}{7}$

   (D) $\dfrac{7}{w}$

   (E) $7 + w$

2. If $p > 1$, which answer choice is greatest?

   (A) $p - 1$

   (B) $p + 1$

   (C) $4p - 1$

   (D) $\dfrac{p}{p+1}$

   (E) $p + \dfrac{1}{p}$

3. Which answer choice gives the number of cents in r dimes, k quarters, and 3 nickels?

   (A) $\dfrac{r}{10} + \dfrac{k}{25} + 3$

   (B) $\dfrac{r}{10} + \dfrac{k}{25} + 15$

   (C) $r + 25k + 3$

   (D) $10r + 25k + 15$

   (E) $10r + 25k + 3$

4. If x is less than 0, and y is greater than 1, which of the following is GREATEST?

(A) $x - y$

(B) $\dfrac{x-y}{2}$

(C) $\dfrac{1}{x}$

(D) $\dfrac{1}{y}$

(E) $y - x$

(Answers to this drill are found on p. 206)

Strategy #3: If the Question Asks for the Value of a Variable, Plug in Answer Choices

On the SSAT, it is often easier to plug in answer choices and see what works. If the question asks for the value of a variable, you can plug in answer choices. You may also find this strategy helpful on word problems. After all, this is a multiple-choice test, so one of those answers has to work!

- If they ask for the value of a variable, plug in answer choices
- Can often use this strategy on word problems
- This is a multiple-choice test!

For this strategy, keep in mind that a variable is not always a letter. The problem might define x as the number of cars, or it might just ask you what the number of cars is. Either way, it is still asking for the value of a variable and you can use this strategy.

- A variable may not always be a letter, it can be any unknown quantity

Whenever a question asks for the value of a variable, whether it is a letter or something like the number of bunnies, one of those answer choices has to work. Since this is a multiple-choice test, you just have to figure out which one. Ruling out is one of our most important strategies and this scenario is just another example of how valuable a tool ruling out can be.

- Remember the mantra: Ruling out is good

Here are the steps for using this strategy:

Step 1: Put your answer choices in order from least to greatest if they are not already in that order

They usually are already in order, but the SSATB sometimes mixes things up.

Step 2: Plug the middle answer choice into the problem to see if it works

The exception to this rule is if the question asks what is the least number or greatest number. If they ask for the least number, start with the least number, and if they ask for the greatest number, then start with the largest number.

- Usually we start in middle
- If they ask for the least number, start with the least number
- If they ask for the greatest number, start with the largest number

Step 3: If the middle choice does not work, go bigger or smaller depending on what you got for the middle answer choice

Here is an example:

1. A fence is going to be built around a rectangular cow pasture. The width of the fenced-in area is to be half the length of the fenced-in area. If the farmer uses exactly 24 yards of fencing, what is the width of the fenced in area?

    (A) 1 yard
    (B) 2 yards
    (C) 3 yards
    (D) 4 yards
    (E) 8 yards

In this case, the answer choices are already in order (they usually are), so we can skip step 1 and go right to step 2.

Step 2: Plug in the middle answer choice

In this case, we make the width equal to 3 in order to test out answer choice C. If the width was 3 yards, then the length would be 6 yards. If we add 2 widths and 2 lengths, then we would get a perimeter of 18 yards. The problem tells us that the distance around should be 24, however, so we know that choice C does not work. Not only do we know that choice C does not work, but we also know that we need a greater width in order to get a perimeter of 24 yards.

Step 3: Go bigger or smaller if the middle answer choice did not work

Next, we make the width 4 yards in order to test out choice D. If the width was 4 yards, then the length would be 8 yards. If we add 2 widths and 2 lengths to get the perimeter, then the perimeter in this case would be 24 yards. That is exactly the distance around that the problem gave us, so we know that choice D is correct.

For the following drill, try plugging in answer choices to see what works. Even if you know how to solve another way, you need to practice this strategy because there will be a time when you need it to bail you out.

Drill #3

1. There are six tables available at a restaurant. Each table can seat up to five people. There are ten people waiting in line. What is the maximum number of tables that can have only one person?

   (A) 2
   (B) 3
   (C) 4
   (D) 5
   (E) 6

2. Gertrude has 17 baseball cards. Sam has 11 baseball cards. How many baseball cards must Gertrude give to Sam if they are going to have the same number of baseball cards?

   (A) 2
   (B) 3
   (C) 4
   (D) 5
   (E) 6

3. If $q > 6$, then $3q + 5$ could be

   (A) 20
   (B) 21
   (C) 22
   (D) 23
   (E) 24

4. Which answer choice could be the value of X if $\frac{1}{6} + X > 1$?

(A) $\frac{1}{6}$

(B) $\frac{1}{3}$

(C) $\frac{1}{2}$

(D) $\frac{5}{6}$

(E) $\frac{11}{12}$

(Answers to this drill are found on p. 206)

Strategy #4: If You Can, Find a Range that the Answer Should Fall Within

Since you are not allowed to use a calculator on this test, try to see if you can at least figure out what two numbers an answer should fall in between.

- No calculator + multiple choice test = find a range

Here is an example:

1. $90 - 6\frac{7}{18} =$

(A) $82\frac{11}{18}$

(B) $83\frac{11}{18}$

(C) $84\frac{7}{18}$

(D) $84\frac{11}{18}$

(E) $85\frac{11}{18}$

To solve this problem, you could do a lot of math. Or you could figure out what the answer should fall in between and then use the fact that this is a multiple-choice test to your advantage.

The number $6\frac{7}{18}$ falls in between 6 and 7. $90 - 6 = 84$ and $90 - 7 = 83$. That tells you that your answer should fall in between 83 and 84. Only answer choice B does, so that is the correct answer.

For the following drill, try to find a range and then rule out rather than computing an exact answer.

Drill #4

1. $54 - 5\frac{3}{5} =$

   (A) $47\frac{3}{5}$

   (B) $48\frac{2}{5}$

   (C) $49\frac{2}{5}$

   (D) $49\frac{3}{5}$

   (E) $50\frac{3}{5}$

2. 8 percent of 150 is

   (A) 6
   (B) 8
   (C) 10
   (D) 12
   (E) 15

(Answers to this drill are found on p. 206)

Those are the basics that you need to know for the math section. As you go through the content sections, you will learn content and the strategies that work for specific problem types.

Answers to Math Strategies Drills

Drill #1
1. C
2. D

Drill #2
1. E
2. C
3. D
4. E

Drill #3
1. D
2. B
3. E
4. E

Drill #4
1. B
2. D

Math Content Sections

We have covered the basic strategies for the math section. Now, we are going to take a look at some of the problem types that you will see on this test.

On the SSAT, sometimes the math to solve a problem is not that hard. However, the tough part of that problem might be recognizing what direction to go and what concept is being tested.

Doing well on the math section is often a matter of decision making. You need to decide what type of problem you are working on as well as what the most efficient way to solve will be.

Each lesson will:

- Teach you the facts that you need to know
- Show you how those facts are tested
- Give you plenty of practice

That is the book's side of the bargain, but you also have to keep up your end of the deal.

As you work through the content always ask yourself:

- What makes this problem unique?
- How will I recognize this problem in the future?

You are on your way to crushing the SSAT math section!

Math Fundamentals

Now let's put the fun in fundamentals.

If you are one of those students who think that math basics are no laughing matter, not to worry. You really don't have to know a lot of definitions or equations. The SSAT is testing your ability to reason and recognize concepts, not your ability to memorize.

This section will teach you what you need to know, just what you need to know, and nothing more.

This section will cover:

- Different kinds of numbers that you need to know
- How to interpret equation/inequality language
- The math facts that you will need to know
- Negative numbers – adding and subtracting
- Converting units
- Place value
- Questions that explicitly test PEMDAS
- Probability

Different Kinds of Numbers

On the SSAT, you will need to know what some different kind of numbers are. They include:

- Integer
- Whole number
- Positive
- Negative
- Even
- Odd
- Consecutive

Integers and whole numbers are very similar. Simply put, they are numbers that do not have decimals or fractions. For example, 0, 1, 2, and 3 are all integers as well as whole numbers. The difference is that integers include negative numbers. On this test, however, they don't really require you to know the difference between integers and whole numbers. You just need to know that if they ask for an integer or a whole number, the correct answer cannot have a fraction or decimal.

- If they ask for integer or whole number, no decimals or fractions

Positive numbers are those that are greater than zero. Negative numbers are those that are less than zero. The only tricky thing about positive and negative numbers is that zero is neither positive nor negative. The SSAT is not likely to ask you if zero is positive or negative, but they might tell you that a variable is positive, in which case you have to know that it can't equal zero.

- Zero is neither positive nor negative

Even numbers are those integers that are evenly divisible by 2. That means that you can divide even numbers into groups of two with nothing left over. Odd numbers are those that cannot be evenly divided by 2. By this definition, zero is an even number because it can be divided by two with nothing left over. Even numbers are 0, 2 4 6, and so on. Odd numbers are 1, 3, 5, and so on.

- Zero is an even number

Consecutive numbers are simply integers that are next to each other when you count. For example, 1 and 2 are consecutive numbers. There are also consecutive even numbers and consecutive odd numbers. These are just the numbers that would be next to each other if you counted by twos. For example, 2 and 4 are consecutive even numbers and 1 and 3 are consecutive odd numbers. The SSAT is not going to ask you if numbers are consecutive, but they will ask you to apply this information. If you see the words "consecutive even numbers" or "consecutive odd numbers", circle them because it is really easy to do just plain consecutive numbers and forget about the even or odd.

- Consecutive just means in a row
- Look out for consecutive even and consecutive odd numbers because it is easy to forget the even or odd part

On the SSAT, they don't directly test these definitions. They are not going to ask you which of the following numbers is positive. But they will ask you to apply the information.

Here is an example of how these concepts may be tested:

1. If the average of five consecutive whole numbers is 22, what is the greatest of the numbers?

    (A) 18
    (B) 20
    (C) 22
    (D) 23
    (E) 24

When we have consecutive numbers, this means that they are all in a row if you were counting. This also means that the middle number is also the average of the numbers (this works as long as there is an odd number of numbers, which is how the SSAT tests this concept). Since there are five numbers, the average (22) is the third number. Since we are looking for the greatest number, we want to count up to the fifth number. The third number is 22, the fourth number is 23, and the fifth number is 24. Since 24 is the greatest number, choice E is correct.

Interpreting Equation / Inequality Language

On the SSAT, you may see language that describes in words what you often see written as an equation or inequality.

You just have to translate these words into an equation or inequality in order to solve.

Here is a cheat sheet for some of what you may see:

If the test says:	Then it can be written as:
X is between 3 and 5	$3 < X < 5$
X is greater than 6	$X > 6$
X is less than 10	$X < 10$

The thing that you need to keep in mind about between, greater than, and less than is that they don't include the numbers themselves. For example, if X is between 3 and 5, then it cannot be either 3 or 5.

Here is an example of how these concepts are tested:

1. M is a whole number that is between 5 and 8. M is also between 6 and 13. Which of the following is M?

   (A) 5
   (B) 6
   (C) 7
   (D) 7.5
   (E) 8

If we drew out a number line, we would see that our number has to be bigger than 6 and smaller than 8. Because the problem uses the word between we know that 6 or 8 cannot be included. That leaves us with choices C and D. However, the problem also says that M is a whole number. The number 7.5 is not a whole number, so choice D is out. Choice C is correct.

There will also be times when the wording gives hint as to what operation should be completed.

Here is a guide to some of the language you may see:

If the test says:	Then it can be written as:
...of...	Multiply
...how many more...	Find the difference (subtract)
...how many times...	Divide
...sum...	Add
...difference...	Subtract
...divisible by...	Divide and look for a number that does not leave a remainder
...into how many...	Divide

Once again, the test usually asks you to apply this information.

Here are some examples of how this information is tested:

2. On Wednesday, Sheila had sold 324 boxes of cookies. Her goal was to sell 410 boxes by Sunday. How many more boxes of cookies must she sell between Wednesday and Sunday?

   (A) 34
   (B) 76
   (C) 86
   (D) 410
   (E) 734

The question uses the words how many more, so we know we need to subtract, or find the difference.

If we subtract $410 - 324$, then we get 86, so choice C is correct.

Here is another example of a question that tests your ability to apply equation language:

3. Tommy brought a cake to school for his birthday. There are 12 kids in his class. If he wants every student to get an equal number of pieces of cakes with none left over, into how many pieces could he cut his cake?

   (A) 6
   (B) 18
   (C) 20
   (D) 36
   (E) 40

This question uses the words "into how many", so we know that we have to divide. It also tells us that he wants each student to have the same number of pieces of cake, so we are looking for a number that is divisible by 12, since there are twelve students. The only answer choice that is evenly divisible by 12 is choice D, so it is correct.

The Math Facts You Need to Know

Don't worry, you don't need to learn a lot of math facts for this test.

It is helpful to know:

1. Multiplication/division facts up to 12
2. Single digit addition/subtraction facts
3. Multiples of 15 (15, 30, 45, 60, 75, 90)
4. Multiples of 25 (25, 50, 75, 100, and so on)

We won't take the time to go over these facts here, but if you are rusty on your facts, be sure to practice them. There are a ton of good apps out there and it doesn't really matter which one you choose. You just want to make sure that these facts are automatic for you since no calculators are allowed on the SSAT.

It can also be helpful to know some basic divisibility rules. You don't absolutely have to know these as long as you can do the problems out by hand. It can save you time if you know divisibility rules, however.

Here are some of the easier rules. There are rules for numbers divisible by 7 and 8, but they are hard to remember and therefore not so helpful!

If …	Then it is divisible by …
the number is even	2
you add up all the digits of the number and the result is divisible by 3 (example: $231 = 2 + 3 + 1 = 6$ and 6 is divisible by 3)	3
the last two digits of your number are divisible by 4 (example: 549,624 and 24 is divisible by 4)	4
the number ends in 0 or 5	5
the number is divisible by both 2 and 3	6
you add up all the digits and the result is divisible by 9 (example: $3,726 = 3 + 7 + 2 + 6 = 18$ and 18 is divisible by 9)	9
the number ends in 0	10

You should also know that if a number is divisible by the factors of a number it is also divisible by that number. For example, if a number is divisible by 5 and 3, it is also divisible by 15.

Here is an example of how divisibility could be tested:

1. If $j + k$ is divisible by 5, which answer choice is also divisible by 5?

   (A) $(j \times k) + 5$

   (B) $j + (5 \times k)$

   (C) $(5 \times j) + k$

   (D) $(2 \times j) + (2 \times k)$

   (E) $\dfrac{j+k}{5}$

To solve this problem, let's plug in our own numbers since there are variables in the answer choices. Let's make $j = 2$ and $k = 3$.

If we plug into answer choices, we get:

   (A) $(j \times k) + 5 = (2 \times 3) + 5 = 11$

   (B) $j + (5 \times k) = 2 + (5 \times 3) = 17$

   (C) $(5 \times j) + k = (5 \times 2) + 3 = 13$

   (D) $(2 \times j) + (2 \times k) = (2 \times 2) + (2 \times 3) = 10$

   (E) $\dfrac{j+k}{5} = \dfrac{2+3}{5} = \dfrac{5}{5} = 1$

Since only answer choice D gives us a number that is divisible by 5, it is the correct answer.

Math facts are not directly tested on the SSAT, but you will be required to apply them as you solve other problem types.

You will also need to know how to do the basic operations. You will need to add, subtract, multiply (including multi-digit numbers), and divide (including long division). We aren't going to work on that here, but if your skills are rusty, be sure to do a little practice.

The trick to SSAT questions that test math facts and basic operations is that you often have to figure out exactly what they are testing. The SSAT is much more about application than just listing facts.

Here are some examples of questions that you might see that test math facts and operations:

2. The perimeter of Figure 1 is 42. If all of the sides are of equal length, then the length of one side is

    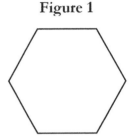

    Figure 1

    (A) 4
    (B) 5
    (C) 6
    (D) 7
    (E) 8

Nowhere does this problem use the word division, but you must divide in order to figure out the side length. Since the total distance around the six sides is 42, we divide 42 by 6 to get the length of each side. The answer is 7, so the correct answer is choice D.

Sometimes we have to think about whether to round up or round down.

3. Grace needs to buy 23 t-shirts for her class. The t-shirts come in packages of 10. How many packages must she buy?

    (A) 1
    (B) 2
    (C) 3
    (D) 4
    (E) 5

The trick to this problem is that Grace has to buy more t-shirts than she needs. If we divide 23 by 10, then we get 2 with remainder 3. However, we can't not have enough t-shirts, so with this problem type, the remainder tells us to round up. The correct answer is C.

Another problem type that requires you to use your math facts involves questions that ask you to multiply two numbers and then divide by a different number.

Here is what that type of question looks like:

4. Five students are each chipping in $6 to buy their teacher a gift. If a sixth student decided to contribute, how much would each student pay in order to share the cost?

    (A) $1
    (B) $3
    (C) $5
    (D) $6
    (E) $8

To solve this problem, we first have to figure out the total cost of the gift. Since there were five students and they each gave $6, we can figure out that the gift cost $30. This $30 is now being split among six students, so we divide 30 by 6. This tells us that each student would have to contribute $5. Answer choice C is correct.

Negative Numbers – Adding and Subtracting

One way to approach these problems is just to draw out a number line and remember to move to the right for adding and to the left for subtracting.

For example, let's say that we have to do the following problem:

$$-7 + 15 =$$

First, we draw out the number line and mark -7.

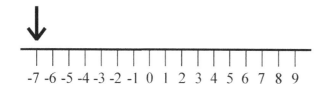

Now, because we are adding, we move 15 spots to the right.

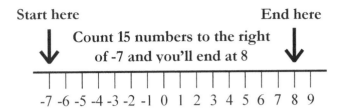

We can now see that the answer is 8.

When we use a number line, we have to remember a couple of rules. Here are the basics:

- If we add a negative number, it is the same as subtracting that positive number.

  Example: $3 + (-5) = 3 - 5 = -2$

- If we subtract a negative number, then it is the same as adding the positive number.

  Example: $3 - (-2) = 3 + 2 = 5$

We will do a couple of examples of this problem type:

1. Calculate: $(-14) + (-8) + 32$
   - (A) -54
   - (B) 10
   - (C) 26
   - (D) 32
   - (E) 54

To answer this question, let's think of the number line. We are starting at negative 14. Now we have to subtract 8 since adding a negative number is the same as subtracting that positive number. That means we must move 8 spaces to the left of -14. We are now at -22. Now we have to add 32, or move 32 spaces to the right. It takes us 22 spaces to get back to 0, and then we have to move an additional 10 to the right so that we have moved a total of 32 spaces. We are left at positive 10 for an answer. Choice B is correct.

2. $4 + 12 - (-14) =$

   (A) -2
   (B) 2
   (C) 4
   (D) 22
   (E) 30

In order to answer this question, we have to remember that subtracting a negative number is the same as adding that positive number. This means that our problem is really just $4 + 12 + 14$, which is equal to 30. Answer choice E is correct.

Often the negative number questions are phrased as word problems and you have to figure out what to do.

Here is an example of how this concept might be tested.

3. At 5 A.M., the temperature on top of Mt. Washington was 8 degrees below zero. By 10 A.M., the temperature had risen by 15 degrees. What was the temperature on top of Mt. Washington at 10 A.M.?

   (A) 23° below zero
   (B) 7° below zero
   (C) 7° above zero
   (D) 8° above zero
   (E) 15° above zero

We can use a number line to solve. We will start at $-8°$ and then move to the right since the temperature increased.

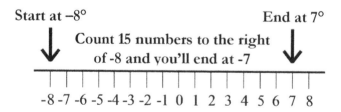

The correct answer is choice (C).

Conversion Questions – What You Need to Know and How to Spot Them

The SSAT also loves to include problems that require you to convert between units. The trick to these problems is generally not that the conversion is hard, but rather that it is easy to not notice that the conversion needs to be done! Watch out for problems that use multiple units, such as feet and yards, in the same problem.

- If you see units, circle them to make sure that you are finding the answer in the correct units

You don't need to memorize a lot of conversions. You basically need to know:

- 12 inches = 1 foot
- 3 feet = 1 yard
- The basics of the metric system
  - 1,000 milli-units = 1 base unit (ex: 1,000 mg = 1 g)
  - 100 centi-units = 1 base unit (ex: 100 cm = 1 m)
  - 1,000 base units = 1 kilo-unit (ex: 1,000 m = 1 km)
- Basic time conversions
  - 60 seconds in a minute
  - 60 minutes in an hour

That's not so bad, right?

Here are a couple of examples of how this concept is tested:

1. A piece of string must be cut into 4-inch pieces. If the string is 3 feet long, how many pieces will the string be cut into?

   (A) 3
   (B) 4
   (C) 7
   (D) 8
   (E) 9

We are talking inches and feet in this problem. Let's convert the 3 feet into inches. Since 1 foot equals 12 inches, that means 3 feet equals 36 inches. The string is 36 inches long and has to be cut into 4-inch pieces. So how many 4-inch pieces can the 36-inch string be cut into? Divide 36 by 4, and you get 9 pieces that are each 4 inches long. The correct answer is choice E.

2. The Smiths want to build a fence around their yard. The perimeter of their yard is 504 feet. The fencing comes in pieces that are 8 yards long. How many pieces of fencing will the Smiths need in order to build their fence?

    (A) 21
    (B) 48
    (C) 63
    (D) 120
    (E) 504

We are talking feet and yards in this problem. The perimeter is 504 feet, so let's convert this to yards. There are 3 feet in 1 yard. We divide 504 feet by 3 to get 168 yards for the perimeter. Now the question is how many pieces of fence do they need? One piece of fence is 8 yards, and they need enough pieces of fence for 168 yards. Divide 168 yards by 8 yards, and you see you need 21 pieces of fencing. Answer choice A is correct.

3. One piece of candy weighs 43 mg. If a box contains 150 pieces of candy, then the whole box of candy weighs how many grams?

    (A) 5.45
    (B) 545
    (C) 6.45
    (D) 645
    (E) 6,450

To solve this problem, we first have to multiply 43 by 150 in order to get the number of mg. If we do this, the result is 6,450 mg. The trick here is to not choose answer choice E! The problem doesn't ask for mg, it asks for grams. In order to convert 6,450 mg to grams, we have to divide by 1000. This tells us that the box weighs 6.45 grams, so answer choice C is correct.

Here is an example that requires you to convert between different units of time.

4. John is raking leaves and can fill $\frac{3}{5}$ of a cart every minute. How many carts can he fill in an hour?

   (A) 12
   (B) 18
   (C) 24
   (D) 36
   (E) 48

In order to solve, we first have to convert an hour into 60 minutes so that the problem has all the same units. Then, we multiply $\frac{3}{5}$ times 60 in order to figure out how many carts John can fill in 60 minutes. This gives us that 36 carts can be filled in an hour, so answer choice D is correct. If you had trouble with multiplying $\frac{3}{5}$ times 60, be sure to review the fractions section.

The SSATB may also ask you to do questions that require you to convert between units of different systems. Don't worry, the test question will give you the conversion factor for these less common conversions.

- The test question will give you the conversion factor if you need to convert between the different systems

In order to answer these questions, we can use proportions.

- Can use a proportion to solve

For example, let's say the question tells us that there are 28 grams in one ounce and then asks us how many ounces 84 grams is equal to. We can use x to represent the number of ounces and set up a proportion.

$$\frac{28\ g}{1\ oz} = \frac{84\ g}{x\ oz}$$

Now we can use cross-multiplying to solve:

$$28x = 84 \times 1$$

$$x = 3$$

Now we know that 3 ounces is equal to 84 g.

Here are a couple of examples for you to try:

5. Jill is running a 5-km race. She is wearing a watch that tells her that she has run 2.48 miles. How much farther does she have to run? (1 km = 0.62 mi.)
    (A) 0.62 miles
    (B) 1.24 miles
    (C) 1.48 miles
    (D) 2.52 miles
    (E) 3.1 miles

Our first step in answering the question is to figure out how many miles are in a 5K race. We can use a proportion for this:

$$\frac{1 \text{ km}}{0.62 \text{ mi.}} = \frac{5 \text{ km}}{x \text{ mi.}}$$

Now we can cross-multiply and solve:

$$1 \times x = 5 \times 0.62$$

$$x = 3.1 \text{ miles}$$

This tells us that the total distance she needs to run is 3.1 miles. We are not done yet, though. The question asks for how much farther she needs to run, so we need to subtract the distance she has run (2.48 miles) from the total that she needs to run (3.1 miles). We get that she has 0.62 miles left to run, so answer choice A is correct.

6. In order to travel on a certain road, a truck plus its cargo must weigh less than 10 tons (one ton is equal to 2,000 pounds). If the truck alone weighs 2,000 kg, then what is the largest mass of cargo that the truck could carry? (1 kg = 2.2 pounds)

   (A) 12,000 pounds
   (B) 14,500 pounds
   (C) 15,600 pounds
   (D) 16,800 pounds
   (E) 20,000 pounds

We have to do a couple of conversions here. First, we have to figure out the total permissible weight in pounds (and not tons).

$$\frac{1 \text{ ton}}{2{,}000 \text{ pounds}} = \frac{10 \text{ tons}}{y \text{ pounds}}$$

$$y = 20{,}000 \text{ pounds}$$

Now that we know the permissible weight in pounds, we have to figure out what the empty truck weighs in pounds.

$$\frac{2{,}000 \text{ kg}}{x \text{ pounds}} = \frac{1 \text{ kg}}{2.2 \text{ pounds}}$$

$$x = 4{,}400 \text{ pounds}$$

Now we have to subtract the weight of the truck from the total weight allowed in order to find the mass of cargo that the truck could carry.

$$20{,}000 - 4{,}400 = 15{,}600 \text{ pounds}$$

Answer choice C is correct.

Place Value – Just the Important Stuff

Another basic concept that is tested is place value.

Consider the number 354. This number is really made up of 3 separate numbers: The "4" is 4 ones. The "5" is 5 tens, and the "3" is 3 hundreds. These 3 numbers are added up as 4 + 50 + 300 to get 354. Here is a chart to help you remember place values.

We will use the number 457,208.196 as an example.

4	5	7	2	0	8	.	1	9	6
Hundred thousands	Ten thousands	Thousands	Hundreds	Tens	Ones	Decimal point	Tenths	Hundredths	Thousandths

Look at the digit 2, which is in the hundreds place. It represents a value of 200, because it represents 2 hundreds which is 200. Similarly, the digit 5 represents 5 ten thousands, so its value is 50,000.

The number 829 is really the result of adding three numbers together: 8 hundreds (800) plus 2 tens (20) plus 9 ones (9).

Another way to think of the number 829 is: $(8 \times 100) + (2 \times 10) + (9 \times 1)$.

The first type of question you may see has a number written out in words and then asks you for the numerical equivalent, or vice versa. The trick to these questions is to remember that if a place value is not mentioned then it must be marked with a 0 in the numerical equivalent. Similarly, if one of the digits of a number is zero, then that place value should not appear in the written out equivalent. Also, if you see the word "and", it indicates a decimal point.

- If a place value is not mentioned, it needs to be marked with a zero
- If one of the digits of a number is 0, then that place value should not be mentioned in the written out equivalent
- The word "and" indicates a decimal point

Here are a couple of samples for you to try:

1. Which number is equivalent to three thousand forty-seven and fourteen thousandths?

    (A) 3,047.014
    (B) 3,047.14
    (C) 3,407.014
    (D) 3,407.14
    (E) 3,470.014

This one is pretty straight-forward. We just need to remember that because the hundreds place is not mentioned, there should be a 0 in that place. Only answer choices A and B have a 0 in the hundreds place, so we can rule out choices C, D, and E. Now we just have to recognize that for decimals, the last digit should go in the place value mentioned. In this case we have 14 thousandths, so the 1 should go in the hundredths place and the 4 should go in the thousandths place. Answer choice A is correct.

2. Which is equivalent to 10,030.27?

    (A) ten thousand three hundred and twenty-seven
    (B) ten thousand thirty twenty-seven
    (C) ten thousand three hundred twenty-seven
    (D) ten thousand thirty and twenty-seven hundredths
    (E) ten thousand three hundred and twenty-seven hundredths

All of our answer choices begin with ten thousand, so we can't use that to rule anything out. The next number is 30, so we know we are looking for an answer choice that begins with ten thousand thirty. That leaves us with choices B and D. Answer choice B doesn't even make sense – thirty and twenty have the same place value so they can't appear in the same number. Answer choice D is correct.

462.3<u>4</u>1

3. In the above number, what is the value of the underlined digit?

    (A) 4 hundredths
    (B) 4 tenths
    (C) 4 ones
    (D) 4 tens
    (E) 4 hundreds

In the above question, the underlined digit is in the hundredths place. That means that the value of the 4 is 4 hundredths, so answer choice A is correct.

The next type of question you may see asks you to decide which number or digit has the greatest value in numbers that have decimal points. The trick to these questions is that you have to remember the place value and not just the value of a digit. For example, a 6 in the hundreds place is really worth 600 and not 6.

Here are a couple of examples for you to try:

4. In the number 304,598.27, which digit has the greatest value?

   (A) 3
   (B) 4
   (C) 5
   (D) 7
   (E) 9

We have to remember that the further to the left that a digit appears, the greater its value (unless it is a zero). Since 3 is the furthest digit to the left, the correct answer is choice A.

5. Which of the following is greater than 3.78?

   (A) 3.09
   (B) 3.80
   (C) 3.43
   (D) 3.71
   (E) 3.55

If we look at the answer choices, we want to evaluate them from left to right since digits further to the left are greater in value. All the answer choices begin with 3, so we can't use that to eliminate any answers. In the next place to the right (the tenths place), we are looking for a number with a tenths digit greater than 7. If we look at answer choice B, that is the only choice with a tenths digit greater than 7. Answer choice B is correct.

Here is another place value problem that may look a little different from how you have seen place value tested before.

6. $4\overline{)436} =$

(A) $\dfrac{4}{4} + \dfrac{3}{4} + \dfrac{6}{4}$

(B) $\dfrac{4}{4} \times \dfrac{3}{4} \times \dfrac{6}{4}$

(C) $\dfrac{400}{4} \times \dfrac{30}{4} \times \dfrac{6}{4}$

(D) $\dfrac{400}{4} + \dfrac{30}{4} + \dfrac{6}{4}$

(E) None of these expresses $4\overline{)436}$

This problem doesn't want you to do long division. It wants you to use the idea of place value to rewrite the long division problem into a place value problem. The number 436 is really the same thing as 4 hundreds plus 3 tens plus 6 ones, or 400 + 30 + 6. So when we divide 436 by 4, we can think of the division problem like this:

$$\frac{436}{4} = \frac{400}{4} + \frac{30}{4} + \frac{6}{4}$$

We can see that answer choice D is correct.

Questions that Explicitly Test PEMDAS

You may see a question on the SSAT that tests whether or not you recognize when to apply the order of operations, or PEMDAS. The trick to these questions is to see what they are really testing rather than just jumping in and solving from left to right. These questions are usually just a string of calculations.

- If you see a question that is essentially a string of calculations, it is testing whether you WILL apply PEMDAS and WON'T just solve from left to right

Here are a couple of examples:

1. Evaluate: $36 - 5(4) + 35 \div 7$
   - (A) 7
   - (B) 21
   - (C) 22
   - (D) 23
   - (E) 35

The key to this question is that we have to remember that multiplication and division are done before addition and subtraction, so we have to multiply 5 by 4 and divide 35 by 7 before we do the other operations.

$$36 - 5(4) + 35 \div 7 = 36 - 20 + 5 = 21$$

Answer choice B is correct.

2. Evaluate: $60 - (4^2) \div 2 + 6$
   - (A) 28
   - (B) 36
   - (C) 45
   - (D) 58
   - (E) 68

In order to answer this question, we have to first take care of the exponent within the parentheses.

$$60 - (4^2) \div 2 + 6 = 60 - 16 \div 2 + 6$$

Now we have to take care of the division:

$$60 - 16 \div 2 + 6 = 60 - 8 + 6$$

Now we can perform any addition or subtraction:

$$60 - 8 + 6 = 58$$

Answer choice D is correct.

Probability

You may see a basic probability question on the SSAT. You aren't likely to see a complicated question with multiple events. Also, you may see a question that uses the word "probability" but is mainly testing another concept.

Probability is the chance that something will happen out of a total number of events. For example, let's say that there are 10 marbles in a bag and three of them are yellow. We would say that the probability of choosing a yellow marble is 3 out of 10. The key to these questions is figuring out how many total events there are and then figuring out how many of these events are the ones we are looking for.

Here are a couple of examples:

1. A deck of cards is labeled 1-25. If a card is chosen at random, what is the probability that the number on the card will be divisible by both 2 and 3?

   (A) $\dfrac{1}{25}$

   (B) $\dfrac{3}{25}$

   (C) $\dfrac{4}{25}$

   (D) $\dfrac{1}{5}$

   (E) $\dfrac{2}{5}$

This question may use the word "probability", but it is mainly testing divisibility rules. In order for a number to be divisible by both 2 and 3, it must also be divisible by 6. The numbers divisible by 6 but less than 25 are 6, 12, 18, and 24. This means that out of 25 events, 4 of them are the ones we are looking for. The probability of choosing a number divisible by both 2 and 3 is therefore $\dfrac{4}{25}$, or answer choice C.

2. If w is an integer and $2 < w < 17$, then what is the probability that w is divisible by 4 but NOT divisible by 3?

(A) $\dfrac{1}{7}$

(B) $\dfrac{3}{14}$

(C) $\dfrac{1}{5}$

(D) $\dfrac{1}{2}$

(E) $\dfrac{4}{7}$

First, we can determine that there are 14 integers between 2 and 17. Then, we can list out the numbers between 2 and 17 that are factors of 4. This gives us 4, 8, 12, 16. Now we have to eliminate the numbers that are also a factor of 3. Since 12 is also a factor of 3, we can take 12 off of our list. We are left with 3 numbers out of a total of 14 numbers between 2 and 17. Answer choice B is correct.

Be sure to complete the practice set for more of these types of problems!

Math Fundamentals Practice Set

1. K is an integer. K is between three and seven. K is also less than five. What is the value of K?

    (A) 3
    (B) 4
    (C) 4.5
    (D) 5
    (E) 6

2. $7\overline{)406}$ =

    (A) $\dfrac{4}{7} + \dfrac{6}{7}$

    (B) $\dfrac{4}{7} + \dfrac{0}{7} + \dfrac{6}{7}$

    (C) $\dfrac{400}{7} + \dfrac{0}{7} + \dfrac{6}{7}$

    (D) $\dfrac{400}{7} \times \dfrac{6}{7}$

    (E) $\dfrac{40}{7} + \dfrac{6}{7}$

3. If $6 < j < 25$, what is the probability that j is divisible by both 4 and 6?

    (A) $\dfrac{1}{10}$

    (B) $\dfrac{1}{9}$

    (C) $\dfrac{3}{20}$

    (D) $\dfrac{2}{9}$

    (E) $\dfrac{1}{3}$

4. $3 - (6 + 2) \div 4$

   (A) $-\dfrac{1}{4}$

   (B) 1

   (C) $\dfrac{5}{4}$

   (D) 4

   (E) 8

5. A basketball team was four points behind their opponents with a minute left in the game. The team then scored nine points in the last minute and their opponents did not score any more points. How many points did the team win by?

   (A) 1 point
   (B) 2 points
   (C) 4 points
   (D) 5 points
   (E) 9 points

6. Janice measures the length of her running stride and finds it to be 4 feet. She runs around a track measuring 220 yards. How many strides did she run?

   (A) 55
   (B) 110
   (C) 165
   (D) 220
   (E) 880

7. Evaluate: $-14 + 8 - 3$

   (A) -25
   (B) -9
   (C) -3
   (D) 2
   (E) 25

8. In the number 479,265.38, which digit has the least value?

   (A) 2
   (B) 3
   (C) 5
   (D) 8
   (E) 9

9. We can express the product 6×952 as

   (A) $(6 \times 900) + (6 \times 50) + (6 \times 2)$
   (B) $(6 \times 900) \times (6 \times 50) \times (6 \times 2)$
   (C) $(6 + 900) \times (6 + 50) \times (6 + 2)$
   (D) $(6 + 900) + (6 + 50) + (6 + 2)$
   (E) None of the above

10. Kim plans to buy balloons for a party. She wants one balloon for the back of each chair and there a total of 27 chairs at the party. If the balloons come in packages of six, how many packages of balloons must she buy?

   (A) 4
   (B) 5
   (C) 6
   (D) 8
   (E) 9

11. A bag hook can hold a maximum of 15 pounds without being pulled off the wall. If the bag itself weighs 20 oz., then what is the greatest mass that can be added to the bag before the hook is pulled off of the wall?
   (1 pound=16 ounces)

   (A) 220 ounces
   (B) 200 ounces
   (C) 150 ounces
   (D) 100 ounces
   (E) 5 ounces

12. Which number is equivalent to five thousand thirty-two and twenty-six thousandths?

    (A) 5,302.26
    (B) 5,302.026
    (C) 5,032.026
    (D) 5,032.26
    (E) 5,002.326

13. In the number 253.874, what is the value of the underlined digit?

    (A) 8 hundredths
    (B) 8 tenths
    (C) 8 oneths
    (D) 8 ones
    (E) 8 tens

14. The Smith family is saving up for a vacation. Four children are contributing $5 per week in order to reach their weekly goal. If a fifth child also contributed, how much would each child have to pay in order to reach their weekly goal?

    (A) $1
    (B) $3
    (C) $4
    (D) $5
    (E) $7

15. There are balls labeled $4 - 20$ in a bag. If a ball is drawn at random, what is the probability that the number on the ball will be divisible by both 2 and 3?

    (A) $\dfrac{3}{5}$

    (B) $\dfrac{1}{2}$

    (C) $\dfrac{2}{5}$

    (D) $\dfrac{5}{17}$

    (E) $\dfrac{3}{17}$

16. Which number is greater than 4.62?

    (A) 4.32
    (B) 4.61
    (C) 3.63
    (D) 4.70002
    (E) 3.0009

17. A bottle holds 2 L of soda. If it is evenly divided among 20 small cups, how many mL would be in each cup?

    (A) $\dfrac{1}{10}$

    (B) $\dfrac{2}{10}$

    (C) 2

    (D) 10

    (E) 100

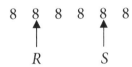

18. The digit 8 in place R has a value that is how many times the value of the digit 8 in place S?

    (A) 1
    (B) 10
    (C) 100
    (D) 1,000
    (E) 10,000

19. Evaluate: $4 + 2 \times 3 - (-7)$

    (A) 11
    (B) 17
    (C) 20
    (D) 24
    (E) 25

20. Which answer is equivalent to 9,602.078?

   (A) nine thousand six hundred two and seventy-eight thousandths
   (B) nine thousand six hundred twenty and seventy-eight
   (C) nine thousand six hundred twenty and seventy-eight hundredths
   (D) nine thousand six hundred two and seventy-eight hundredths
   (E) nine thousand six hundred two and seventy-eight tenths

Answers to Math Fundamentals Practice Set

1. B	11. A
2. C	12. C
3. B	13. B
4. B	14. C
5. D	15. E
6. C	16. D
7. B	17. E
8. D	18. D
9. A	19. B
10. B	20. A

Fractions and Decimals

On the SSAT, you will need to be able to:

1. Compare fractions
2. Place fractions on a number line (including improper fractions)
3. Add and subtract fractions
4. Multiply fractions
5. Add and subtract mixed numbers and whole numbers
6. Solve inequalities that have fractions
7. Convert fractions into decimals
8. Basic operations with decimals

There are some basic rules that you need to know for fractions on the SSAT. They won't be tested directly, but you will need them in order to solve other questions correctly. They are:

1. You can multiply or divide the numerator (top number) as long as you multiply or divide the denominator (bottom number) by the SAME number. This allows us to create *equivalent fractions* – or fractions that are equal in value.
2. If you want to add or subtract fractions, you have to get the same bottom number (or common denominator). Use *equivalent fractions* to do that. You then add or subtract the top numbers, but keep the same bottom number (common denominator).
3. If you want to multiply fractions, you multiply across the top and then across the bottom (you DON'T figure out a common denominator).

Creating Equivalent Fractions

The cardinal rule for equivalent fractions is that if you multiply the top by some number, you must also multiply the bottom by the same number in order for the value of the fraction to remain the same. This also works when you divide the top and bottom by the same number. You can NOT add or subtract the same number from both the top and the bottom and keep the same value, however.

For example:

$$\frac{1}{2} \times \frac{2}{2} = \frac{2}{4}$$ Since we multiplied the numerator (top number) and denominator (bottom number) by the same number, we know that $\frac{1}{2} = \frac{2}{4}$

$$\frac{1+2}{2+2} = \frac{3}{4}$$ Since we added the same number to the numerator and denominator, $\frac{1}{2}$ is NOT equal to $\frac{3}{4}$

Comparing Fractions

Some questions will ask you to compare fractions to a particular fraction. In other words, you will be asked which fraction is greater than or less than another fraction.

In order to do this, you need to get a common denominator. Rather than looking for a denominator that all of the answer choices go into, it is easier to set up a different equivalent fraction for each answer choice. These equivalent fractions should be equal to the fraction in the question and have the same denominator as the answer choice so that they can be easily compared.

- Set up an equivalent fraction for each answer choice

Take a look at this example:

1. Which of the following fractions is less than $\frac{1}{4}$?

(A) $\frac{10}{40}$

(B) $\frac{4}{8}$

(C) $\frac{5}{16}$

(D) $\frac{3}{20}$

(E) $\frac{7}{24}$

To solve, make a chart:

Answer choice	Equal to $\frac{1}{4}$	Which is smaller?
(A) $\frac{10}{40}$	$\frac{10}{40}$	Equal
(B) $\frac{4}{8}$	$\frac{2}{8}$	$\frac{1}{4}$
(C) $\frac{5}{16}$	$\frac{4}{16}$	$\frac{1}{4}$
(D) $\frac{3}{20}$	$\frac{5}{20}$	Answer choice!
(E) $\frac{7}{24}$	$\frac{6}{24}$	$\frac{1}{4}$

From my chart, I can see that only choice D is smaller than $\frac{1}{4}$, so choice D is correct.

Here is another one for you to try:

2. Which of the following fractions is greater than $\frac{2}{3}$?

(A) $\frac{8}{12}$

(B) $\frac{7}{14}$

(C) $\frac{7}{9}$

(D) $\frac{11}{18}$

(E) $\frac{1}{6}$

Again, let's create our chart!

Answer choice	Equal to $\frac{2}{3}$	Which is greater?
(A) $\frac{8}{12}$	$\frac{8}{12}$	Equal
(B) $\frac{7}{14}$	See note	$\frac{2}{3}$
(C) $\frac{7}{9}$	$\frac{6}{9}$	Answer choice!
(D) $\frac{11}{18}$	$\frac{12}{18}$	$\frac{2}{3}$
(E) $\frac{1}{6}$	$\frac{4}{6}$	$\frac{2}{3}$

Note: 14 isn't divisible by 3, so equivalent fractions won't work easily. But we can see that $\frac{7}{14}$ is equal to one-half, so we know it has to be less than $\frac{2}{3}$.

We can see that answer choice C is correct.

You may also see questions that ask you to put fractions in order. For these questions, the test writers usually choose fractions that are relatively easy to find a common denominator for. You can use equivalent fractions to rewrite the fractions with a common denominator and then put them in order.

Here is one of these questions for you to try:

3. Write the following fractions in order from least to greatest: $\dfrac{7}{10}, \dfrac{2}{3}, \dfrac{3}{5}$

(A) $\dfrac{7}{10}, \dfrac{2}{3}, \dfrac{3}{5}$

(B) $\dfrac{7}{10}, \dfrac{3}{5}, \dfrac{2}{3}$

(C) $\dfrac{2}{3}, \dfrac{7}{10}, \dfrac{3}{5}$

(D) $\dfrac{2}{3}, \dfrac{3}{5}, \dfrac{7}{10}$

(E) $\dfrac{3}{5}, \dfrac{2}{3}, \dfrac{7}{10}$

To answer this question, we first have to find a common denominator. The least common multiple of 10, 3, and 5 is 30 so that will be our common denominator.

$$\frac{7}{10} = \frac{7 \times 3}{10 \times 3} = \frac{21}{30}$$

$$\frac{2}{3} = \frac{2 \times 10}{3 \times 10} = \frac{20}{30}$$

$$\frac{3}{5} = \frac{3 \times 6}{5 \times 6} = \frac{18}{30}$$

From this, we can see that $\dfrac{3}{5}$ is the least fraction. Since only answer choice E has $\dfrac{3}{5}$ as the least fraction, it is the correct answer choice.

Fractions on a Number Line (Including Improper Fractions)

You may also see questions that ask you to place a fraction in the appropriate place on a number line. These are just comparing fraction questions – you have to decide the range that a fraction falls within. The only thing to look out for is improper fractions – you have to remember to convert these into mixed numbers before placing them on a number line.

- Look out for improper fractions – you need to convert them into mixed numbers before you can place them on number lines

Here are a couple questions for you to try:

1. Use the following number line to answer the question.

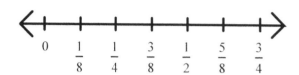

$\dfrac{5}{16}$ falls between which of the following two numbers on the number line?

(A) $\dfrac{1}{8}$ and $\dfrac{1}{4}$

(B) $\dfrac{1}{4}$ and $\dfrac{3}{8}$

(C) $\dfrac{3}{8}$ and $\dfrac{1}{2}$

(D) $\dfrac{1}{2}$ and $\dfrac{5}{8}$

(E) $\dfrac{5}{8}$ and $\dfrac{3}{4}$

In order to answer this question, we need to use common denominators. We can convert the answer choices into equivalent fractions that have 16 as a denominator. Looking at answer choice A, $\dfrac{1}{8}$ and $\dfrac{1}{4}$ are equivalent to $\dfrac{2}{16}$ and $\dfrac{4}{16}$. $\dfrac{5}{16}$ is greater than $\dfrac{4}{16}$, so A is not the correct answer. Looking at choice B, $\dfrac{1}{4}$ and $\dfrac{3}{8}$ are equivalent to $\dfrac{4}{16}$ and $\dfrac{6}{16}$. $\dfrac{5}{16}$ falls between those two values, so answer choice B is correct.

2. Use the following number line to answer the question.

$\dfrac{11}{4}$ falls between which of the following two numbers from the number line?

(A)   0 and $\dfrac{1}{2}$

(B)   1 and $1\dfrac{1}{2}$

(C) $1\dfrac{1}{2}$ and 2

(D)   2 and $2\dfrac{1}{2}$

(E) $2\dfrac{1}{2}$ and 3

To solve this problem, we first need to convert the improper fraction $\dfrac{11}{4}$ into a mixed number. To do this, we can break $\dfrac{11}{4}$ into $\dfrac{4}{4} + \dfrac{4}{4} + \dfrac{3}{4} = 2\dfrac{3}{4}$. Once we have done this conversion, we can see that the value is between $2\dfrac{1}{2}$ and 3. Answer choice E is correct.

To Add or Subtract Fractions

We use equivalent fractions to get the same bottom number, otherwise known as a common denominator.

We then add (or subtract) across the top and keep the common denominator as the denominator in our answer.

For example, let's say our problem looks like this:

$$\dfrac{1}{2} + \dfrac{2}{3} = ?$$

We are looking for a number that both denominators go into, or are factors of. 2 and 3 both go into 6, so 6 will be our common denominator.

$$\frac{1}{2} \times \frac{3}{3} = \frac{3}{6}$$ We use equivalent fractions to get a common denominator

$$\frac{2}{3} \times \frac{2}{2} = \frac{4}{6}$$

We can now add the equivalent fractions:

$$\frac{3}{6} + \frac{4}{6} = \frac{7}{6}$$ We add across the top but keep the common denominator

We aren't quite done yet. We now have a fraction where the top number is bigger than the bottom number (an improper fraction). To fix this, we can break apart the fraction.

$$\frac{7}{6} = \frac{6}{6} + \frac{1}{6}$$ We break the fraction apart so that we can see how many "ones" we have and what fraction is left.

Finally, we can create a mixed number as an answer.

$$\frac{6}{6} + \frac{1}{6} = 1 + \frac{1}{6} = 1\frac{1}{6}$$

For adding fractions, you generally have to find a common denominator. However, keep in mind that this is a multiple-choice test. Sometimes you can use ruling out to get to the right answer choice.

- Before you do the work of finding a common denominator, see if you can estimate or rule out answer choices

Here are a few examples for you to try:

1. Evaluate: $\dfrac{1}{5} + \dfrac{1}{6} + \dfrac{1}{20}$

   (A) $\dfrac{5}{12}$

   (B) $\dfrac{12}{11}$

   (C) $\dfrac{15}{12}$

   (D) $\dfrac{21}{20}$

   (E) $\dfrac{37}{20}$

For this question, first we will look at the answer choices before we jump into solving. Only one of our answer choices is less than one, so let's see if we can estimate whether the answer should be less than or greater than one. If we visualize a circle cut into 5 pieces, a circle cut into 6 pieces, and a circle cut into 20 pieces, we can see that each of those pieces would be very small. If we combined one piece from each circle, it would clearly still be less than a full circle. Only answer choice A can work, so we choose that and move on.

2. Evaluate: $\dfrac{5}{6} + \dfrac{11}{15}$

   (A) $1\dfrac{1}{3}$

   (B) $1\dfrac{1}{2}$

   (C) $1\dfrac{17}{30}$

   (D) $2\dfrac{1}{3}$

   (E) $2\dfrac{1}{2}$

If we look at our answer choices for this one we can see that there is no easy shortcut. We can see that our answer should be greater than one, but less than 2 since each individual fraction is greater than $\frac{1}{2}$ but less than 1. However, there are three answer choices in that range so we have to find a common denominator and do the math:

$$\frac{5}{6} + \frac{11}{15} = \frac{5 \times 5}{6 \times 5} + \frac{11 \times 2}{15 \times 2} = \frac{25}{30} + \frac{22}{30} = \frac{47}{30}$$

The problem now is that we have an improper fraction. We need to break apart that fraction to find the equivalent mixed number.

$$\frac{47}{30} = \frac{30}{30} + \frac{17}{30} = 1\frac{17}{30}$$

Answer choice C is correct.

3. Evaluate: $\frac{1}{6} + \frac{1}{5} + \frac{1}{4} + \frac{1}{3} + \frac{1}{2}$

(A) $\frac{1}{720}$

(B) $\frac{1}{20}$

(C) $\frac{5}{20}$

(D) $\frac{7}{20}$

(E) $\frac{29}{20}$

First, we will look at our answer choices. We can see that only one answer choice is greater than 1. Now if we look at the question, without doing the hard work of finding a common denominator, we can see that $\frac{1}{4} + \frac{1}{3} + \frac{1}{2}$ alone is greater than 1, so our total answer must be greater than 1. Answer choice E is correct.

To Multiply Fractions

We can simply multiply across the top and across the bottom.

For example:

$$\frac{1}{2} \times \frac{2}{3} = \frac{2}{6}$$

We then have to reduce the fraction since there is a number that goes into both the numerator and denominator. We use our rule of equivalent fractions (do the same to the top and bottom), only this time we are dividing.

$$\frac{2 \div 2}{6 \div 2} = \frac{1}{3}$$

Our final answer is $\frac{1}{3}$.

For multiplying fractions, we need to remember that we do NOT find a common denominator. We just multiply across the top and across the bottom. We also need to remember that the word "of" indicates multiplication. Finally, if you have to multiply several fractions, first see if you can cross-cancel to make the math easier.

- Do NOT find a common denominator for multiplying fractions
- If you see "of", that tells you to multiply
- See if you can cross-cancel

Here are a couple of problems for you to try:

1. Evaluate: $\frac{5}{6} \times \frac{6}{7} \times \frac{7}{8}$

    (A) $\frac{1}{2}$

    (B) $\frac{5}{8}$

    (C) $\frac{18}{21}$

    (D) $\frac{35}{21}$

    (E) $\frac{8}{5}$

In order to answer this question, we could multiply out and then reduce the answer. However, that is a lot of work with no calculator! Instead, we will cross-cancel. We can cancel the 6's and the 7's. This leaves us with:

$$\frac{5}{6} \times \frac{6}{7} \times \frac{7}{8} = \frac{5}{1} \times \frac{1}{1} \times \frac{1}{8} = \frac{5}{8}$$

Answer choice B is correct.

2. $\frac{3}{5}$ of $\frac{2}{3}$ is equal to which fraction?

(A) $\frac{6}{5}$

(B) 1

(C) $\frac{4}{5}$

(D) $\frac{3}{5}$

(E) $\frac{2}{5}$

To answer this question, we need to remember that the word "of" tells us to multiply. This means that our problem is really:

$$\frac{3}{5} \times \frac{2}{3}$$

Now we cross-cancel the 3's and are left with:

$$\frac{1}{5} \times \frac{2}{1} = \frac{2}{5}$$

Answer choice E is correct.

The next problem type is multiplying a whole number and a fraction.

Here is an example:

$$6 \times \frac{2}{3}$$

The key to this is to make the whole number into a fraction. The way we do this is just to put the whole number over 1 since that does not change the value of the whole number.

Now it looks like this:

$$\frac{6}{1} \times \frac{2}{3}$$

It is now a basic fraction multiplication problem. But before you multiply, notice that you can cross-cancel. The 6 on top and the 3 on the bottom both can be evenly divided by 3, and so the cancellation would look like this:

$$\frac{\cancel{6}^{2}}{1} \times \frac{2}{\cancel{3}_{1}} = \frac{4}{1} = 4$$

Here's a problem for you to try:

$$3 \times \frac{11}{15} =$$

3. Which of the following is equal to the above calculation?

   (A) $2\frac{1}{5}$

   (B) $2\frac{3}{5}$

   (C) $2\frac{11}{15}$

   (D) $3\frac{1}{5}$

   (E) $3\frac{11}{15}$

In order to solve, we have to first put the 3 over 1 so that we are multiplying two fractions. Then we use cross-cancelling since we don't have a calculator and want to keep the numbers smaller. We are left with an improper fraction, so we have to convert that into a mixed number. The math would look like this:

$$3 \times \frac{11}{15} = \frac{\overset{1}{\cancel{3}}}{1} \times \frac{11}{\underset{5}{\cancel{15}}} = \frac{11}{5} = \frac{5}{5} + \frac{5}{5} + \frac{1}{5} = 2\frac{1}{5}$$

The correct answer is (A).

On the actual SSAT, they might give you a problem that looks like the following:

4. All of the following calculations have the same result EXCEPT

(A) $1 \times \dfrac{1}{5}$

(B) $2 \times \dfrac{1}{10}$

(C) $3 \times \dfrac{2}{15}$

(D) $4 \times \dfrac{1}{20}$

(E) $5 \times \dfrac{2}{50}$

In order to answer this question, we can use cross-cancelling. If we cross-cancel (and reduce on answer choice E), then we can see that all of the answer choices are equal to $1 \times \dfrac{1}{5}$ except for choice C. Since this is an EXCEPT question, choice C is the correct answer.

Here is one for you to try on your own:

5. All of the following calculations have the same result EXCEPT

   (A) $1 \times \dfrac{1}{3}$

   (B) $2 \times \dfrac{1}{6}$

   (C) $3 \times \dfrac{1}{9}$

   (D) $4 \times \dfrac{1}{12}$

   (E) $6 \times \dfrac{1}{24}$

In order to solve this one, we just use cross-cancelling. If we do this, we get that all of the answer choices are equal to $1 \times \dfrac{1}{3}$ except for choice E, so choice E is the correct answer.

Adding and Subtracting Mixed Numbers and Whole Numbers

You may see a problem that asks you to subtract a mixed number, like $45\dfrac{2}{3}$, from a whole number like 100.

For example:

$$100 - 45\dfrac{2}{3} = ??$$

We can't do this problem as written because we must change the whole number into a mixed number. What we will do is borrow 1 from the 100 and make that 1 into the fraction $\dfrac{3}{3}$.

This is how it would look:

$$100 = 99\frac{3}{3}$$

Now all we do is subtract the whole number part and the fraction part to get the final answer.

$$99\frac{3}{3} - 45\frac{2}{3} = 54\frac{1}{3}$$

Here is an example of how this skill could be tested on the SSAT:

1. $40 - 6\frac{2}{9} =$

   (A) $33\frac{2}{9}$

   (B) $33\frac{7}{9}$

   (C) $34\frac{2}{9}$

   (D) $34\frac{7}{9}$

   (E) $46\frac{2}{9}$

First, we have to borrow to rewrite the 40 as $39\frac{9}{9}$. Here is what the math looks like:

$$40 - 6\frac{2}{9} = 39\frac{9}{9} - 6\frac{2}{9} = 33\frac{7}{9}$$

The correct answer is (B).

Here is another type of problem that deals with adding mixed numbers:

$$3\frac{2}{5} + 5\frac{2}{5} + 7\frac{3}{5}$$

There is a hard way to do this problem and an easy way. Let's do it the easy way. We will just break up each fraction into a whole number part and a fraction part and then use regrouping.

Here is what that looks like:

$$3\frac{2}{5} + 5\frac{2}{5} + 7\frac{3}{5} =$$
$$3 + \frac{2}{5} + 5 + \frac{2}{5} + 7 + \frac{3}{5}$$

Since it is all addition, we are allowed to use the commutative property. This lets us put all the whole numbers together and all the fractions together:

$$3 + 5 + 7 + \frac{2}{5} + \frac{2}{5} + \frac{3}{5}$$

Now we can combine like terms:

$$15 + \frac{7}{5} = 15\frac{7}{5}$$

If you are thinking that the final answer looks a bit strange, you are correct. We have to convert the improper fraction $\frac{7}{5}$ into a proper fraction.

We do this by breaking apart the fraction to get "ones" and a fraction that is left over:

$$\frac{7}{5} = \frac{5}{5} + \frac{2}{5} = 1 + \frac{2}{5}$$

Now the answer is:

$$15\frac{7}{5} = 15 + 1 + \frac{2}{5} = 16\frac{2}{5}$$

Here is one to try:

2. $8\frac{1}{7} + 3\frac{4}{7} + 7\frac{3}{7} =$

    (A) $18\frac{1}{7}$

    (B) $18\frac{6}{7}$

    (C) $19\frac{4}{7}$

    (D) $20\frac{1}{7}$

    (E) None of these

Our first step in solving this problem is to use regrouping to get all of the whole numbers together and all of the fractions together.

It would look like this:

$$8\frac{1}{7} + 3\frac{4}{7} + 7\frac{3}{7} = 8 + \frac{1}{7} + 3 + \frac{4}{7} + 7 + \frac{3}{7} = 8 + 3 + 7 + \frac{1}{7} + \frac{4}{7} + \frac{3}{7}$$

Now we can combine like terms and reduce to get:

$$18 + \frac{8}{7} = 18 + \frac{7}{7} + \frac{1}{7} = 19\frac{1}{7}$$

The correct answer is choice E.

Solving Inequalities with Fractions

This type of problem combines basic algebra and fractions because we have to solve an inequality involving x and a fraction. Remember the inequality signs:

"$>$" means "greater than"
"$<$" means "less than"

The important thing to remember when answering these questions is that if they ask us for the value of a variable, then we plug in answer choices.

Here is an example of what this type of question could look like on the SSAT:

1. If $X + \dfrac{1}{5} > 1$, which of the following could equal X?

   (A) $\dfrac{1}{3}$

   (B) $\dfrac{1}{2}$

   (C) $\dfrac{2}{3}$

   (D) $\dfrac{4}{5}$

   (E) $\dfrac{9}{10}$

We are looking for the answer choice that we can add to $\dfrac{1}{5}$ and the result will be bigger than 1. We can see that choices are in order from least to greatest. If we plug in $\dfrac{4}{5}$, or answer choice D, we can see that the answer would be equal to 1. However, we need the result to be bigger than 1. Only answer choice E is greater than answer choice D, so it must be the correct answer.

Here is one for you to try:

2. Which of the following could NOT be the value of M if $M + \dfrac{1}{4} < 1$?

(A) $\dfrac{1}{3}$

(B) $\dfrac{2}{3}$

(C) $\dfrac{1}{2}$

(D) $\dfrac{3}{5}$

(E) $\dfrac{3}{4}$

In order to solve this one, we are looking for an answer choice that when added to $\dfrac{1}{4}$ would give us a result that was NOT less than one (you did remember to circle that NOT so that you wouldn't forget it, right?). Let's start with answer choice E because we already have a common denominator. If we add $\dfrac{1}{4}$ and $\dfrac{3}{4}$, then we get 1. This tells us that choice E is correct since it is equal to 1 and not less than 1.

Converting Fractions into Decimals

Another task is to convert fractions to decimals. To convert $12\dfrac{3}{7}$ into a decimal could look tough, but first think of it as $12 + \dfrac{3}{7}$. Now, ignore the 12 for a while and just look at the fraction part, $\dfrac{3}{7}$. To convert this into a decimal, it's just a division problem.

$$
\begin{array}{r}
0.428 \\
7\overline{)3.000} \\
\underline{28} \\
20 \\
\underline{14} \\
60 \\
\underline{56}
\end{array}
$$

We can stop the division and round the answer to 0.43. Remember – this is a multiple-choice test!

So we now have the whole number part 12 plus the fraction part of $\frac{3}{7}$, which is the decimal .43 (rounded), so we say that $12\frac{3}{7} = 12.43$.

Here is a problem for you to try on your own:

1. Which of the following is equal to $12\frac{5}{8}$?

    (A)   12.25
    (B)   12.625
    (C)   12.75
    (D)   12.875
    (E)   15.625

Ignore the 12, and just do the long division with the fraction part.

$$8\overline{)5.000} \quad .625$$

The decimal answer to the fraction part is .625. Now just add this to the whole number 12 to get 12.625. The correct answer is B.

On the real SSAT, they are likely to ask you to combine adding mixed numbers and converting fractions into decimals.

Here is what an actual SSAT question may look like:

2. $5\frac{2}{3} + 3\frac{1}{3} + 2\frac{1}{3} =$

    (A)   10.66
    (B)   11
    (C)   11.33
    (D)   11.66
    (E)   12.33

In order to solve this problem, we first have to regroup and combine like terms. This looks like:

$$5 + \frac{2}{3} + 3 + \frac{1}{3} + 2 + \frac{1}{3} = 10\frac{4}{3}$$

Now we have to take care of the improper fraction:

$$10\frac{4}{3} = 10 + \frac{3}{3} + \frac{1}{3} = 11 + \frac{1}{3} = 11\frac{1}{3}$$

If we look at the answer choices, we can see that they are in decimal form, however. We can use long division to figure out that $\frac{1}{3}$ is about .33. If we add that to the 11, we get 11.33, or answer choice C.

Basic Operations with Decimals

The SSAT has very few problems that simply require a calculation. Performing basic operations with decimals is one of those problem types, however.

We are going to cover how to perform addition, subtraction, multiplication, and division with decimals. Then we will give you a couple of harder word problems that ask you to put it all together.

To add and subtract with decimals, you have to line up the decimals and then add or subtract as usual. Just remember to mark the decimal point in your final answer.

- Just line up the decimals and then add or subtract as usual

For example, let's say we need to add $54.231 + 3.27$:

```
   5  4  .  2  3  1
+     3  .  2  7
-----------------------
   5  7  .  5  0  1
```

We just lined up the decimal points and then added as usual. (Note that we needed to carry a 1 over to the next place when we added 7 and 3).

As always, we need to keep in mind that this is a multiple-choice test. Before we jump into solving, we need to look at the answer choices. They may be far enough apart that we can estimate.

- Look at your answer choices first, you may be able to estimate

Here are a couple of problems for you to try:

1. $443.3 + 51.9 + 43.6 + 311.2 =$
   - (A) 700
   - (B) 750
   - (C) 800
   - (D) 850
   - (E) 900

We certainly could jump right in and do the calculation. However, if we look at our answer choices, they are pretty far apart. We can just round off and estimate!

$$443.3 + 51.9 + 43.6 + 311.2 \approx 450 + 50 + 50 + 300 = 850$$

Now we know that answer choice D is correct.

2. Evaluate the expression $69.81 - 3.5$
   - (A) 65.31
   - (B) 65.81
   - (C) 66.31
   - (D) 66.86
   - (E) 67.31

For this question, the answer choices are close together so we need to do the actual math. We just need to make sure that we line up the decimal point.

```
    6   9  .  8   1
 −      3  .  5
-----------------------
    6   6  .  3   1
```

Answer choice C is correct.

Decimal multiplication is straightforward if you remember one rule:

- If you move the decimal point to the right when you begin the problem, you will move it to the left when you get the answer.

Here are the steps for multiplying decimals:

1. If any of the numbers in your question have decimal points, move the decimal point to the right. Keep track of how many decimal places you moved in total!
2. Multiply these numbers together.
3. Take the answer that you get and then move the decimal place back to the left the same number of spaces that you moved it to the right before multiplying.

Here is an example:

$34 \times 0.03 =$

Step 1: Move the decimal place to the right – and keep track of the number of spaces moved.

34×3 We moved the decimal place on the second number two spots to the right – we need to remember that

Now we can use multiplication with whole numbers.

$34 \times 3 = 102$

Our next step is to move the decimal back two spaces to the left to get our final answer.

$$34 \times 0.03 = 1.02$$

In the first step, we moved the decimal two places to the right, so now we move it two places to the left in the final answer

Here are a couple of examples of how this concept is tested on the SSAT:

3. $50 \times 0.004 =$

(A) 0.02
(B) 0.2
(C) 2.0
(D) 20.0
(E) 200.0

We move the decimal point 3 places to the right, to make the problem 50×4, and the answer is 200. Now move the decimal point 3 places to the left for the answer, and you get .200, or 0.2 as the answer. The correct answer is B.

4. $12 \times 0.056 =$

(A) 0.672
(B) 0.683
(C) 0.784
(D) 0.823
(E) 0.973

To answer this question, we first have to get rid of the decimal in the second number. We will move the decimal three places to the right so that our problem becomes 12×56, which is equal to 672. Now we have to move the decimal point back three places to the left to get our answer. Our final answer is 0.672, or answer choice A.

To divide decimals, we need to move over the decimal point for both numbers until there is no decimal needed. The trick is that we must move the decimal the same number of places for both the divisor and the dividend. Remember that we might need to add zeroes in order to do that.

* Move the decimal the same number of places in the divisor and the dividend
* That might require us to add zeroes

For example, let's say that we are doing the problem $147.12 \div 61.3$. Another way to write this problem is:

$$\frac{147.12}{61.3}$$

Now we have to move the decimal two places to the right for BOTH numbers. The bottom number only has one number to the right of the decimal, so we will need to add a zero in order to move the decimal point two places.

$$\frac{147.12}{61.3} = \frac{14712}{6130}$$

We then have to do long division and wind up with 2.4 as an answer.

Here are a couple of problems for you to try:

5. Divide 114.224 by 5.9.

    (A) 18.46
    (B) 18.97
    (C) 19.24
    (D) 19.36
    (E) 19.45

In order to perform this operation, our first steps are to rewrite the problem and then get rid of the decimal points.

$$\frac{114.224}{5.9} = \frac{114224}{5900}$$

If we do the long division, we get 19.36 as an answer. Answer choice D is correct.

6. Evaluate: $236.25 \div 18.9$

    (A) 1.25
    (B) 12.5
    (C) 125
    (D) 1,250
    (E) 4,465

If we look at the answer choices for this problem, we can see that the answers are all very far apart. We only need to figure out the approximate answer, so we can round off and estimate.

$$\frac{236.25}{18.9} \approx \frac{200}{20} = 10$$

We know that our answer must be around 10 and only answer choice B comes close. Choice B is the correct answer.

Those are the basics that you need to know for the harder fraction and decimal problems. Be sure to complete the following practice set in order to reinforce what you have learned.

Fractions and Decimals Practice Set

1. $300 - 150\frac{4}{11} =$

   (A) $149\frac{4}{11}$

   (B) $149\frac{7}{11}$

   (C) 150

   (D) $150\frac{4}{11}$

   (E) $150\frac{7}{11}$

2. $7\frac{2}{3} + 4\frac{1}{3} + 6\frac{1}{3} =$

   (A) $17\frac{1}{3}$

   (B) $17\frac{4}{9}$

   (C) $18\frac{1}{3}$

   (D) $18\frac{4}{9}$

   (E) 19

3. Write the following fractions in order from greatest to least:

$$\frac{3}{5}, \frac{5}{6}, \frac{11}{15}$$

    (A) $\frac{3}{5}, \frac{11}{15}, \frac{5}{6}$

    (B) $\frac{3}{5}, \frac{5}{6}, \frac{11}{15}$

    (C) $\frac{5}{6}, \frac{3}{5}, \frac{11}{15}$

    (D) $\frac{5}{6}, \frac{11}{15}, \frac{3}{5}$

    (E) $\frac{11}{15}, \frac{3}{5}, \frac{5}{6}$

4. $\frac{2}{5} + \frac{1}{3} + \frac{1}{2} =$

    (A) $\frac{4}{10}$

    (B) $\frac{1}{2}$

    (C) $\frac{7}{10}$

    (D) $\frac{29}{30}$

    (E) $\frac{37}{30}$

5. All of these are equal EXCEPT

    (A) $4 \times \dfrac{3}{4}$

    (B) $6 \times \dfrac{1}{2}$

    (C) $8 \times \dfrac{3}{8}$

    (D) $10 \times \dfrac{1}{6}$

    (E) $48 \times \dfrac{1}{16}$

6. Which of the following could be the value of x if $\dfrac{6}{11} + x > 1$?

    (A) $\dfrac{2}{7}$

    (B) $\dfrac{7}{30}$

    (C) $\dfrac{8}{19}$

    (D) $\dfrac{13}{37}$

    (E) $\dfrac{19}{29}$

7. $\dfrac{1}{2}$ of $\dfrac{3}{5}$ is equal to

    (A) $\dfrac{1}{5}$

    (B) $\dfrac{3}{10}$

    (C) $\dfrac{2}{5}$

    (D) $\dfrac{1}{2}$

    (E) $\dfrac{3}{5}$

8. $237.6 + 51.07 + 5.43 + 8.12 =$

   (A) 299.24

   (B) 300.32

   (C) 301.48

   (D) 302.22

   (E) 306.53

9. $10.0 \times 0.007 =$

   (A) 0.07

   (B) 0.70

   (C) 7.00

   (D) 70.00

   (E) 700.00

10. $30 \times 0.2 =$

   (A) 0.06

   (B) 0.60

   (C) 6.00

   (D) 60.00

   (E) 600.00

11. $15.0 \times 0.003 =$

   (A) 0.00045

   (B) 0.0045

   (C) 0.045

   (D) 0.45

   (E) 45

12. Use the following number line to answer the question.

$\frac{9}{7}$ falls between which of the following two numbers from the number line?

(A) 0 and $\frac{1}{2}$

(B) 1 and $1\frac{1}{2}$

(C) $1\frac{1}{2}$ and 2

(D) 2 and $2\frac{1}{2}$

(E) $2\frac{1}{2}$ and 3

13. $3\frac{2}{3} + 2\frac{1}{3} + 4\frac{2}{3} =$

(A) 5.33

(B) 6.33

(C) 7.67

(D) 9.67

(E) 10.67

14. All of the following products have the same value EXCEPT

(A) $2 \times \frac{3}{5}$

(B) $4 \times \frac{3}{10}$

(C) $5 \times \frac{3}{10}$

(D) $6 \times \frac{3}{15}$

(E) $10 \times \frac{3}{25}$

15. Which fraction is greater than $\frac{2}{3}$?

    (A) $\frac{5}{7}$

    (B) $\frac{3}{7}$

    (C) $\frac{1}{2}$

    (D) $\frac{5}{9}$

    (E) $\frac{7}{12}$

16. Evaluate: $\frac{7}{8} + \frac{5}{6}$

    (A) $1\frac{1}{5}$

    (B) $1\frac{3}{10}$

    (C) $1\frac{7}{11}$

    (D) $1\frac{15}{24}$

    (E) $1\frac{17}{24}$

17. $90 - 4\frac{4}{9} =$

    (A) $85\frac{5}{9}$

    (B) $84\frac{4}{9}$

    (C) $84\frac{5}{9}$

    (D) $85\frac{4}{9}$

    (E) $85\frac{2}{3}$

18. If $\dfrac{3}{5} + X < 1$, which of the following could NOT be the value of X?

(A) $\dfrac{1}{6}$

(B) $\dfrac{2}{7}$

(C) $\dfrac{2}{5}$

(D) $\dfrac{1}{4}$

(E) $\dfrac{1}{10}$

19. Evaluate: $\dfrac{3}{4} \times \dfrac{8}{11} \times \dfrac{22}{35}$

(A) $\dfrac{24}{1540}$

(B) $\dfrac{66}{1540}$

(C) $\dfrac{10}{35}$

(D) $\dfrac{12}{35}$

(E) $\dfrac{9}{10}$

20. $\dfrac{4}{5} \div \dfrac{8}{25} =$

    (A) $\dfrac{32}{125}$

    (B) $\dfrac{85}{125}$

    (C) $1\dfrac{1}{2}$

    (D) $2\dfrac{1}{5}$

    (E) $2\dfrac{1}{2}$

Answers to Fractions and Decimals Practice Set

1. B
2. C
3. D
4. E
5. D
6. E
7. B
8. D
9. A
10. C

11. C
12. B
13. E
14. C
15. A
16. E
17. A
18. C
19. D
20. E

Percent Problems

Percent problems are really just glorified fraction and decimal problems.

On the SSAT you will have to:

1. Determine percent shaded in a figure
2. Find the percent of a number or work backwards to find the original number when a percent is given
3. Answer questions that mix fractions and percents
4. Find how much interest is earned on a certain amount of money
5. Take multiple percent increases and decreases

Keep in mind that "per" means "out of" and "cent" means "hundred". Therefore, "percent" means "out of a hundred".

Percent Shaded Problems

You may see a question that has a figure placed over a grid and then asks you what percent of the figure is shaded.

The steps to answering these questions are easy:

1. Count the total number of grid boxes within the figure.
2. Count how many of those boxes are shaded.
3. Write a fraction with $\dfrac{\text{\# of boxes shaded}}{\text{total number of boxes}}$
4. Use equivalent fractions to find the percent:

$$\frac{\text{\# of boxes shaded}}{\text{total number of boxes}} = \frac{\text{percent}}{100}$$

Since these questions are straightforward, we will do just one of them:

1. What is the percentage that is shaded in the following figure?

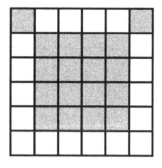

(A) 18%
(B) 20%
(C) 36%
(D) 50%
(E) 67%

Our first step is to figure out how many total smaller squares there are. There are 6 rows across and 6 columns down, so we can multiply $6 \times 6 = 36$ and see that there are 36 total squares. Now we have to count the number of squares that are shaded. There are 18 shaded squares.

Now we will use a proportion.

$$\frac{18}{36} = \frac{x}{100}$$
$$1800 = 36x$$
$$50 = x$$

We can see that answer choice D is correct.

How to Find the Percent of a Number

The easiest way to solve percent problems is to use equivalent fractions and cross-multiplying.

Here is the basic setup:

$$\frac{\text{part}}{\text{whole}} = \frac{\text{percent}}{100}$$

For example, let's say that we wanted to find 15% of 60.

First, we set up the equivalent fraction and plug in what we have been given.

$$\frac{x}{60} = \frac{15}{100}$$

Now we use cross-multiplying to solve.

$$100x = 15 \times 60$$
$$100x = 900$$
$$\div 100 \quad \div 100$$
$$x = 9$$

Here are some examples of how this could be tested:

1. 16 is 5 percent of what number?

    (A) 80
    (B) 160
    (C) 250
    (D) 320
    (E) 350

To solve, we can create equivalent fractions and then use cross-multiplying.

$$\frac{16}{x} = \frac{5}{100}$$

We can then cross multiply and solve for x.

$$5x = 1600$$
$$\div 5 \quad \div 5$$
$$x = 320$$

Since we got 320 for x, answer choice D is correct.

2. 14 is what percent of 40?
    (A) 15%
    (B) 25%
    (C) 35%
    (D) 40%
    (E) 45%

To answer this question, we simply set up an equivalent fraction:

$$\frac{\text{part}}{\text{whole}} = \frac{\text{percent}}{100}$$

Now we just plug in the information given:

$$\frac{14}{40} = \frac{\text{percent}}{100}$$

We can use cross-multiplying to solve:

$$14 \times 100 = 40 \times \text{percent}$$
$$1400 = 40 \times \text{percent}$$
$$35 = \text{percent}$$

Answer choice C is correct.

3. 12 is 40 percent of what number?

    (A) 4.8
    (B) 12
    (C) 24
    (D) 30
    (E) 48

Again, we can set up the equivalent fractions. It is just important to recognize that the piece of the fraction we are missing in this case is the "whole" number.

$$\frac{\text{part}}{\text{whole}} = \frac{\text{percent}}{100}$$

$$\frac{12}{\text{whole}} = \frac{40}{100}$$

$$12 \times 100 = 40 \times \text{whole}$$

$$1200 = 40 \times \text{whole}$$

$$30 = \text{whole}$$

Answer choice D is correct.

You may also see word problems that ask you to apply these basics. The key is to always return to the basic formula for percent and use equivalent fractions.

Here is an example for you to try:

4. If there are 3 white eggs and 4 brown eggs in a basket, about what percent of eggs in the basket are white?

    (A) 43%
    (B) 54%
    (C) 60%
    (D) 75%
    (E) 90%

In order to answer this question, we have to remember that the "whole number" will include both the brown eggs and the white eggs.

$$\frac{3 \text{ white eggs}}{3 \text{ white eggs} + 4 \text{ brown eggs}} = \frac{\text{percent}}{100}$$

$$\frac{3}{7} = \frac{\text{percent}}{100}$$

$$3 \times 100 = 7 \times \text{percent}$$

$$\approx 43 \text{ percent}$$

Answer choice A is correct.

Since you cannot use a calculator on this test, sometimes it is easier to find 10% of a number and then use that to find the answer.

To find 10% of a number, you just move the decimal place one spot to the left.

For example:

10% of 12.36 = 1.236

You can even use 10% to find other percentages, or a range in which the answer should fall.

Let's say you have to find 15% of 18.

First, you find 10% of 18. You do this by moving the decimal to the left one place.

10% = 1.8

Then you find 5% by taking half of 10%.

$$5\% = \frac{1}{2} \text{ of } 1.8 = 0.9$$

Now we add 10% of 18 and 5% of 18 to get 15% of 18.

$$\begin{array}{r} 10\% = 1.8 \\ + \, 5\% = 0.9 \\ \hline 15\% = 2.7 \end{array}$$

Here are some examples of problems that would allow us to use this strategy:

5. Of the following, which is closest to 15% of $11.95?

   (A) $1.50
   (B) $1.80
   (C) $2.10
   (D) $2.50
   (E) $3.00

First, we round $11.95 to $12 since the problem uses the words "closest to". Then, to find 10% of $12, we move the decimal one spot to the left. Therefore, 10% of 12 is 1.2. We use that to find 5% and add them together to get 15%.

$$
\begin{array}{r}
10\% \text{ of } 12 = 1.2 \\
+\ 5\% \text{ of } 12 = 0.6 \\
\hline
15\% \text{ of } 12 = 1.8
\end{array}
$$

This tells us that answer choice B is correct.

6. Julia has $350 in her bank account. If she takes out 30% of her money, how much money will she still have in her bank account?

   (A) $105
   (B) $245
   (C) $285
   (D) $320
   (E) $455

The key to this question is that it is a multi-step problem and we have to be sure that we don't stop before we find what they are asking for.

First, we have to find the amount withdrawn:

$$
\frac{\$ \text{ taken out}}{350} = \frac{30}{100}
$$
$$
\$ \text{ taken out} = \$105
$$

Now we have to subtract that amount from what she started with to get her new balance:

$350 − $105 = $245

Answer choice B is correct.

Some percent questions will ask you to solve for a variable and then use the value of that variable to solve another percent problem.

Here is an example of how these questions could look:

7. When 20 percent of y is 21, what is 10 percent of $2y$?

    (A) 21
    (B) 42
    (C) 50
    (D) 96
    (E) 105

To answer this question, we have to first solve for y. Let's use our equivalent fraction method.

$$\frac{21}{y} = \frac{20}{100}$$
$$21 \times 100 = 20 \times y$$
$$2100 = 20y$$
$$\div 20 \quad \div 20$$
$$y = 105$$

Since we now know that $y = 105$, it is easy to see that $2y = 210$. Now, let's find 10% of 210. We use our 10% shortcut, move the decimal over one place, and get 21 as our answer. Answer choice A is correct.

A trick to the above problem type is that the test writers often compose these questions so that we don't have to go through solving for the variable.

If you look at the previous problem, you will notice that 20 percent of y is the same as 10 percent of $2y$.

Remember that the word "of" means multiply. If we translate 20 percent of y into equation language, we get:

$$\frac{20}{100} \times y$$

If we do the same thing with 10 percent of 2y, then we get:

$$\frac{10}{100} \times 2y$$

If we break up the 2y, then we get:

$$\frac{10}{100} \times 2 \times y \text{ which is equal to } \frac{20}{100}y$$

This allows us to see that 10 percent of $2y$ should be the same as 20 percent of y, or equal to 21.

Here is a problem for you to try on your own:

8. If 80 percent of $2b$ is 36, what is 40 percent of $4b$?

    (A)   40
    (B)   18
    (C)   36
    (D)   50
    (E)   72

If we use our trick of setting up equations and comparing before solving, we can see that 80 percent of $2b$ is equal to 40 percent of $4b$. This tells us that 40 percent of $4b$ would also be equal to 36, so answer choice C is correct.

You may also see a very similar type of question. In these problems, you are given one percentage and then are asked to calculate a different percentage. The key to these questions is that we don't solve for the original number and then find the new percent – that would take way too long! Think about how you can manipulate what you are given instead.

- If you have to go from one percentage to another, do not go through all the work to find the original number

Here are a couple of examples for you to try:

9. If 20% of a number is 60, then what is 50% of that same number?

(A) 50
(B) 60
(C) 120
(D) 130
(E) 150

Instead of finding the original number, let's work with what we have. Knowing that 50% is equal to 20% plus 20% plus 10% (or half of 20%), we can use addition to get the answer:

$$
\begin{aligned}
20\% &= 60 \\
20\% &= 60 \\
10\% &= 30 \\
\hline
50\% &= 150
\end{aligned}
$$

Answer choice E is correct.

10. If 18 is 60% of a number, then what is 40% of that same number?

(A) 12
(B) 18
(C) 24
(D) 30
(E) 36

We could certainly do the math on this one. Or we could just look at the answer choices. We know that 40% of a number must be less than 60% of that same number. Only answer choice A is less than 18, so it is the correct answer choice.

Questions that Mix Fractions and Percents

You may also see questions that mix fractions and percents. The key to these questions is just to keep returning to the basics.

Here are a couple for you to try:

1. In a class, there are 20 girls and 30 boys. One quarter of the girls play the cello and 60% of the boys play the cello. How many total students in the class play the cello?

    (A) 5
    (B) 12
    (C) 18
    (D) 23
    (E) 40

In order to answer this question, we have to figure out separately how many boys and how many girls play the cello. We have to remember that the word "of" means to multiply:

$$\frac{1}{4} \text{ of the girls} = \frac{1}{4} \times 20 = 5 \text{ girls}$$

$$60\% \text{ of the boys} = \frac{60}{100} \times 30 = 18 \text{ boys}$$

Now we add 5 and 18 and get that a total of 23 students play the cello. Answer choice D is correct.

2. There are 30 students in a class. Three fifths of them are girls. Of the girls, 50% have blue eyes. How many girls are there in the class with blue eyes?

    (A) 6
    (B) 9
    (C) 12
    (D) 18
    (E) 25

First, we have to use the fraction to figure out how many girls there are.

$$\frac{3}{5} \times 30 = 18 \text{ girls in the class}$$

Now we have to find 50% of 18 girls. Since 50% is equal to one half, the easiest thing to do is just to take half of 18. We find that there are 9 blue-eyed girls in the class. Answer choice B is correct.

Interest Problems

A special type of percent problem is questions that ask you how much interest was earned on a bank account.

If the question tells you that the account earns 5% or 10% interest, then we can use our 10% shortcut. However, the test often gives a percent interest that doesn't work so well with the 10% shortcut.

Here is an example of what an interest problem looks like on the SSAT:

1. Sam has a savings account with $15,000 in it. If he earns 8 percent interest on it per year, how much will he earn in one year?
   (A) $800
   (B) $900
   (C) $1,000
   (D) $1,100
   (E) $1,200

In order to solve this problem, we first have to set up the equation. We can think of the question as asking us to find 8 percent of $15,000. Remember that the word "of" means multiply.

Our equation looks like this:

$$\frac{8}{100} \times 15,000 = ?$$

Since we don't have a calculator, we want to cancel zeroes before solving. We can cancel two zeroes from the top and the bottom, so we are left with:

$$8 \times 150$$

This is equal to $1,200, so answer choice E is correct.

Here is another one for you to try – remember to pay close attention to the wording of the question!

2. Carl has a bank account with $12,400 in it. He earns 5 percent interest per year. After one year, how much money will he have in his account?
    (A) $620
    (B) $1,240
    (C) $12,400
    (D) $13,020
    (E) $13,640

Since we are looking for 5% of a number, we can use our 10% trick. To find 10% we just move the decimal one place to the left, so 10% of $12,400 is $1,240. 5% is half of that, or $620. Now, we have to add that to $12,400 since the question is asking for the total amount in the account, not just the interest earned (answer choice A is a trap). If we add $12,400 and $620, we get $13,020, so answer choice D is correct.

Taking Multiple Percent Increases and Decreases

On the SSAT, they may ask you to do more than one percent increase or decrease calculation. The trick to these questions is that you take the first percent off and then you have to take the next percent off of the new number. You can't just add the percentages together.

- Don't just add percentages together
- You have to take the second percent increase or decrease from the new number

For example, let's say we have the following problem:

1. A sweater usually costs $20. It was marked down 20% for a sale. It was then marked down an additional 10% for final clearance. What was the new price?

    (A) $20.00
    (B) $16.00
    (C) $14.40
    (D) $14.00
    (E) $17.00

To solve this problem, we can't just add 20% and 10% to get 30% off. We have to first take 20% off of $20. If we use our 10% trick, we can easily find that the 20% of $20 is $4. So our price is $16 after the 20% discount. Now we have to take an additional 10% off of $16. 10% of $16 is only $1.60, not $2. If we take $1.60 off of $16, we are left with $14.40, so answer choice C is correct.

Here is an example for you to try:

(Keep in mind that interest earns interest, so we can't just add percentages)

2. Sarah deposited $16,500 in a bank account that earns 5% interest per year. After two years, how much money does she have?

    (A) $18,125.50
    (B) $18,150.00
    (C) $18,191.25
    (D) $18,250.00
    (E) $18,500.00

Our first step is to find 5% of $16,500. Since it is 5%, we can find 10% and take half of that. 10% of $16,500 is $1,650, so 5% of $16,500 is $825. We need to add this to her balance before we figure out how much interest she earned the next year. This gives us that her new balance of $17,325. Now we find 5% of that number, which is $866.25. If we add this to her balance, we get that she now has $18,191.25, so answer choice C is correct.

Sometimes, they will give you percent problems with no starting number, so we plug in 100 to make our lives easier.

- If they give you a percent problem with no starting amount, plug in 100

Here is an example of how this could look on the test:

3. The price of a book is increased by 20%. It is then decreased by 20%. The new price is what percent of the original price?

 (A) 90%
 (B) 80%
 (C) 96%
 (D) 100%
 (E) 104%

If we plug in 100 for the original price of the book, our job is easy. If we increase the price by 20%, we get a new price of $120. We then have to take 20% off of the *new price*. This gives a final price of $96. Since we started with a price of 100, the new price is 96% of the original price. Answer choice C is correct.

Here is one for you to try on your own:

4. If I take a number and increase it by 30% of its original value, and then take this new number and decrease it by 30% of its value, the final result will be what percent increase or decrease from my original number?

 (A) 30% decrease
 (B) 9% decrease
 (C) 0% change
 (D) 9% increase
 (E) 30% increase

To solve this problem, let's use 100 for the original number. When we increase it by 30%, we get 130. If we take 30% of 130, we get 39. Since 130 − 39 = 91, our final number is 91, which is a 9% decrease from 100. Answer choice B is correct.

Now you know what you need to do well on the percent questions! Be sure to do the practice set.

Percent Problems Practice Set

1. If 80 percent of d is 12, what is 40 percent of $2d$?

    (A) 8
    (B) 10
    (C) 12
    (D) 18
    (E) 24

2. Lance has $13,500 in his savings account and that account earns 8% interest per year. How much interest will he earn in a year?

    (A) $997
    (B) $1,080
    (C) $1,093
    (D) $1,180
    (E) $1,198

3. What percentage of the following figure is unshaded?

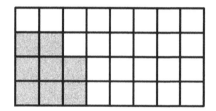

    (A) 8%
    (B) 25%
    (C) 62%
    (D) 75%
    (E) 92%

4. If there are 6 chocolate bars and 14 fruit chews in a candy jar, what percent of the candies are chocolate bars?

    (A) 6%
    (B) 20%
    (C) 30%
    (D) 43%
    (E) 70%

5. 9 is 30 percent of

    (A) 30
    (B) 15
    (C) 35
    (D) 45
    (E) 60

6. George has $3,400 in his savings account. If he earns 5% interest per year, how much interest will he earn in two years?

    (A) $170
    (B) $178.50
    (C) $340.25
    (D) $344
    (E) $348.50

7. Carlos has a collection of 80 miniature cars. If he donates 40% to charity, then how many cars does he have remaining?

    (A) 4
    (B) 8
    (C) 16
    (D) 32
    (E) 48

8. There are 15 boys and 10 girls in Vicki's class. If 60% of boys play soccer and 70% of girls play soccer, then how many total children in Vicki's class play soccer?

    (A) 13
    (B) 16
    (C) 19
    (D) 22
    (E) 25

9. If 60 percent of *y* is 25, what is 30 percent of 2*y*?

(A) 25
(B) 30
(C) 50
(D) 60
(E) 75

10. 24 is 40 percent of

(A) 44
(B) 50
(C) 54
(D) 60
(E) 64

11. If 9 is 15% of a number, then what is 70% of that same number?

(A) 135
(B) 70
(C) 60
(D) 54
(E) 42

12. 16 is 20% of what number?

(A) 80
(B) 84
(C) 96
(D) 100
(E) 104

13. 18 is what percent of 120?

(A) 8%
(B) 12%
(C) 15%
(D) 20%
(E) 36%

Answers to Percent Problems Practice Set

1. C
2. B
3. D
4. C
5. A
6. E
7. E
8. B
9. A
10. D
11. E
12. A
13. C

Ratios

On the Upper Level SSAT, you may see ratio problems. The important thing to remember about a ratio is that it compares part to part. A fraction gives you a part out of a whole.

- Ratio compares part to part
- Fraction gives you a part out of a whole

For example, let's say we have a fruit bowl with just apples and oranges. The ratio of apples to oranges is 4 to 3 (we could also write this ratio as 4:3 or $\frac{4}{3}$). This tells us that for every 4 apples there are 3 oranges. We can turn these figures into fractions as well. We can see that 4 out of a total of 7 pieces of fruit are apples and express this by saying that $\frac{4}{7}$ of the pieces of fruit are apples. A fraction is just a ratio that compares one part to the whole.

- Ratios can be written as "part to part", for example: 2 to 3
- Ratios can also be written as "part:part", for example: 2:3
- Ratios may also sometimes look like a fraction, for example: $\frac{2}{3}$
- A fraction is really a ratio that compares a part to the whole, for example: $\frac{2}{5}$ and $\frac{3}{5}$

On the Upper Level SSAT, there are a few different types of ratio problems that you may see. They include:

- Creating and reducing a ratio when given the parts
- Finding a part to part ratio given a part to whole ratio
- Using a part to part ratio to determine a possible total quantity
- Using a ratio to determine actual quantities

Creating and Reducing a Ratio when Given the Parts

Some questions on the SSAT may give you parts to work with and then ask for a ratio.

There are two things to keep in mind with this type of question:

1. Make sure you keep your parts in the right order. For example, if they ask for the ratio of red marbles to green marbles, make doubly sure you don't write the ratio as green marbles to red marbles.
2. A ratio can be reduced just like a fraction can be reduced. For example, if our ratio is 4:2, we can divide both sides by the same number (2), and get 2:1. Since we divided both sides by the same number, the ratio 4:2 is equivalent to the ratio 2:1.

Here are some examples of these types of questions for you to try:

1. Harold has a bag with 6 red marbles, 4 yellow marbles, 8 green marbles, and 2 pink marbles. What is his ratio of red marbles to all the marbles that he has?

   (A) 3:10
   (B) 10:3
   (C) 3:4
   (D) 2:3
   (E) 3:2

To answer this question, we first have to figure out the total number of marbles that he has. If we add $6 + 4 + 8 + 2$, we get that Harold has a total of 20 marbles. Now we can set up our ratio. The ratio of red marbles to total marbles is 6 to 20. However, that is not one of our answer choices because we must reduce that ratio. If we divide both 6 and 20 by 2, we get that the ratio of red marbles to total marbles is 3 to 10, or answer choice A.

2. Clara has 10 blue shirts and 15 red shirts. What is her ratio of red shirts to blue shirts?

   (A) $\dfrac{10}{25}$

   (B) $\dfrac{25}{10}$

   (C) $\dfrac{5}{10}$

   (D) $\dfrac{2}{3}$

   (E) $\dfrac{3}{2}$

In this question, we have to make sure that we put the parts in the right order. The shirts are given as number of blue shirts and then number of red shirts. However, the question asks for the ratio of red to blue, so we have to make sure that we put the numbers in the right order. The ratio of red to blue shirts is $\frac{15}{10}$. Now we have to reduce this ratio. If we divide both 15 and 10 by 5, we get that the ratio of red to blue shirts is $\frac{3}{2}$, or choice E.

Some questions are a little more involved because they require you to do a conversion and then figure out a ratio. Just make sure that you have all the parts in the same units before you figure out the ratio. Be particularly careful with questions that ask for the ratio of areas because the ratio of areas is NOT equal to ratio of sides. To find the ratio of areas, we have to square the ratio of the side lengths.

- Make sure all the parts have the same units
- Remember that the ratio of areas is not equal to the ratio of sides – we have to square the ratio of the sides to get the ratio of the area

Here are a few examples for you to try:

3. What is the ratio of 3 yards to 6 feet?
   (A) 3 to 6
   (B) 3 to 2
   (C) 3 to 18
   (D) 2 to 1
   (E) 1 to 3

Our first step is to convert all of the measurements into the same unit. If we multiply the number of yards by 3 (since there are 3 feet in a yard), we get that 3 yards is equivalent to 9 feet. This means that our ratio is really 9 feet to 6 feet. If we reduce 9 to 6, we get a final ratio of 3 to 2, or answer choice B.

4. Find the ratio of 2 ft. 4 in. to 1 yd.

   (A) 1:2
   (B) 2:3
   (C) 3:2
   (D) 7:9
   (E) 9:7

Our first step is to convert both measurements into the same unit. The easiest unit to use in this case is inches since our first measurement has both feet and inches. If we convert the 2 feet part of the first measurement into inches, we get 24 inches. We then have to add in the 4 inches to get a total of 28 inches for the first measurement. Now we have to convert one yard into inches. There are 3 feet in one yard and 12 inches in each foot, so we do the following calculation:

$$1 \; yard \left(\frac{3 \; feet}{1 \; yard}\right)\left(\frac{12 \; inches}{1 \; foot}\right) = 36 \; inches$$

Now we now we are looking for the ratio of 28 inches to 36 inches. The next step is simply to divide both parts by 4 to get a ratio of 7 to 9. Answer choice D is correct.

5. The side length of square *FGHI* is 3 in. The side length of square *WXYZ* is 5 in. What is the ratio of the area of square *FGHI* to the area of square *WXYZ*?

   (A) 3 to 5
   (B) 3 to 8
   (C) 5 to 3
   (D) 9 to 25
   (E) 9 to 64

To find the area of each square, we must square the side length (or multiply it by itself). That means that the area of square *FGHI* is $3 \times 3 = 9$ and the area of square *WXYZ* is $5 \times 5 = 25$. The ratio of the areas is therefore 9 to 25, or answer choice D.

6. The perimeter of square *ABCD* is 16 cm. The perimeter of square *LMNP* is 20 cm. What is the ratio of the area of square *ABCD* to the area of square *LMNP*?

   (A) 4:5
   (B) 4:9
   (C) 10:15
   (D) 16:24
   (E) 16:25

For this question, we have to remember to first convert from perimeter to side length. (In actuality, the ratio of side lengths is equal to the ratio of the perimeters, but on this test we can't use a calculator so it is better to find side lengths so that the calculations do not become too complicated). We find that the side length of square *ABCD* is 4 cm and the side length for square *LMNP* is 5 cm. Now we square each of these numbers to find the areas. The ratio of the areas is therefore 16 to 25, or answer choice E.

Even more difficult are questions that don't give you hard numbers, but rather ask you to compare quantities. If you get a question that asks you to determine a ratio without giving you real quantities, simply plug in your own numbers. Be particularly careful with questions that ask for the ratio of areas because the ratio of areas is NOT equal to ratio of sides.

 • If you have to determine a ratio without hard numbers, plug in your own numbers

Here are a couple of examples of this type of problem:

7. One number is four times as large as a second number. What is the ratio of the first number to the second number?

   (A) 1:2
   (B) 1:4
   (C) 1:5
   (D) 4:1
   (E) 5:1

To answer this question, let's just plug in our own numbers. The question tells us that the first number is four times as large as the second number. So let's make the first number equal to 4 and the second number equal to 1. Therefore, our ratio is 4:1 or answer choice D.

8. A rug company produces circular rugs in three sizes. The radius of the medium-sized rug is twice the radius of the smallest rug. The radius of the largest rug is twice the radius of the medium-sized rug. What is the ratio of the area of the largest rug to the area of the smallest rug?

   (A)   16:4
   (B)   16:1
   (C)   4:1
   (D)   1:4
   (E)   1:16

Note: The area of a circle is given $A = \pi r^2$, where r is the radius. This equation will NOT be given to you on the actual test but we want you to be able to answer this ratio question.

To answer this question, we can plug in our own numbers for the radii. To make our life easy, let's make the radius of the smallest rug 1. If we multiply this by 2, we get that the radius of the medium-sized rug is 2. Then we multiply 2 (radius of the medium-sized rug) by 2 to get that the radius of the largest rug is 4. Now we use the area formula to find the area of the smallest and largest rugs.

$$A \text{ of smallest rug} = \pi r^2 = \pi(1^2) = 1\pi$$
$$A \text{ of largest rug} = \pi r^2 = \pi(4^2) = 16\pi$$

We now know that the ratio of area of the largest rug to the area of the smallest rug is 16π to 1π. We can reduce this ratio, however, since both sides can be divided by π. This leaves us with a ratio of 16 to 1, or answer choice B.

Finding a Part-to-Part Ratio Given a Part-to-Whole Ratio

Sometimes a question will give you what is essentially a part to whole fraction and ask you to convert it into a part to part ratio. The key to this type of question is to remember that the part given was included in the whole, so we need to subtract it out to get the other part.

- If you are given a part to whole fraction, remember to subtract out the part given

These are straightforward so we will just do a couple of examples:

1. A softball team won 15 games out of 25 played and there were no ties. What is the ratio of games won to games lost?
    (A) 5 to 3
    (B) 5 to 2
    (C) 3 to 5
    (D) 3 to 2
    (E) 2 to 3

To answer this question, we must first figure out how many games the team lost. If there were a total of 25 games we simply subtract off the 15 games that they won to get that they lost 10 games. Our ratio of games won to lost is therefore 15 to 10. Now we just have to reduce that fraction. If we divide both sides by 5, we get a final ratio of 3 to 2, so answer choice D is correct.

2. A bouquet of flowers has 24 total stems. There are 6 marigolds, 8 petunias, and the rest are carnations. What is the ratio of marigolds to carnations?
    (A) $\dfrac{3}{5}$

    (B) $\dfrac{4}{5}$

    (C) $\dfrac{1}{4}$

    (D) $\dfrac{1}{3}$

    (E) $\dfrac{2}{5}$

Our first step is to figure out how many carnations we have. To find this out, we must subtract the number of marigolds and petunias from the total number of flowers. Since $24 - 6 - 8 = 10$, we know there must be 10 carnations. The ratio of marigolds to carnations is therefore 6 to 10. We must divide both sides by 2 in order to reduce the ratio and get 3 to 5. Since answer choice A expresses the ratio 3 to 5 as a fraction, that is the correct answer.

Using a Part-to-Part Ratio to Determine a Possible Total Quantity

You may see a question that asks you to use a ratio to determine what a total quantity could be. These questions always use something you can't have a partial piece of, such as eggs or people. The trick to these questions is that you have to turn the ratios into part-to-whole fractions and then look for the answer that is evenly divisible by the denominator – otherwise you would wind up with part of an egg or part of a person, which would be bad.

- Turn ratios into part to whole fractions
- Look for the answer choice that is evenly divisible by the denominator of these part to whole fractions

Here are a couple of examples:

1. A basket contains only white and brown eggs. The ratio of white to brown eggs is 2 to 3. Which could be the total number of eggs in the basket?
   (A) 2
   (B) 3
   (C) 18
   (D) 20
   (E) 24

The key to answering this question is that we have to turn the ratios into part-to-whole fractions. If we add the two "pieces" of the ratio together, we get a total of 5 eggs. This means that 2 out of every 5, or $\frac{2}{5}$, of the eggs are white. Since only answer choice D is divisible by 5, that is the correct answer. (If you multiplied any of the other answer choices by $\frac{2}{5}$ you would wind up with a partial egg.)

2. The ratio of boys to girls in a class is 3 to 5. What could be the total number of students in the class?
   (A) 10
   (B) 12
   (C) 15
   (D) 20
   (E) 24

Our first step is to convert the part-to-part ratio into a part-to-whole fraction. If we add the "pieces" of the ratio, we get that there is a total of 8 students. This means that $\frac{3}{8}$ of the class are boys and $\frac{5}{8}$ are girls. Since only answer choice E is divisible by 8, it is the correct answer.

Using a Ratio to Determine Actual Quantities

Finally, you may see a ratio question that asks you to use a part to part ratio to determine a total quantity. For these questions, you can use the same trick of turning the part to part ratio pieces into fractions. You can use those fractions to solve for another piece of the ratio or for the total.

- Turn the ratio into fractions
- Use those fractions to solve for quantities

Here are a couple of questions for you to try:

1. There are red and blue marbles in a jar. The ratio of red to blue marbles is 4 to 5. If there are a total of 81 marbles in the jar, how many of them are red?

    (A) 9
    (B) 36
    (C) 45
    (D) 54
    (E) 81

Our first step is to use the ratio to find what fraction of the marbles are red. If we add up the parts of the ratio, we get that there is a total of 9 parts. Since 4 out of those 9 parts are red, we know that $\frac{4}{9}$ of the marbles are red. Now we just multiply the total number by the fraction that is red.

$$\frac{4}{9} \times 81 = 36$$

Answer choice B is correct.

2. In a box of chocolates there are marshmallow, caramel, and nut-filled chocolates. The ratio of marshmallow to caramel to nut-filled chocolates is 3:5:6. If there are 20 caramel chocolates, how many nut-filled chocolates are there?

    (A) 12
    (B) 20
    (C) 24
    (D) 36
    (E) 56

For this question, we have to use a part to find the whole and then work back to a different part. Our first step is to add up the parts and get that there are total of 14 parts. This means that $\frac{3}{14}$ of the chocolates are marshmallow-filled, $\frac{5}{14}$ are caramel-filled, and $\frac{6}{14}$ are nut-filled. Now we have to use a proportion to solve for the total number of chocolates.

$$\frac{5 \ caramel \ chocolates}{14 \ total \ chocolates} = \frac{20 \ caramel \ chocolates}{x \ total \ \# \ of \ chocolates}$$

If we solve for x, we get that there is a total of 56 chocolates. Now we just have to find $\frac{6}{14}$ of 56. Since the word "of" indicates that we should multiply, we calculate $\frac{6}{14} \times 56 = 24$. Answer choice C is correct.

Those are the basics that you need to know about ratios. Be sure to complete the practice set to reinforce your learning!

Ratio Practice Set

1. What is the ratio of 1 hour 6 minutes to 2 hours?

    (A) 1:2

    (B) 2:3

    (C) 2:5

    (D) 11:20

    (E) 65:120

2. A company produces square tiles in three sizes. The side of the medium-sized tile is three times the side length of the smallest tile. The side length of the largest tile is three times the side length of the medium-sized tile. What is the ratio of the area of the smallest tile to the area of the largest tile?

    (A) 1 to 81

    (B) 1 to 27

    (C) 1 to 9

    (D) 27 to 1

    (E) 81 to 1

3. In a class of 24 students, there are 16 boys. What is the ratio of boys to girls?

    (A) 1:2

    (B) 2:1

    (C) 2:3

    (D) 3:2

    (E) 3:5

4. The number represented by w is three times as large as the number represented by y. What is the ratio of y^2 to w^2?

    (A) 27 to 1

    (B) 9 to 1

    (C) 3 to 1

    (D) 1 to 3

    (E) 1 to 9

5. There are red and green marbles in a jar. If the ratio of red to green marbles is 2 to 5, which could be the total number of marbles in the jar?

    (A) 5
    (B) 10
    (C) 21
    (D) 30
    (E) 36

6. Klein has 15 pens and 20 pencils. Find his ratio of pens to pencils.

    (A) $\dfrac{3}{7}$

    (B) $\dfrac{4}{7}$

    (C) $\dfrac{3}{5}$

    (D) $\dfrac{3}{4}$

    (E) $\dfrac{4}{5}$

7. A bowl contains yellow candies and blue candies. The ratio of yellow candies to blue candies is 2 to 3. If there are a total of 25 candies in the bowl, how many of them are yellow?

    (A) 2
    (B) 3
    (C) 10
    (D) 15
    (E) 25

Answers to Ratio Practice Set

1. D
2. A
3. B
4. E
5. C
6. D
7. C

Average Problems

Average problems on the SSAT aren't so bad because they fall into very predictable categories.

The types of problems you will see include:

1. Averages of consecutive numbers
2. Weighted averages
3. Applying the definition of an average
4. Average problems that use rate

Average problems on the SSAT use the following equation:

$$\frac{\text{sum of numbers}}{\text{number of numbers}} = \text{average}$$

Sometimes you will have to manipulate the equation to get:

$$\text{sum of numbers} = \text{number of numbers} \times \text{average}$$

Consecutive Number Average Problems

Sometimes they will give you an average for consecutive whole numbers, consecutive odd numbers, or consecutive even numbers.

You should rejoice when you see these problems – as long as you know the problem type, consecutive number average problems are super easy.

The only potential trick is forgetting what kind of numbers they are using (consecutive, consecutive even, or consecutive odd) or forgetting whether they are asking for the smallest number or the greatest number. Circle what kind of numbers they are looking for and what they are asking for and you will be just fine.

- Circle what kind of numbers are being used (consecutive, consecutive even, or consecutive odd)
- Circle what they are asking for (smallest or greatest number)

Here is an example of how a question could look on the SSAT:

1. The average of three consecutive odd numbers is 11. What is the smallest
    number?
    (A) 9
    (B) 10
    (C) 11
    (D) 12
    (E) 13

First of all, did you remember to circle "consecutive odd" and "smallest number?"
Good. Consecutive number problems are pretty easy – the average is just the
middle number. The strategy for this is just to draw a blank for each number.
Insert the average in the middle blank and find what they are looking for.

For the above example:

    1. Draw a blank for each number: _____ _____ _____

    2. Insert the average in the middle: _____ __11__ _____

    3. Find what they are looking for: __9__ __11__ _____

Since the smallest number is 9, answer choice A is correct.

Here is another one for you to try:

2. If the average of five consecutive whole numbers is 12, what is the largest
    one?
    (A) 7
    (B) 10
    (C) 12
    (D) 14
    (E) 17

For this problem, we draw out five slots and then put twelve in the middle. We then fill in the other slots like so:

$$\underline{} \quad \underline{} \quad \underline{} \quad \underline{} \quad \underline{}$$
$$ 12 13 14$$

From this, it is clear to see that 14 is the largest number, so answer choice D is correct.

Weighted Average Problems

Sometimes you have to find a total average given the average of a couple of groups. What you need to do is use the following equation to find the sum of each group:

sum of group = number of numbers × average

Then use the average equation again to find the total average.

$$\frac{\text{sum of group 1} + \text{sum of group 2}}{\text{total number of numbers}} = \text{overall average}$$

This is called a weighted average. You don't need to remember this term, you just need to know NOT to add the two averages together and divide by 2.

Here is an example of how this is tested on the SSAT:

1. The average test score for two students was 88. The average test score for another three students was 92. What was the average of all the test scores?

   (A) 88
   (B) 89.6
   (C) 90
   (D) 90.4
   (E) 92

In order to solve this problem, first we have to find the sum of the scores of each group.

sum of students who scored 88 = # *of students × average* = 2 × 88 = 176

sum of students who scored 92 = # *of students × average* = 3 × 92 = 276

Now we add the two sums together to get the total sum of the student's scores.

$$sum\ of\ group\ 1 + sum\ of\ group\ 2 = total\ sum$$
$$176 + 276 = 452 = sum\ of\ all\ the\ students\ scores$$

Now, to get the average of all the students, we simply divide the sum of their scores by the total number of students.

$$\frac{452}{5} = 90.4$$

The correct answer choice is D.

Now here is another one for you to try:

2. The average height of four students is 64 inches. The average height of a different set of two students is 68 inches. What is the average height of all six students?

   (A) 64.5
   (B) 65
   (C) 65.33
   (D) 66.45
   (E) 67

To solve this problem, we first have to figure out the sum of all the heights. If we multiply 4 times 64, we get that the sum of the heights of the students who are 64 inches tall on average is 256. Then, to find the sum of the students who are 68 inches tall on average, we multiply 2 times 68 to get 136. Now we add 256 and 136. This tells us that the sum of the heights of all the students in 392. If we divide that sum by the total number of students (6), we get that the average height is 65.33 inches, or choice C.

Applying the Definition of an Average

These problems generally ask you to apply the following two concepts:

- If you have only two numbers, the difference between each number and the average will be the same
- If you have only two numbers, the sum of those numbers will be twice the average

Here is one way that this question may look on the actual SSAT:

1. If two numbers, T and N, have an average of 80, and T is less than N, then which of the following must be true?

   (A) $T = 80 + N$
   (B) $80 - T = N - 80$
   (C) $T + N = 80$
   (D) $N - T = 40$
   (E) $T = 80$ and $N = 80$

Which answer choice shows that the difference between the average and each number is the same? Choice B does, so that is the correct answer. If that is confusing, you can also make up your own numbers and plug them in to see which answer choice works. Since the average must be right in the middle, we could make T equal to 75 and N equal to 85. Plug those numbers into the equations and see which answer choice gives you a true equation.

Here is another one for you to try:

2. If W and X have an average of 60 and X is less than W, which of the following must be true?

   (A) $W + X = 120$
   (B) $W - X = 30$
   (C) $W = 60$ and $X = 60$
   (D) $W = 60 + X$
   (E) $W + X = 60$

To answer this question, we have to apply the fact that the sum of two numbers is equal to twice their average. Since the average is 60, the sum of W and X has to be 120, so answer choice A is correct.

Average Problems that Use Rate

There are two types of these problems:

1. Problems that give you an average time or length for a segment and then ask for a total
2. Problems that give you a total time and distance and ask for rate

The first problem type is the easiest. To solve these problems, we just have to use:

$$sum = \# \ of \ numbers \times average$$

The only potential trick to these questions is that we often have to convert between units. Not hard, you just have to remember to do it.

- Remember to convert any minutes over 60 into hours and minutes
- Remember to convert any inches over 12 into feet and inches

Here is an example of how this question could look on the test:

1. Sally completed in a triathlon (a race with three segments) and her average time for each of the segments was 1 hour and 42 minutes. What was her total time?
   - (A) 2 hours 30 minutes
   - (B) 3 hours 42 minutes
   - (C) 4 hours 42 minutes
   - (D) 5 hours 6 minutes
   - (E) 6 hours

To solve this question, we have to multiply the average segment length by the number of segments.

If we do the hours and minutes separately, we get:

$$1 \ hour \times 3 \ segments = 3 \ hours$$
$$42 \ minutes \times 3 \ segments = 126 \ minutes$$

Now, the issue is that we have to convert the minutes into hours and minutes:

$$126 \ minutes = 60 \ minutes + 60 \ minutes + 6 \ minutes =$$
$$2 \ hours \ 6 \ minutes$$

Now we add back in the three hours from the first part of the problem and we get 5 hours and 6 minutes, or answer choice D.

Here is another one for you to try:

2. A piece of rope was cut into four pieces. The average length of each piece was 4 feet 7 inches. What was the length of the original piece of rope?

(A) 17 feet 10 inches
(B) 18 feet 4 inches
(C) 19 feet 14 inches
(D) 20 feet 2 inches
(E) 24 feet

To solve this problem, let's handle the feet and inches separately.

$$4 \ feet \times four \ pieces = 16 \ feet$$
$$7 \ inches \times four \ pieces = 28 \ inches$$

Now we have to change the 28 inches into feet and inches.

$$28 \ inches = 12 \ inches + 12 \ inches + 4 \ inches = 2 \ feet + 4 \ inches$$

If we combine the feet, we get that the total length must be 18 feet and 4 inches, so choice B is correct.

The trickiest average problems on the SSAT are those that ask you to figure out an average rate.

In order to do these problems, you have to divide the total miles by the number of hours to get the average rate. The test often asks for a range of speeds, so make sure that you figure out the speed for both the shortest possible time and the longest possible time.

- Figure out the speed for both times given

The trick to these questions is that it is really tempting to just figure out one speed and then look at the answers. The problem with this is that the shorter the period of time, the higher the average speed. It is better just to do the math for each of the times.

- Don't try to take a shortcut

Here is an example of how this type of question looks on the SSAT:

3. A bus driver drove 125 miles and it took him between 2½ and 3 hours. His average speed, in miles per hour, was between

   (A) 42 and 50
   (B) 50 and 54
   (C) 54 and 58
   (D) 58 and 60
   (E) 60 and 64

To solve this problem, we have to first divide 125 by 2.5 (miles per hour means miles divided by hours). If we do this we get 50, so we know that one of the speeds must be 50 mph. That tells us that it must be answer choice A or B. To find the other end of the range, we can divide 125 by 3. We don't even need to do out the whole problem, we just need to do enough to see whether it could be 42 or 54. If we do long division, the first digit we get in the answer is a 4, so choice A is correct.

Here is another one for you to try:

4. A ferry took between 1.5 and 2 hours to go 40 miles. The ferry's average speed on this trip must have been between (answers given in miles per hour)

   (A) 15 and 20
   (B) 20 and 27
   (C) 27 and 32
   (D) 32 and 40
   (E) 40 and 45

To solve this problem, we first divide 40 by 1.5 to get one end of our range. If we do that we get roughly 27, so we know it must be answer choice B or C. To get the other end of our range, we divide 40 by 2 to get 20, so answer choice B is correct.

Now you know all the average problem types, and how to solve them! Complete the following practice set to reinforce what you have learned.

Average Problem Practice Set

1. According to Figure 1, what was the average number of children in a classroom from 1990 to 1993?

   (A) 20
   (B) 22.5
   (C) 24
   (D) 25
   (E) 26

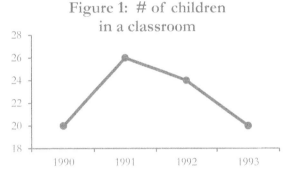

Figure 1: # of children in a classroom

2. If D and F are two numbers whose average is 50, and D is less than F, which of the following must be true?

   (A) $D - 50 = F - 50$
   (B) $D = 50 \ and \ F = 50$
   (C) $D + F = 50$
   (D) $D + F = 100$
   (E) $F - D = 50$

3. Sally's trip to the state fair took between two and two and a quarter hours to get there. If the state fair was 90 miles away, her average speed, in miles per hour, must have been between:

   (A) 35 and 40
   (B) 38 and 42
   (C) 40 and 45
   (D) 42 and 50
   (E) 45 and 50

4. Luke has to write a ten-page paper. After three weeks, he has only written 2 pages. The paper is due in 3 days. How many pages must he write, on average, per day?

   (A) 2

   (B) $2\frac{1}{3}$

   (C) $2\frac{2}{3}$

   (D) 3

   (E) 8

5. If the average of five consecutive even numbers is 22, what is the smallest one?

   (A) 17
   (B) 18
   (C) 20
   (D) 22
   (E) 27

6. Sarah scored an average of 90 on her first four tests. If she scores a 100 on her fifth test, what will her new average be?

   (A) 90
   (B) 90.5
   (C) 91
   (D) 92
   (E) 95

Answers to Average Problem Practice Set

1. B
2. D
3. C
4. C
5. B
6. D

Solving Equations & Inequalities

The basic goal of solving equations is to get a variable by itself – or to isolate it.

There are two basics for isolating a variable:

1. Use PEMDAS, but in reverse.
2. Do the opposite operation in each step

What does this mean to reverse the order of PEMDAS? It means if there is addition or subtraction, we take care of that first. Then we look for any multiplication or division, followed by exponents and parentheses.

Here is a basic example:

(In each step, notice that we do the *opposite* operation in order to simplify the equation.)

$$x + 2 = 4 \qquad \text{The left side has \textit{addition}, so we must \textit{subtract}.}$$
$$\underline{-2 \quad -2}$$
$$x = 2 \qquad \text{The problem is solved, the value of } x \text{ is 2.}$$

Here is another example:

$$\frac{1}{2}x = 7 \qquad \text{The left side has \textit{division} by 2, so we must \textit{multiply} by 2.}$$
$$\underline{\times 2 \quad \times 2}$$
$$x = 14 \qquad \text{The problem is solved, the value of } x \text{ is 14.}$$

Here are a couple of quick ones for you to try. On the actual SSAT, all of the problems are multiple choice, but they also don't ask you questions that ask you just to solve for a variable. We just want to check to make sure you have the basics down before we move on.

Solve for x:

1. $2x + 4 = 14$

2. $\dfrac{1}{3}x - 7 = 3$

Here are the solutions and explanations:

1. $2x + 4 = 14$	Using reverse PEMDAS, look first for subtraction or addition.
$-4 = -4$	We found addition, so we will subtract 4 from both sides.
$2x = 10$	Now we find multiplication, so we must use division.
$\dfrac{2x}{2} = \dfrac{10}{2}$	We divide both sides by 2.
$x = 5$	The problem is solved. The value of x is 5.

2. $\dfrac{1}{3}x - 7 = 3$	Using reverse PEMDAS, look first for subtraction or addition.
$+7 = +7$	We found subtraction, so we will add 7.
$\dfrac{1}{3}x = 10$	Now we find division (multiplying by $\dfrac{1}{3}$ is the same as dividing by 3), so we must use multiplication.
$\times 3 = \times 3$	We multiply both sides by 3.
$x = 30$	The problem is solved. The value of x is 30.

On the SSAT, it is rarely as simple as solving for a variable.

Some of the problem types that you will see are:

1. Solving for a variable
2. Asking for more than just the variable
3. "Could be" questions
4. Setting up an equation and solving
5. Setting up equations using equation language
6. Questions that require solving for numbers that relate to each other
7. Solving for 3 variables

Solving for a Variable

On the SSAT, you may see questions that involve solving for a variable but with a twist. Sometimes you are asked about the process and not the result, sometimes you have to first combine like terms, and so on.

The keys to these questions are:

1. Remember to first combine like terms
2. Don't forget PEMDAS!
3. Make sure that you are answering the question asked

Here are a few for you to try:

1. In order to solve for x in the equation $\frac{x}{3} = -12$, what would you have to multiply both sides by?
   - (A) -36
   - (B) -12
   - (C) -4
   - (D) 3
   - (E) 12

This is one of those questions that looks easy, but it is really a sneaky question. They aren't asking you for the value of x, they are only asking what you would multiply both sides of the equation by in order to isolate x. Since x is currently divided by 3, we would do the opposite and multiply both sides by 3 in order get x by itself. Answer choice D is correct.

2. In the equation $15 - x + 3 = 2x$, what is x equal to?
   - (A) 3
   - (B) 6
   - (C) 9
   - (D) 12
   - (E) 15

Our first step is to combine like terms:

$$15 - x + 3 = 2x$$
$$18 - x = 2x$$
$$\underline{+x \qquad +x}$$
$$18 = 3x$$

Now we divide both sides by 3 and get that $x = 6$. Answer choice B is correct.

3. Solve for x: $3x + 2x - 6x = 5 - 3 + 1$

    (A) -3
    (B) -1
    (C)   1
    (D)   3
    (E)   6

Again, we must first combine like terms:

$$3x + 2x - 6x = 5 - 3 + 1$$
$$-x = 3$$

Now we divide both sides by -1 and get that $x = -3$. Answer choice A is correct.

Asking for More than Just the Variable

These questions ask you to solve for a variable and then use that value to solve another problem.

These aren't hard, you just have to remember to complete all the steps. It is very easy to solve for the variable and then choose that as your answer choice. To get around that, be sure to circle what they are asking for.

- Circle what the question is asking for

Here is what these questions look like on the SSAT:

1. If $5 \times T = 35$, what does $5 + T$ equal?

   (A) 0
   (B) $\frac{1}{7}$
   (C) 1
   (D) 7
   (E) 12

To solve, first we have to find T. It is currently multiplied by 5, so we do the opposite and divide by 5. This gives us that T is equal to 7. We aren't done yet, though, because the question asks for $5 + T$ (you did remember to circle what the question asks for, right?). $7 + 5 = 12$, so answer choice E is correct.

Here is another one for you to try:

2. If $25 \times B = 25$, then $25 + B =$

   (A) 0
   (B) $\frac{1}{25}$
   (C) 1
   (D) 25
   (E) 26

If we first solve for B, we get that $B = 1$. If we plug that into $25 + B$, then we get that the answer is 26, or choice E.

Inequalities

You may also see inequalities, or questions that don't ask you to solve for a variable but rather to figure out the minimum or maximum value of a variable. The only trick is to remember that "<" or ">" does NOT include the numbers themselves but "≤" or "≥" does include the number given. For example, $x > 4$ includes values that are greater than 4, and $x \geq 4$ includes 4 and the values that are greater than 4.

Here are a few basic inequality problems for you to try:

1. Which of the following could be the value of X if $X + \frac{2}{5} < 1$

   (A) $\frac{3}{7}$

   (B) $\frac{3}{5}$

   (C) $\frac{3}{4}$

   (D) 1

   (E) $\frac{3}{2}$

The key to answering this question is to recognize that $X + \frac{2}{5}$ must be less than, and not equal to, 1. If we substitute in $\frac{3}{5}$ for X, $X + \frac{2}{5}$ would be equal to 1. Therefore, the correct answer needs to be less than $\frac{3}{5}$. Only answer choice A is less than $\frac{3}{5}$, so it is the correct answer.

2. Which inequality expresses all possible solutions of $\frac{m}{3} \geq -2$?

   (A) $m \leq -6$
   (B) $m \geq -6$
   (C) $m \leq -5$
   (D) $m \geq -5$
   (E) $m \geq 6$

In order to answer this question, we need to multiply both sides by 3. This results in $3 \times \frac{m}{3} \geq -2 \times 3$, or $m \geq -6$. Answer choice B is correct. We have to be careful not to be tricked by this question. If we were dividing by a negative number, we would have flipped the inequality sign, but just because a negative number shows up in the problem doesn't automatically mean we need to flip the sign.

Here is an example of a question that requires you to flip the inequality sign because we are multiplying or dividing by a negative number:

3. Which inequality represents all possible solutions of $9 - 4x \leq -3$?

    (A) $x \geq -3$
    (B) $x \leq -3$
    (C) $x \geq -\frac{3}{2}$
    (D) $x \geq 3$
    (E) $x \leq 3$

Our first step in answering this question is to subtract 9 from both sides. This leaves us with $-4x \leq -3 - 9$, which is $-4x \leq -12$ when we combine like terms. Now we have to divide both sides by -4. When we multiply or divide an inequality by a negative number, we need to flip the inequality sign. Our inequality becomes $x \geq 3$. Answer choice D is correct.

You may also see inequality questions that have a variable on each side of the inequality sign. We solve these just like we do equations that have a variable on both sides: we move all the variables onto the same side of the inequality when we combine like terms.

Here are a couple of questions to try:

4. Which inequality represents all possible solutions of $4x - 3 \geq 2x + 7$?

    (A) $x \geq -5$
    (B) $x \leq -5$
    (C) $x \geq 5$
    (D) $x \leq 5$
    (E) $x \geq 10$

This inequality has a variable on both sides, so we need to combine like terms. We can do this by subtracting $2x$ from both sides and adding 3 to both sides. Doing this allows us to work with positive numbers and avoid the mistakes that sometimes crop up when working with negative numbers. Our inequality becomes $2x \geq 10$. Now we just divide both sides by 2 and the result is $x \geq 5$. Answer choice C is correct.

5. Which inequality represents all possible solutions of
$30m - 9(5m + 2) \geq -3m + 18$?

(A) $m \geq -3$
(B) $m \leq -3$
(C) $m \geq 0$
(D) $m \leq 3$
(E) $m \geq 3$

Our first step here is to distribute the 9 so that we can get rid of the parentheses:

$30m - 45m - 18 \geq -3m + 18$
$-15m - 18 \geq -3m + 18$

Now we can add $15m$ to each side:

$-18 \geq 12m + 18$

The next step is to subtract 18 from both sides:

$-36 \geq 12m$

Finally, we divide each side by 12:

$-3 \geq m$

Answer choice B is correct.

Finally, we have inequality questions that ask you to combine the solution sets for two different inequalities. The trick to these is to pay attention to the words "or" and "and". The word "or" indicates that the solution set should be all numbers that are in one solution set or the other. The word "and" indicates that the solution set is all numbers that show up in both solution sets (where they overlap).

- "or" indicates all numbers that show up in either solution set
- "and" indicates all numbers that show up in both solution sets

Here are a couple of questions for you to try:

6. Which inequality represents all possible solutions of $3 \leq -2x + 3$ or $4x + 1 \geq 13$?

   (A) $-3 \leq x \leq 0$
   (B) $0 \leq x \leq 3$
   (C) $x \geq -3$ or $x \leq 0$
   (D) $x \geq -3$ or $x \leq -3$
   (E) $x \leq 0$ or $x \geq 3$

We can start by solving the first inequality, remembering to flip the inequality sign when we divide by a negative number:

$$3 \leq -2x + 3$$
$$0 \leq -2x$$
$$0 \geq x$$

Now we can solve to the second inequality:

$$4x + 1 \geq 13$$
$$4x \geq 12$$
$$x \geq 3$$

Since this is an "or" question, the solution set for both inequalities should be included. Answer choice E is correct. Don't be fooled by the fact that $x \leq 0$ looks a little different from the $0 \geq x$ that we came up with. Both inequalities mean x is less than 0 and are equivalent.

7. Which inequality represents all possible solutions for $2x + 3 \geq 5$ and $7 - 2x \leq 3$?

   (A) $x \leq -2$
   (B) $x \leq -1$
   (C) $x \geq 0$
   (D) $x \geq 1$
   (E) $x \geq 2$

First, we need to solve for x in the first inequality:

$$2x + 3 \geq 5$$
$$2x \geq 2$$
$$x \geq 1$$

Now we need to solve for x in the second inequality:

$$7 - 2x \leq 3$$
$$-2x \leq -4$$
$$x \geq 2$$

The question uses the word "and" so we are looking for the solution set that includes the numbers from both sets. Since only numbers greater than or equal to 2 are included in both solution sets, choice E is correct.

"Could Be" Questions

There are two types of could be questions:

1. Questions that tell us that a variable must be greater than (or less than) a number and then ask what the value of an expression with that variable could be
2. Questions that require you to set up an equation and then choose which answer choice would give you a whole number for the variable

The first type of "could be" questions give you an inequality to define the value of a variable and then ask what an expression with that variable could be equal to.
Here is how you solve these types of questions:

1. First, plug into the expression the value that the variable must be greater than/less than.
2. Solve the expression.
3. Choose the answer choice that is greater than (if you had a greater than in the inequality) or less than (if you had a less than in the inequality)

What doesn't work is plugging in the whole number that is one number greater than (or less than) the number in the inequality. To make one of the answer choices work, the value of the variable is generally not a whole number.

- Don't just plug in the next greater (or lesser) whole number

Another trick to these questions is that the correct answer must be either the greatest or least answer choice, otherwise there would be more than one correct answer. If you remember this trick, then you can just choose the greatest answer choice if the variable has to be greater than a number or the smallest answer choice if the variable has to be less than a number. If you don't remember this trick, it is OK, you can still solve using the above method.

- If the variable has to be greater than a number, then choose the largest answer choice
- If the variable has to be less than a number, then choose the smallest answer choice

Here is an example of how these questions look:

1. If $q > 6$, then which of the following could be $3q - 4$?
   - (A) 10
   - (B) 11
   - (C) 12
   - (D) 14
   - (E) 15

In this case, if we plugged in 6 for q in $3q - 4$, we would get 14. Since q has to be greater than 6, our answer must be greater than 14. Only answer choice E works. If you remembered our shortcut, you would have just chosen answer choice E since it is a greater than problem and we should choose the largest answer with greater than problems.

Here is another one for you to try:

2. If $M < 3$, then $2M + 5$ could be
   - (A) 10
   - (B) 11
   - (C) 12
   - (D) 13
   - (E) 14

If we plug in 3 for M, we get that $2M + 5$ is equal to 11. That means that our answer must be less than 11 since M is less than 3. Only answer choice A works.

If you use our shortcut, you would choose the smallest answer since it is a less than problem.

Another type of problem gives you variables and then you have to find a scenario where the variable would be a whole number.

The trick to these problems is to not skim over the term "whole number"!

- Circle the term "whole number" if you see it
- These problems are really testing divisibility

Here is what this type of problem looks like on the SSAT:

3. In the figure above, if h is a whole number, then which of the following could be equal to the length of the entire segment FG?

   (A) 24
   (B) 21
   (C) 18
   (D) 15
   (E) 10

To answer this question, we first have to figure out what the entire length of the segment is in terms of h. If we add the pieces together, we get that the whole segment is $7h$. If h has to be a whole number, then the length of FG has to be divisible by 7. Only answer choice B is divisible by 7, so that is the correct answer.

Here is another one for you to try:

4. In the figure above, if x is a whole number, then which of the following could be equal to the length of QR?

(A) 8
(B) 9
(C) 11
(D) 15
(E) 18

If we add the segments together, we get that the total length is $5x$. Since x is a whole number, then the length of QR must be divisible by 5. Only answer choice D is divisible by 5, so that is the correct answer choice.

Setting Up an Equation and Solving

These questions can often look like geometry questions, but don't be fooled! They are really asking you to set up an equation and then solve for a variable or rearrange the equation.

To solve these problems, there are two helpful things to keep in mind:

1. If they give you information in words and on a picture, mark the information given in words on the picture. This way you will have all the information in one place.
2. You have to use all the information given in a problem. If you are stuck, look for the information that you have not used.

Here is how this type of question can look on the SSAT:

Figure 1:

1. In Figure 1 above, if segment *PR* is 42 inches long then how long is segment *QR*?

   (A)   7 inches
   (B)   10.5 inches
   (C)   14 inches
   (D)   21 inches
   (E)   28 inches

In order to solve this problem, we first have to set up an equation.

We know that:

$$PQ + QR = 42$$

If we substitute in the values that are given for each segment in terms of *N*, we get:

$$2N + 4N = 42$$

Now we just have to combine the *N*s and solve.

$$6N = 42$$
$$\div 6 \quad \div 6$$
$$N = 7$$

We aren't done yet, though. The problem doesn't ask for the value of *N*, it asks us for the length of segment *QR*. Since *QR* is equal to *4N*, we multiply 4×7 and get 28 inches. Answer choice E is correct.

Figure 2:

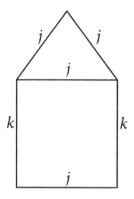

2. In Figure 2 above, the perimeter of the triangle is equal to 18. The perimeter of the quadrilateral region is equal to 26. What is the value of $j + k$?

(A) 6
(B) 12
(C) 13
(D) 18
(E) 24

To answer this question, we have to set up a couple of different equations. We can start with the triangle. We know that the perimeter is 18 and we also know that the perimeter is the sum of the sides.

We can solve for j using this information.

$$j + j + j = 18$$
$$3j = 18$$
$$j = 6$$

Now that we have j, we can solve for k. We know that the perimeter of the quadrilateral is 26, and we also know that the perimeter is the sum of the sides. We can set up the following equation:

$$2j + 2k = 26$$

Then we can substitute in the value that we already found for j and solve.

$$2(6) + 2k = 26$$
$$12 + 2k = 26$$
$$2k = 14$$
$$k = 7$$

We now have $j = 6$ and $k = 7$, so we can figure out that $j + k = 13$ and answer choice C is correct.

Another type of problem that you will see is where they give the values for overlapping line segments.

To solve these problems:

- Mark all the information given on the drawing
- Set up equations so that you can see how all the parts are related

Here is what these questions look like on the test:

<u>Figure 3:</u>

3. In figure 3 above, the distance between B and D is 12. The distance between A and C is also 12. If the distance between C and D is 8, what is the distance between A and B?

   (A) 6
   (B) 7
   (C) 8
   (D) 10
   (E) 12

To solve this equation, the first step is to mark information given. Our picture now looks something like this:

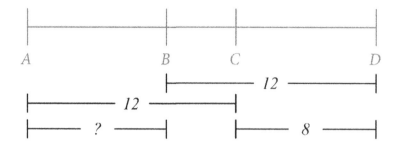

This allows us to set up some equations and solve.

We can see that:

$$BC + CD = 12$$

Since we know that $CD = 8$, we can solve to get that $BC = 4$.

We can also see that:

$$AB + BC = 12$$

Since we know that $BC = 4$, we can solve to get that $AB = 8$.

Since they were asking for the length of AB, we know that answer choice C is correct.

Here is another one for you to try:

(It might look scary, but it is really just the same type of problem)

Figure 4:
(figure not drawn to scale)

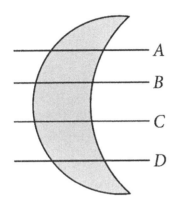

4. In Figure 4, the shaded region is divided by lines A, B, C, and D. The shaded area between lines A and C is 25 square yards. The area of the shaded region between lines B and D is 30 square yards. If the area of the shaded region between lines C and D is 15, then what is the area, in square yards, of the shaded region between A and B?

(A) 10
(B) 15
(C) 20
(D) 25
(E) 35

First, mark the distances on your picture. From that, you can see that:

$$AC = AB + BC = 25$$

We can also see that:

$$BC + CD = BD$$

Since we are given that the area between C and D is 15 and that the area between B and D is 30, it is not hard to figure out that the area between B and C is also 15. Now we can plug this back into our first equation and solve:

$$AB + BC = 25$$
$$AB + 15 = 25$$
$$AB = 10$$

Since AB is equal to 10, answer choice A is correct.

Setting Up Equations Using Equation Language

You may see a question on the SSAT that requires you to translate a written statement into an equation. These questions are not asking you to solve, you just need to set up an equation.

- These questions don't ask you to solve so be sure to look at answer choices before you dive in to calculations

The key to these types of questions is to remember to go through the question word by word.

Here is a table for some of the language that you may see:

If the statement says...	Translate it into...
sum	addition
more than	addition
difference	subtraction
less than	subtraction
product	multiplication
of	multiplication (of does not always mean multiplication, but it often does)
quotient	division
is	equal sign
greater than	> if in an inequality, addition if in an equation
less than	< if in an inequality, subtraction if in an equation (see important rule below)
greater than or equal to	≥
less than or equal to	≤

The only term that is a little tricky is when "less than" is used in an equation (and not an inequality). In this case, the rule is to reverse the order of the numbers and variables. For example, let's say that the question states "x is three less than y". The first part of the statement "x is" would translate into "$x =$". In order to turn "three less than y" into an equation, however, we have to flip the 3 and the y to get "$y - 3$". Our final equation is $x = y - 3$.

- Generally, we can translate from the order that words are given into an equation
- The only language that is tricky is "less than" when it is used in an equation

Here are a couple of questions for you to try:

1. Choose the equation that best represents the following statement: "The sum of 4 times a number and seven is equal to five less than three times another number."
   - (A) $7x + 4 = 5 - 3y$
   - (B) $7x + 4 = 3y - 5$
   - (C) $4x + 4 = 5 - 3y$
   - (D) $4x + 4 = 3y - 5$
   - (E) $4x + 7 = 3y - 5$

To answer this question, we just translate. The words "is equal to" represent our equal sign so let's deal with what comes before it first. We can translate "sum of 4 times a number and seven" into "$4x + 7$". Now we have to deal with the right side of the equation. Since we have the words "less than" in an equation, we need to remember to flip the order. The words "five less than three times another number" translate into "$3y - 5$". If we put all this together, we get $4x + 7 = 3y - 5$, or answer choice E.

2. Which inequality represents the statement "The product of two times a number and three times another number is greater than or equal to fifteen"?
   - (A) $2c \div 3d \leq 15$
   - (B) $2c \div 3d \geq 15$
   - (C) $2c \times 3d \leq 15$
   - (D) $2c \times 3d \geq 15$
   - (E) $2c \times 3c \geq 15$

This question is more straightforward when it comes to setting up the equation. The trick to this one is that the answer choices are all very similar. We need to make sure that we pay attention to the differences between each choice. We are looking for an inequality that indicates that the side with variables is greater than or equal to 15, so we can eliminate choices A and C. We are also looking for a choice with two different variables since our two numbers are different. We can eliminate choice E. Finally, we are looking for a choice with multiplication since we have the word product. Choice B can be eliminated since it has division. Choice D remains and it is the correct answer choice.

You may also see questions that ask you to set up an equation and then solve for the actual number. The trick to these ones is that they often require using some tougher math, unless you remember that you can just plug in answer choices and see what works.

- Keep in mind that we can plug in answer choices to see what work

Here are a couple of questions for you to try:

3. The product of $4n$ and 3 more than n is equal to 72. Which could be a value of n?

   (A) −6
   (B) −4
   (C) 4
   (D) 6
   (E) 8

We can start by translating the words into an equation. The word product tells us to multiply. We can translate "3 more than n" into $3 + n$. Therefore, the product of $4n$ and 3 more than n is equal to 72 can be turned into $4n(3 + n) = 72$. If we were to multiply the terms, it would get into solving a quadratic equation, which may or may not be something you have learned. However, one of the answer choices has to work. Let's try choice A, substituting in −6 for n in the equation $4n(3 + n) = 72$:

$$4n(3 + n) = 72$$
$$4(-6)(3 + -6) = 72$$
$$-24(-3) = 72$$
$$72 = 72$$

Since the equation was true, 72 = 72, when we substituted in –6 for n, answer choice A is correct. We do not need to check the other answer choices since we found one that worked and there is only one right answer per question.

4. The quotient of $4b$ and $b - 4$ is 6. What is the value of b?

    (A) –2
    (B) –4
    (C) 0
    (D) 12
    (E) 24

To answer this question, let's start with setting up an equation. Since quotient is the result of division, our equation is:

$$\frac{4b}{b - 4} = 6$$

In this case, we wouldn't have to use terribly advanced math to solve, so it might be easier just to solve for the variable. We can multiply both sides by $b - 4$ and then solve:

$$4b = 6(b - 4)$$
$$4b = 6b - 24$$
$$-2b = -24$$
$$b = 12$$

When we translated into an equation and then solved for b, the result was 12. Answer choice D is correct.

Questions that Require Solving for Numbers that Relate to Each Other

Finally, we have questions that require you to define one variable in terms of another. These questions may use language like "two numbers whose difference is 4". In this case, one number could be represented by x and the other number could be represented by $x - 4$. You may also see questions that ask you for consecutive numbers, consecutive even numbers, or consecutive odd numbers. To represent consecutive numbers, we can use x, $x + 1$, $x + 2$ and so on. To represent consecutive even or consecutive odd numbers we can use x, $x + 2$, $x + 4$ and so on. The trick to these questions is to underline how the numbers are related and to circle what they are asking for.

- Remember to define one number in terms of the other
- Consecutive numbers can be represented by x, $x + 1$, $x + 2$ and so on
- Consecutive even or odd numbers can be represented by x, $x + 2$, $x + 4$ and so on
- Underline how the numbers are related
- Circle what they are asking for

Here are a couple of questions that ask you to set up equations but not actually solve:

1. The sum of three consecutive odd numbers is 51. Which equation could be used to solve for the value of the smallest of these numbers?

    (A) $x + 1 + 2 = 51$
    (B) $x + 2 + 4 = 51$
    (C) $x + x + 1 + 2 = 51$
    (D) $x + x + 1 + x + 3 = 51$
    (E) $x + x + 2 + x + 4 = 51$

We have to remember to keep straight how the numbers are related. They are consecutive odd numbers, so we can represent them with $x, x + 2,$ and $x + 4$. Answer choice E correctly shows these terms being added together, so it is the correct answer choice.

2. The sum of two numbers, whose difference is 7, is 25. Which equation could be used to find the smaller number?

    (A) $x - 7 = 25$
    (B) $x + 7 = 25$
    (C) $x + (x + 7) = 25$
    (D) $x - (x + 7) = 25$
    (E) $x - (x - 7) = 25$

This question is a little tricky because they are asking us for the smallest number and not the largest number. If we make the smaller number x, then the larger number would be $x + 7$ since the difference between them is 7. Answer choice C correctly represents the sum of x and $x + 7$, so it is the correct answer choice.

Now we will try a couple where not only do you have to set up the equation but you also have to solve:

3. Two numbers have a difference of 8. Their sum is 34. What is the larger of these numbers?

  (A) 8
  (B) 13
  (C) 17
  (D) 21
  (E) 34

To answer this question, let's make the larger number equal to x. This makes the smaller number equal to $x - 8$. Now let's set up an equation and solve:

$$x + (x - 8) = 34$$
$$2x - 8 = 34$$
$$2x = 42$$
$$x = 21$$

Since we set x equal to the larger number, we know that answer choice D is correct.

4. The least minus twice the greatest of three consecutive integers is 6. What is the value of the least of these integers?

  (A) −10
  (B) −6
  (C) 2
  (D) 6
  (E) 10

Our first step is to set up expressions that represent each of the numbers. Since they are consecutive integers, we can represent them with $x, x + 1,$ and $x + 2$. Now we have to translate "the least minus twice the greatest of three consecutive integers is 6" into an equation and solve:

$$x - 2(x + 2) = 6$$
$$x - 2x - 4 = 6$$
$$-x = 10$$
$$x = -10$$

Answer choice A is correct.

Solving for 3 Variables

The next type of problem is one where they give you two equations that have three different variables in them and ask you to solve.

These are trick questions!

The general rules are:

- If you have one variable, you need one equation to solve
- If you have two variables, you need two equations to solve
- If you have three variables, you need three equations to solve

Here is how this question type looks on the test:

1. If $Q + R = 5$ and $R + S = 10$, then what is the value of S?

   (A) 15
   (B) 10
   (C) 5
   (D) 0
   (E) Cannot be determined

This problem has three variables and only two equations, so choice E is correct.

Here is another one for you to try:

2. If $T + V = 7$ and $2V + W = 7$, then what is the value of V?

   (A) 14
   (B) 7
   (C) –7
   (D) –14
   (E) Cannot be determined

Again, three variables with only two equations, so choice E is correct.

One thing to note is that if the question doesn't ask you to solve for the variable, but only to write one variable in terms of another, then the question CAN be answered.

Now you know what you need in order to answer solving equations questions!

Solving Equations Practice Set

1. If $L + K = 16$ and $3K + M = 16$, then what is the value of K?

   (A) 16

   (B) 8

   (C) −8

   (D) −16

   (E) Cannot be determined

Figure 1:

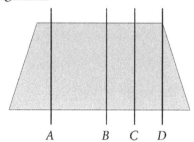

$\quad\quad\quad A \quad\quad\quad B \quad C \quad D$

2. The shaded polygon in Figure 1 is divided by lines A, B, C, and D. The area of the shaded region between A and C is 40 and the area of the shaded region between B and D is 35. If the area between B and C is 15, what is the area of the shaded region between A and D?

   (A) 40

   (B) 45

   (C) 50

   (D) 55

   (E) 60

3. In order to solve for n in the equation $4n = 24$, what would you have to multiply both sides of the equation by?

   (A) −4

   (B) $\dfrac{1}{4}$

   (C) 4

   (D) 6

   (E) 24

4. Solve for y: $2y - 6 + y - 3 = 4 + 4y$

   (A) -13

   (B) $-\dfrac{13}{3}$

   (C) $-\dfrac{5}{7}$

   (D)   3

   (E)   5

5. If $R < 7$, then $3R + 6$ could be

   (A)   26
   (B)   27
   (C)   28
   (D)   29
   (E)   30

Figure 2:

6. In Figure 2 above, segment AC is 35 centimeters long. How long is segment AB?

   (A)   7 cm
   (B)   14 cm
   (C)   21 cm
   (D)   28 cm
   (E)   35 cm

7. In the equation $5c - 6 - 2 = 2c + 1$, what is c equal to?

   (A) -9
   (B) -3
   (C)   1
   (D)   3
   (E)   9

8. Choose the equation that best represents the following statement: "The sum of 3 times a number and six is equal to eight more than five times another number."

    (A) $3 \times 6 = 8 + 5$
    (B) $3n + 6 = 8 - 5p$
    (C) $3n + 6 = 8 + 5p$
    (D) $3n + 6 = 5p - 8$
    (E) $3n + 6 + 8 > 5p$

9. If $20 \times R = 20$, then $20 - R =$

    (A) 0
    (B) 1
    (C) 19
    (D) 20
    (E) 21

10. In Figure 3, the perimeter of the smaller triangle is 15 cm. The perimeter of the quadrilateral below the triangle is 25. What is $x + y$ equal to?

    (A) 10
    (B) 15
    (C) 25
    (D) 27
    (E) 32

Figure 3:

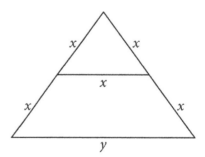

11. Which inequality represents the statement "The product of four times a number and two times another number is greater than or equal to nine"?

    (A) $4 \times 2x \geq 9$
    (B) $4x + 2y \geq 9$
    (C) $4x - 2y > 9$
    (D) $4x > 2y \times 9$
    (E) $4x \times 2y \geq 9$

12. The sum of four consecutive even numbers is 60. Which equation could be used to solve for the smallest of these numbers?

(A) $n + 1 + 2 + 3 = 60$
(B) $n + 2 + 4 + 6 = 60$
(C) $n + n + 2 + n + 4 = 60$
(D) $n + n + 2 + n + 4 + n + 6 = 60$
(E) $4n = 60$

13. If $x > 5$, then $2x + 11$ could be

(A) 17
(B) 18
(C) 19
(D) 21
(E) 22

Figure 4:

14. In Figure 4 above, if f is a whole number, then the length of UV could be

(A) 6
(B) 9
(C) 15
(D) 21
(E) 24

15. The sum of two numbers, whose difference is 11, is 9. Which equation could be used to find the larger of the two numbers?

(A) $p - 11 = 9$
(B) $2p + 11 = 9$
(C) $11p - 9 = p$
(D) $p + 9 = 11$
(E) $p + p - 11 = 9$

16. Two numbers have a difference of 6 and a sum of 42. What is the smaller of the two numbers?

   (A) 6
   (B) 18
   (C) 21
   (D) 24
   (E) 42

17. Twice the greatest number is one more than three times the least number of three consecutive odd numbers. What is the value of the greatest of these numbers?

   (A) 3
   (B) 5
   (C) 7
   (D) 9
   (E) 11

18. Which of the following could be the value of m if $m - \frac{1}{6} \geq 1$?

   (A) $\frac{1}{6}$

   (B) $\frac{1}{2}$

   (C) $\frac{5}{6}$

   (D) 1

   (E) $\frac{7}{6}$

19. Which inequality represents all possible solutions of $8 - 3x \geq -3$?

   (A) $x \leq -\frac{11}{3}$

   (B) $x \geq -\frac{11}{3}$

   (C) $x \leq \frac{11}{3}$

   (D) $x \geq \frac{11}{3}$

   (E) $x \geq \frac{3}{11}$

20. Which inequality represents all possible solutions of
$20m - 4(6m - 4) \leq -10m + 4$?

(A) $m \leq -2$
(B) $m \geq -2$
(C) $m \leq \frac{1}{2}$
(D) $m \leq 2$
(E) $m \geq 2$

21. Which inequality represents all possible solutions of $7 \geq 4n - 1$
and $3 \leq 3 - 2n$?

(A) $0 \geq n$
(B) $2 \geq n$
(C) $2 \leq n$
(D) $0 \geq n$ or $2 \leq n$
(E) $2 \geq n \geq 0$

22. The product of $3y$ and 5 less than y is 18. Which could be a value of y?

(A) -6
(B) -3
(C) 3
(D) 6
(E) 12

23. The quotient of $5c$ and $c + 2$ is 4. What is the value of c?

(A) $\frac{2}{39}$
(B) 3
(C) 6
(D) 8
(E) $\frac{39}{2}$

Answers to Solving Equations Practice Set

1. E		13. E
2. E		14. D
3. B		15. E
4. A		16. B
5. A		17. E
6. C		18. E
7. D		19. C
8. C		20. A
9. C		21. A
10. B		22. D
11. E		23. D
12. D		

Sequences and Patterns

On the SSAT, you are likely to see sequence and pattern questions that use arithmetic sequences. Arithmetic sequences are those that are formed when the same number is added to each term to get the next term.

For example:

2, 5, 8, 11, ...

The above is an arithmetic sequence because we add 3 to each term to get the next term in the sequence.

Keep in mind that the number that we add each time could be negative, meaning that we would essentially subtract from each term to get the next term.

For example:

10, 8, 6, 4, ...

To find each term in this sequence, we add −2, or subtract 2, from the term that comes before it.

On the SSAT, there are three basic types of sequence questions:

- Find the next term
- Use a sequence to predict a term that is not the next term
- Find the sum of a sequence

Find the Next Term

These questions tend to be straightforward. You need to figure out the rule and then apply it to find the next term.

We are going to jump straight to a couple of examples:

1. ____ , 34, 37, 40, 43

   What is the missing number in the sequence above?
   (A) 30
   (B) 31
   (C) 32
   (D) 33
   (E) 46

First, we have to establish the rule. In this case we have to add 3 to get to the next term. The only thing that is tricky about this problem is that we have to reverse the rule to get the missing term since it comes before the other numbers. We subtract 3 from 34 and get that the missing term is 31. Answer choice B is correct.

2. Find the missing term in the sequence below:

$$\frac{1}{6}; \frac{1}{3}; \frac{1}{2}; \frac{2}{3}; \text{—}$$

   (A) $\frac{1}{2}$

   (B) $\frac{2}{5}$

   (C) $\frac{3}{5}$

   (D) $\frac{5}{6}$

   (E) 1

Our first step is to establish the pattern. The trick to this question is that in order to see the pattern, all of our fractions must have a common denominator. If we look at the denominators (6, 3, and 2), we can see that the common denominator is 6. Now let's rewrite our pattern, turning all the fractions into fractions with a denominator of 6.

$$\frac{1}{6}; \frac{2}{6}; \frac{3}{6}; \frac{4}{6}$$

Now we can clearly see that we add $\frac{1}{6}$ each time to get the next term. If we add $\frac{1}{6}$ to $\frac{4}{6}$ then we can determine that the next term is $\frac{5}{6}$ or answer choice D.

Use a Sequence to Predict a Term that is not the Next Term

Sometimes a question will ask you for a term that is not the next term. Maybe you are given the first three terms and then asked to determine what the 30th term would be. It would take too long for us to list out every term until we get to the 30th term, but luckily, we have a formula.

To find a term in an arithmetic sequence we use the equation:

$a_n = a_1 + d(n-1)$
$a_n =$ the term we are looking for
$a_1 =$ the first term
$d =$ the difference between terms
$n =$ the # of the term we want (example: for the 30th term, $n = 30$)

For example, let's say our sequence is 3, 6, 9, 12 and we want to find the 25th term. In this case, $a_1 = 3$ since that is our first term, $n = 25$ since we are looking for the 25th term, and $d = 3$ since we add 3 to get from one term to the next.

Now, we can plug into our equation:

$a_n = a_1 + d(n-1)$
$a_n = 3 + 3(25-1) = 75$

Now we know that the 25th term in this sequence is 75.

You may also be given a term and then asked which number of the sequence the term is. In the above example, they could have told you that a term was 75 and asked what number term it was. In this case, you would plug in 75 for a_n and then solve for n. These questions are usually phrased as word problems in applied situations.

Here are a couple of questions for you to try.

1. On the first day of cookie sales, Pam sold 3 boxes of cookies. On the next day, she sold 6 boxes of cookies, on the next day she sold 9 boxes of cookies, and so on. If this pattern continued, how many cookies would she have sold on Day 20 of cookie sales?

   (A) 12
   (B) 15
   (C) 30
   (D) 45
   (E) 60

To answer this question, we can use our equation:

$$a_n = a_1 + d(n-1)$$

Since we are looking for the actual number of cookies, we will be solving for a_n. We will plug in 3 for a_1 since that is our first term, 3 for d since that is the difference between each term, and 20 for n since we are looking for the 20th term.

$$a_{20} = a_1 + d(n-1) = 3 + 3(20-1) = 60$$

Answer choice E is correct.

2. Anna is saving up for a new bicycle. On the first day, she has $1.50, on the next day she has $2.00, on the next day she has $2.50, and so on. If this pattern continues, and the bicycle costs $50, on what day will she have enough money for the bicycle?

   (A) 97
   (B) 98
   (C) 100
   (D) 150
   (E) 200

We use the same equation for this question, we just have to remember that we are looking for n, which in this case is the number of days.

$$a_n = a_1 + d(n - 1)$$
$$50 = 1.50 + 0.50(n - 1)$$
$$48.50 = 0.50(n - 1)$$
$$97 = n - 1$$
$$98 = n$$

Answer choice B is correct.

Find the Sum of a Sequence

Some questions will ask you to find the sum of an arithmetic sequence.

We also have an equation for finding the sum:

$$S_n = \frac{n(a_1 + a_n)}{2}$$

In this formula, n is the number of the last term included in the sum, a_1 is the first term, and a_n is the last term that is included in the sum. Usually, we have to use the earlier formula to solve for the value of the last term so that we can plug it in for a_n.

Here are a couple of questions for you to try:

1. Harriet is collecting buttons. On the first day, she collects one button. On the second day, she collects two buttons and on the third day she collects 3 buttons. If this pattern continues, how many buttons will Harriet have at the end of 45 days?

   (A) 45
   (B) 135
   (C) 545
   (D) 789
   (E) 1035

To answer this question, we just plug into our equation. For this question, we don't actually have to solve for a_n since the number of buttons collected is the same as the day number, or 45 for the 45th day.

$$S_n = \frac{n(a_1 + a_n)}{2} = \frac{45(1 + 45)}{2} = \frac{2070}{2} = 1035$$

Answer choice E is correct.

2. Naima is collecting pennies. On day 1 she collects 2 pennies. On day 2 she collects 4 pennies and on day 3 she collects 6 pennies. If this pattern continues, what is the value of the pennies that she will have collected after 30 days?

    (A) $8.90
    (B) $9.10
    (C) $9.30
    (D) $9.45
    (E) $9.63

Our first step to answer this question is to figure out how many pennies she will have collected on day 30.

$$a_{30} = a_1 + d(n-1) = 2 + 2(30-1) = 60$$

Now we can use that value to plug into our formula for the sum of a sequence:

$$S_{30} = \frac{n(a_1 + a_n)}{2} = \frac{30(2+60)}{2} = 930$$

We aren't done yet, though. The question asks for the value of the pennies, not how many pennies there were.

$$930 \times \$0.01 = \$9.30$$

Answer choice C is correct.

Those are the basics that you need to know for sequence and pattern questions. Be sure to complete the practice set.

Sequences and Patterns Practice Set

1. Justin sold 5 candy bars on day 1 of a competition. The next day he sold 9 candy bars and the day after that he sold 13 candy bars. If this pattern continued, and the contest lasted for 16 days, how many candy bars did Justin sell during the competition?

   (A) 65
   (B) 355
   (C) 424
   (D) 560
   (E) 1120

2. Find the missing term in the following arithmetic sequence:

   24, _____, 36

   (A) 26
   (B) 28
   (C) 30
   (D) 32
   (E) 34

3. Myra is collecting marbles. On the first day, she collects 3 marbles. On day 2 she collects 6 marbles and on day 3 she collects 9 marbles. If this pattern continues, how many marbles will she collect on day 11?

   (A) 33
   (B) 35
   (C) 36
   (D) 39
   (E) 42

4. $\frac{1}{4}$; $\frac{1}{2}$; $\frac{3}{4}$; 1; ____

What is the fifth term in the sequence above?

(A) $\frac{3}{4}$

(B) $1\frac{1}{4}$

(C) $1\frac{1}{2}$

(D) $1\frac{3}{4}$

(E) 2

5. Lara is saving nickels. On the first day, she saves one nickel. On the second day, she saves two nickels and on the third day she saves three nickels. How much money will she have saved after 20 days?

(A) $8.50

(B) $9.20

(C) $9.55

(D) $10.45

(E) $10.50

Answers to Sequences and Patterns Practice Set

1. D
2. C
3. A
4. B
5. E

Linear Equations & Functions

We have already covered some linear equation questions in the "Solving Equations" chapter. In this section, we will cover how to rearrange an equation without solving for a variable. We will also cover slope as well as functions.

In this section:

- Interpreting variables in linear equations
- Rearranging linear equations
- Slope
- Definition of functions
- Solving functions

Interpreting Variables in Linear Equations

A linear equation is the equation of a straight line. In practical terms, this means that there are no exponents greater than 1 in the equation. For example, $h = 4g - 7$ is linear but $h = 4g^2 - 7$ is not.

One form of a linear equation is $y = mx + b$, where m is the slope and b is the y-intercept. In practical terms, the slope gives the rate by which something varies. For example, let's say the number of miles driven (d) varies according to the number of hours driven (h). Our equation is $d = hx$. As h increases, so does d. The y-intercept gives the constant value, or value that does not vary. It is generally the "starting point". For example, let's say the number of miles from home (m) varies according to the number of hours driven (h), but we started driving 50 miles from home. In this case, our equation is $m = hx + 50$.

Here are a couple of questions for you to try:

1. The expression $300 + 2m$ represents the total dollar amount that it costs to rent a truck to drive m miles. What does 2 represent in this equation?

   (A) the cost to drive 300 miles
   (B) the cost when 0 miles have been driven
   (C) the cost of each additional mile driven
   (D) the cost after 2 miles have been driven
   (E) the total cost of a rental to drive 1 mile

In the expression, the 2 is the coefficient of the variable amount (or the number of miles driven). This means that every time 1 more mile is driven, the cost increases by \$2. Answer choice C is correct.

2. The equation $b = 400 - 10x$ can be used to find b, or the amount of money that Paolo has in his bank account after x weeks. Which scenario is best supported by this equation?

   (A) Paolo had \$10 in his account at the start of the time period.
   (B) Paolo had \$400 in his account after 10 weeks.
   (C) Paolo had \$10 in his account to start with and deposits \$400 week.
   (D) Paolo had \$400 in his account to start and deposits \$10 a week.
   (E) Paolo had \$400 in his account to start and withdraws \$10 a week.

If we look at the equation, 400 is the constant value or y-intercept. This means that at 0 weeks, Paolo had \$400 in his bank account. The number -10 is the coefficient of the variable so it represents the slope or rate of change. Since it is negative, the balance decreases by \$10 each week. Since Paolo had \$400 in his account to begin and then that amount was decreased by \$10 each week, we can easily eliminate choices A, B, and C. Choice D ignores the negative sign and is incorrect. Answer choice E is correct because it accurately represents the situation given.

Rearranging Linear Equations

You may also see questions that don't ask you to solve for a variable but rather ask you to rearrange an equation to isolate a variable. You just need to follow our rules of doing PEMDAS in reverse, doing the opposite operation to move a term to the other side of an equation, and do the same thing to both sides.

To manipulate an equation to isolate a variable:

- use reverse PEMDAS
- use the opposite operation to move a term to the other side of the equation
- do the same thing to both sides of an equation

For example, let's say we have the equation $14 = 3x + y$ and the question asks which expression represents x.

Our first step is to look for anything added or subtracted (the last steps in PEMDAS). The side of the equation with x has a y added to it, so we do the opposite of addition of and subtract y from both sides:

$$14 - y = 3x + y - y$$
$$14 - y = 3x$$

Now we see if there is anything multiplied or divided. The x is multiplied by 3 so we divide both sides by 3:

$$\frac{14 - y}{3} = \frac{3x}{3}$$

Our final answer is:

$$\frac{14}{3} - \frac{y}{3} = x$$

Here are a couple of questions for you to try:

3. If $12 + 3a = 4b$, which expression represents a?

    (A) $\frac{3}{4}b - 4$

    (B) $\frac{3}{4}b + 4$

    (C) $\frac{4}{3}b - 4$

    (D) $\frac{4}{3}b + 4$

    (E) $\frac{4}{3}b - 12$

Let's start with the original equation: $12 + 3a = 4b$. To isolate a, the first step is to subtract 12 from both sides. The result is $3a = 4b - 12$. Now we can divide all of the terms by 3. The result is $a = \frac{4}{3}b - 4$. Answer choice C is correct.

4. To convert between degrees Fahrenheit and degrees Celsius, the formula $\frac{5}{9}(F - 32) = C$ can be used. Which is the result of solving this equation for F?

    (A) $F = \frac{9}{5}C + 32$

    (B) $F = \frac{9}{5}C - 32$

    (C) $F = \frac{5}{9}C + 32$

    (D) $F = \frac{5}{9}C - 32$

    (E) $F = \frac{9}{5}C + \left(32 \times \frac{9}{5}\right)$

The first step is to multiply both sides of the equation by $\frac{9}{5}$ in order to eliminate the $\frac{5}{9}$ on the left side of the equation. The result is $F - 32 = \frac{9}{5}C$. Now we have to add 32 to each side and it becomes $F = \frac{9}{5}C + 32$. Answer choice A is correct.

Slope

Solving for a variable becomes particularly important when a question asks for slope. The easiest way to identify the slope of a line from its equation is to put it into the form $y = mx + b$, where m is the slope.

Let's say we are given the equation $2x + 3y = 6$. If we want to find the slope of the line, first we can subtract $2x$ from both sides, and the result is $3y = -2x + 6$. Note that we put the term with x in it first so that it is easier to see the $y = mx + b$ form. Now we divide all the terms by 3, and the resulting equation is $y = -\frac{2}{3}x + 2$. The slope of our line is $-\frac{2}{3}$.

There are a few important equations and facts that you should know about using slope on the SSAT:

1. $y = mx + b$
   This is the slope-intercept form of the equation of a line. It is the most helpful for the SSAT. Any equation can be rearranged into this form where m is the slope and b is the y-intercept.

2. $m = \dfrac{y_2 - y_1}{x_2 - x_1}$
   This is the equation that we can use to find slope when we are given two points, (x_1, y_1) and (x_2, y_2).

3. Perpendicular lines have slopes that are negative reciprocals.
   To find negative reciprocals, you flip the fraction and change the sign. For example, if a line has a slope of $\dfrac{1}{2}$, then the slope of a line perpendicular to this line would be -2.

4. Parallel lines have the same slope.

Here are a couple of questions for you to try that test these facts:

1. Find the slope of a line that is perpendicular to $4x + 5y = 12$.
   (A) -4
   (B) $-\dfrac{5}{4}$
   (C) $\dfrac{4}{5}$
   (D) $\dfrac{5}{4}$
   (E) 5

Our first step in answering this question is to put the equation into $y = mx + b$ form:

$$4x + 5y = 12$$
$$5y = -4x + 12$$
$$y = -\frac{4}{5}x + \frac{12}{5}$$

Now we know that the slope of the line given is $-\frac{4}{5}$. To find the slope of a line that is perpendicular, we just take the negative reciprocal of $-\frac{4}{5}$. The slope of the perpendicular line is $\frac{5}{4}$, or answer choice D.

2. The points $(4, 6)$ and $(t, 5)$ are on a line that is perpendicular to the line $y = 4x - 7$. Which of the following is the value of t?

   (A) 1
   (B) 2
   (C) 4
   (D) 6
   (E) 8

Since we see the word *perpendicular*, we know that we should be looking at slope. Since our line is perpendicular to $y = 4x - 7$, its slope is $-\frac{1}{4}$. Now we can plug that into our equation for slope:

$$m = \frac{y_2 - y_1}{x_2 - x_1}$$
$$-\frac{1}{4} = \frac{6 - 5}{4 - t}$$
$$-\frac{1}{4} = \frac{1}{4 - t}$$

We can see that the bottom of the fraction needs to be equal to -4 in order to make the entire fraction equal to $-\frac{1}{4}$. Therefore, $t = 8$. Answer choice E is correct.

Functions

A function relates each element of a set to exactly one element of another set. In practical terms, that means that for every input there has to be exactly one output. We can think of a function as rule that tells us what to do to the input in order to produce an output. We use notation such as $f(x)$ or $g(x)$. For example, $f(x) = x + 4$ means that for every input x, we add 4 to get the output.

- For every input of a function, there should be exactly one output
- A function is a rule that tells us what must be done to the input in order to produce the output

Here are a couple of questions that test the definition of a function:

1. The table below shows ordered pairs.

x	y
4	3
7	m
n	8
10	9

Which value of a variable would prevent the relation from being a function?

(A) $m = 3$
(B) $m = 4$
(C) $m = 6$
(D) $n = 6$
(E) $n = 4$

By definition, for each input there can be exactly one output (not more than one). In this case, if $n = 4$, there would be two outputs: 3 and 8. Therefore the relation would no longer be a function. Answer choice E is correct.

2. Which identifies the outputs of the function given by the ordered pairs (2, 5), (4, 11), and (7, 20)?

   (A) $\{5, 11, 20\}$
   (B) $\{5, 11\}$
   (C) $\{5\}$
   (D) $\{2, 4, 5\}$
   (E) $\{2\}$

We can think of the output of a function as being the y-values in a standard ordered pair. Therefore, the outputs of this function are 5, 11, and 20 and answer choice A is correct.

Solving Functions

Solving functions is relatively easy once you know how the notation works. There are two important rules to remember:

1. It is the letter in front of the parentheses that tells you what function to use. For example, $f(x)$ is different from $g(x)$, but $f(a)$ is not different from $f(b)$.
2. To apply a function rule, we plug in the given inputs to each side of the function. For example, if the function is defined as $f(x) = x + 2$, then $f(4) = 4 + 2$.

Here are a couple of problems for you to try:

3. Which is the value of $f(-5)$ if $f(x) = x^2 - 3x + 4$?

   (A) 14
   (B) 20
   (C) 36
   (D) 44
   (E) 48

In order to find $f(-5)$, we substitute in -5 for x in $x^2 - 3x + 4$. It becomes $(-5)^2 - 3(-5) + 4$. This is equal to $25 + 15 + 4$, or 44. Answer choice D is correct.

4. What is the value of $h(4) - j(3)$ if $h(x) = x^2 - 3$ and $j(x) = x + 4$?

   (A) 1
   (B) 6
   (C) 7
   (D) 9
   (E) 20

In order to answer this question, we first have to determine the value of $h(4)$ and $j(3)$:

$$h(4) = 4^2 - 3 = 16 - 3 = 13$$
$$j(3) = 3 + 4 = 7$$

Now we can substitute in those values for $h(4)$ and $j(3)$:

$$h(4) - j(3) = 13 - 7 = 6$$

Answer choice B is correct.

Now you have learned all about linear equations and functions! Be sure to complete the practice set to reinforce what you have learned.

Practice Set for Linear Equations & Functions

1. Which of the following is the graph of $y = -2x + 3$?

   (A)
   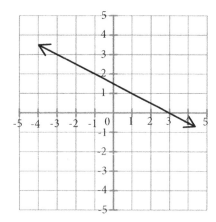

   (B)
   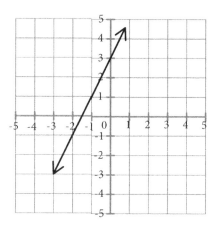

   (C)
   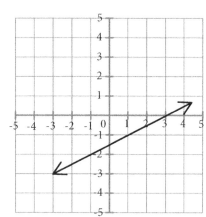

   (D)
   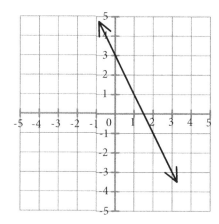

   (E)
   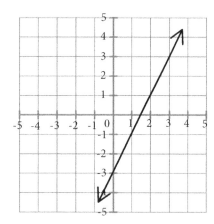

2. The ordered pairs $(4,11)$, $(2, -1)$, and $(6, 31)$ are ordered pairs in a relation. Which ordered pair, if added to the list of ordered pairs, would make the relation NOT a function?

   (A) $(2, 5)$
   (B) $(7, 44)$
   (C) $(3, 4)$
   (D) $(1, -4)$
   (E) $(5, 20)$

3. A pool is slowly being drained of water. The amount of water remaining in the pool can be found using the expression $500 - 3m$, where m is the number of minutes that the pool has been draining. Which scenario fits this expression?

   (A) The pool has 500 gallons of water left after 3 minutes.
   (B) The pool is draining at the rate of 500 gallons every minute.
   (C) Every three minutes, one gallon of water drains from the pool.
   (D) It will take 500 minutes to drain the entire pool.
   (E) The pool had 500 gallons of water in it before any was drained.

4. Find the slope of the line perpendicular to the line $x - y = 2$.

   (A) $\dfrac{1}{2}$
   (B) $-\dfrac{1}{2}$
   (C) 1
   (D) -1
   (E) 2

5. What is the value of $f(6) - f(4)$ if $f(m) = 3m - 1$?

   (A) 2
   (B) 5
   (C) 6
   (D) 8
   (E) 10

6. What is the value of $h(-7)$ if $h(x) = x^2 - 2x + 5$?

   (A) 70
   (B) 68
   (C) 40
   (D) 35
   (E) 30

7. If $3r = 5s - 7$, which expression represents s?

   (A) $\frac{3}{5}r + \frac{7}{5}$

   (B) $\frac{3}{5}r - \frac{7}{5}$

   (C) $\frac{3}{5}r + 7$

   (D) $3r + 7$

   (E) $3r - 7$

8. Two points, C and D, are on a line, E, with a slope of 3. Which of the following could be the coordinates of points on a line that is perpendicular to line E?

   (A) $(0, 0)$ and $(2, 6)$
   (B) $(-6, 2)$ and $(0, 0)$
   (C) $(1, -1)$ and $(2, 8)$
   (D) $(-4, 3)$ and $(3, 3)$
   (E) $(0, 0)$ and $(3, 3)$

9. Line b has the equation $3x - 2y = 6$. If it passes through the point $(0, w)$, what is the value of w?

   (A) -6
   (B) -5
   (C) -3
   (D) 3
   (E) 6

10. A function contains the ordered pairs (3, 5), (7, 9), and (10,12). Which set shows the inputs for this function?

  (A) {5}
  (B) {5, 9, 12}
  (C) {3}
  (D) {3, 7}
  (E) {3, 7, 10}

Answers to Practice Set for Linear Equations & Functions

1. D
2. A
3. E
4. D
5. C
6. B
7. A
8. B
9. C
10. E

Advanced Algebra

On the Upper Level SSAT, some problems may require you to know advanced algebra topics.

The types of problems that you may see include:

- Factors and multiples
- Plugging in for variables with exponents
- Operations with monomials and polynomials
- Simplifying expressions with negative exponents
- Simplifying expressions that have negative numbers and exponents
- Radicals
- Factoring and quadratic equations

Exponents play an important role in this section. Exponents tell us to multiply a number by itself (and how many times to do that!).

For example:

$$2^2 = 2 \times 2 = 4$$
$$2^3 = 2 \times 2 \times 2 = 8$$
$$w^4 = w \times w \times w \times w$$

Factors and Multiples

Factors are numbers that another number can be divided by without a remainder. For example, the factors of 8 are 1,2,4, and 8. It is important to note that 1 and the number itself are always factors of a number.

- Factors are numbers that another number can be divided by with no remainder
- 1 and the number itself are factors

Multiples are numbers are the numbers that are the product of a number and other whole numbers. For example, the multiples of 8 are 8, 16, 24, 32, and so on. Multiples do not end.

- Multiples are the product of a number and other whole numbers
- Multiples do not end

One concept that you will see tested on the SSAT is the greatest common factor. The greatest common factor is the largest number that is a factor of the numbers given. We find it by listing the factors of the numbers given and looking for the largest number they have in common.

- Greatest common factor is the largest number that is a factor of all the numbers given
- Find the greatest common factor by listing all the factors and looking for the largest number that each list of factors has

Here is a basic problem using real numbers:

1. What is the greatest common factor of 36, 54, and 60?
   (A) 2
   (B) 6
   (C) 9
   (D) 18
   (E) 60

Let's go ahead and list the factors for each number:

36: 1, 2, 3, 4, 6, 9, 12, 18, 36
54: 1, 2, 3, 6, 9, 18, 27, 54
60: 1, 2, 3, 4, 5, 6, 10, 12, 15, 20, 30, 60

If we look for the largest number that shows up in each list of factors, we can see that the greatest common factor is 6. Answer choice B is correct.

We can also find the greatest common factor for expressions with variables. We have to look at each part of the expressions individually. For example, we need to find the greatest common factor of the whole number portion and then the greatest common factor for each variable. The trick for finding the greatest common factor for each variable is to look for the term that has the lowest exponent for that variable. Keep in mind that if a variable does not show up in one of the terms, it essentially has an exponent of 0 and should not show up in the greatest common factor.

To find the greatest common factor for terms with variables:

- Find the greatest common factor of the whole number portion
- Find the greatest common factor for each variable, which is the lowest exponent for that variable among all the terms
- If a variable is not in one of the terms, it should not be in the greatest common factor at all

Here are a couple of examples for you to try:

2. What is the greatest common factor of $12m^6, 36m^9, 18m^{15}$?

    (A) $6m^6$
    (B) $6m^{15}$
    (C) $12m^6$
    (D) $12m^{15}$
    (E) $36m^{15}$

First, we need to look at the whole number portions of each term: 12, 36, and 18. The greatest factor that all three have in common is 6. Therefore, the whole number portion of our greatest common factor is 6, and choice A or B must be correct. Now we need to look at the variable part. They all have the same variable, m, so m must be included in our greatest common factor. The lowest exponent for m is 6, so m^6 should show up in our greatest common factor. If we combine the two parts, 6 and m^6, our greatest common factor is $6m^6$, and answer choice A is correct.

3. Which is the greatest common factor of $30x^3y^4, 45x^2y^2$, and $60xy^4z$?

    (A) $3xy^2$
    (B) $6xy^2z$
    (C) $15xy^2$
    (D) $15x^3y^4z$
    (E) $60xy^2z$

To find the greatest common factor, we first need to look for the greatest common factor of the whole number portions. Rather than listing the factors, one way we can approach this is to start with the largest answer choice and, if that doesn't work, go smaller – remember that this is a multiple-choice test and our only options for the greatest common factor are the answer choices. If we look at choice E, which has 60 as the whole number portion, 60 is not a factor of 30 and 45, so choice E is incorrect. Now let's look at choices C and D – 15. The number 15 is a factor of 30, 45, and 60. We know that choice C or D must be correct. Now let's look at the variables. Choice D includes z as a factor, but z is not present in the first two terms, so it cannot be in the greatest common factor, and choice D can be eliminated. Answer choice C is correct.

Another concept that you may see tested is least common multiple. To find the least common multiple, you simply list the multiples and look for the smallest number that the lists have in common. Keep in mind that this is a multiple-choice test – one way to approach these questions is to start with the smallest answer choice and see if it is a multiple of all the numbers given. If not, move on to the next smallest answer choice, and so on.

- Least common multiple is the smallest multiple that all of the numbers have in common
- Use the multiple-choice answers- start with the smallest number, see if it works, and then move on to the next biggest number if it doesn't

Here is a basic question to try that uses real numbers:

4. What is the least common multiple of 3, 5, and 12?
    (A) 9
    (B) 12
    (C) 30
    (D) 60
    (E) 120

Let's start with looking at the smallest answer choice – 9. Since 9 is not a multiple of 5 or 12, we can eliminate choice A. Now let's look at choice B. The number 12 is not a multiple of 5, so choice B can also be ruled out. If we look at choice C, 30 is not a multiple of 12, so choice C is not correct. Now let's look at choice D – 60 is a multiple of 3, 5, and 12, so choice D is correct. Note that if you chose E, 120 is a multiple of 3, 5, and 12, but it is not the least number that is a multiple of all 3 so it is not the least common multiple.

You can also have least common multiple questions using variables. For these, you need to find the least common multiple of each whole number portion and then the least common multiple of the exponents for each variable. In the case of a variable, the least common multiple is the greatest exponent, and if a variable shows up in any of the terms then it must show up in the least common multiple.

To find the least common multiple in terms with variables:

- Find the least common multiple of the whole number portion
- Find the least common multiple of the exponents for each variable (the greatest exponent for each variable)
- All variables that are in any of the terms must be in the least common multiple

Here are a couple of questions for you to try:

5. What is the least common multiple of $4m^2$ and $6m^3$?

    (A) $12m^3$
    (B) $12m^6$
    (C) $24m^3$
    (D) $24m^5$
    (E) $24m^6$

The first portion we need to look at is the whole number portion. We can see from the answer choices that it must be either 12 or 24. Since 4 and 6 are factors of both numbers, but 12 is less than 24, 12 must be part of the least common multiple, and choice A or B must be correct. Now we need to find the least common multiple of m^2 and m^3. Since m^3 is a multiple of m^2 (m^3 is just m^2 multiplied by another m), m^3 should be part of the least common multiple, and choice A is correct.

6. What is the least common multiple of $2x^2y^4z$ and $8x^3y$?

    (A) $2x^3y^4$
    (B) $4x^3y^4z$
    (C) $8x^3y^4$
    (D) $8x^3y^4z$
    (E) $16x^3y^4z$

We can look first at the whole number portions of the terms: 2 and 8. The least common multiple of 2 and 8 is 8 because a number is a multiple of itself and 8 is also a multiple of 2. Answer choice C or D must be correct. Now we look at the exponents. We can see that the difference between the two answer choices is whether z should be in the least common multiple. Since z does show up in at least one term, it belongs in the least common multiple, and choice D is correct.

Plugging In for Variables with Exponents

The most basic problems ask you to plug in for a variable and then use exponents to solve.

We will just do a couple of examples here:

1. If $c = 4$ and $d = 6$, then what is the value of $3c^2 - d$?

    (A) 6
    (B) 4
    (C) 0
    (D) 10
    (E) 42

In order to answer this question, we have to plug in the values that we have been given for c and d.

$$3c^2 - d = 3(4)^2 - 6$$

Now we have to remember to use PEMDAS to solve. In this particular case, it is important that we remember to first deal with squaring the 4 before we multiply it by 3.

$$3(4)^2 - 6 = 3 \times 16 - 6 = 48 - 6 = 42$$

Answer choice E is correct.

2. Calculate $2w^2 + z^3$ when $w = 3$ and $z = 2$.

    (A) 8
    (B) 16
    (C) 26
    (D) 34
    (E) 44

We follow the same process to solve this problem, remembering to use PEMDAS.

$$2w^2 + z^3 = 2(3)^2 + (2)^3$$
$$(2 \times 9) + 8 = 18 + 8 = 26$$

Answer choice C is correct.

Operations with Monomials and Polynomials

Some questions will ask you to combine like terms and then simplify with expressions that have variables with exponents.

For these questions, you first need to look at whether the problem has addition/subtraction or multiplication/division.

- Look first at whether the problem has addition/subtraction or multiplication/division

The basic rules for addition and subtraction questions are:

- For us to be able to combine two terms, they must have the same variables
- To be combined, two expressions must also have the same exponents for the same variables

Here are some examples:

$$x^2 + x^2 = 2x^2$$

Because the x is squared in both terms, they can be combined.

$$x^2 + x^3$$

These two terms CANNOT be combined since x^2 and x^3 do not have the same exponent.

A little more complicated is when we have terms with more than one variable. For these terms, they can only be combined:

1. If they have the same variables
2. If each variable has the same exponent in both terms

Here are some examples:

$$2x^2y^3 + 3x^2y^3 = 5x^2y^3$$

In this case, both terms have x^2 and y^3, so we can combine the terms.

$$2x^2y^3 + 3x^3y^2$$

In this case, we CANNOT combine the terms because the first term has x^2 and y^3 while the second term has x^3 and y^2.

On the SSAT, you are likely to see problems that are more involved than these. There are a few things you need to remember for these problems:

1. Use PEMDAS – when you see parentheses, pay close attention to whether or not you need to distribute a negative sign before combining like terms
2. You can only combine terms if they have the same variables and the same exponents for each variable

Here are a couple of examples for you to try:

1. Combine and simplify the expression $(2y^3 + 4y + 7) - (y^3 - y^2 + 2y - 4)$.
   (A) $y^3 - y^2 + 6y + 3$
   (B) $y^3 - y^2 + 2y + 3$
   (C) $y^3 - y^2 + 6y + 11$
   (D) $y^3 + y^2 + 2y + 11$
   (E) $y^3 + 5y^2 + y + 11$

For us to answer this question, we first need to distribute the subtraction sign to the terms in the second set of parentheses:

$$2y^3 + 4y + 7 - y^3 + y^2 - 2y + 4$$

Now we can use the commutative property to move around the terms – remember that each term must take with it the sign in front of it:

$$2y^3 - y^3 + y^2 + 4y - 2y + 7 + 4$$

Now we can easily combine like terms to get:

$$y^3 + y^2 + 2y + 11$$

Answer choice D is correct.

2. Simplify the expression $(2x^2 + 3x^2y^2 + 6y^2) - (x^2 - 2x^2y + 3y^2)$.
   (A) $x^2 + 3x^2y^2 + 2x^2y + 3y^2$
   (B) $x^2 + 5x^2y^2 - 3y^2$
   (C) $x^2 + 5x^2y - 3y^2$
   (D) $3x^2 + 3x^2y^2 + 2x^2y - 3y^2$
   (E) $3x^2 + 3x^2y^2 + 2x^2y + 9y^2$

Our first step is to rewrite the expression, distributing the subtraction sign to the terms in the second set of parentheses:

$$2x^2 + 3x^2y^2 + 6y^2 - x^2 + 2x^2y - 3y^2$$

Now we can use the commutative property to rearrange the terms:

$$2x^2 - x^2 + 3x^2y^2 + 2x^2y + 6y^2 - 3y^2$$

We can now combine like terms – but remember that we can only combine the terms if they have the same variables and each variable has the same exponent:

$$x^2 + 3x^2y^2 + 2x^2y + 3y^2$$

Answer choice A is correct.

You may also see a question that requires you to simplify expressions that use multiplication or division. Let's start with questions that ask you to multiply monomials with the same variable raised to various exponents. In this case, you simply add the exponents.

- If multiplying monomials with the same variable, add the exponents

For example:

$$n^4 \times n^3 = n^7$$

We can also multiply terms with multiple variables by breaking apart the terms and using the commutative property to combine like terms.

For example:

$$4a^2b^3 \times 5a^4b^5$$

First, we break apart the terms:

$$4 \times a^2 \times b^3 \times 5 \times a^4 \times b^5$$

Now we use the commutative property to reorder the terms:

$$4 \times 5 \times a^2 \times a^4 \times b^3 \times b^5$$

Now we combine like terms, adding the exponents for each variable:

$$20a^6b^8$$

We can also raise a term with an exponent to another exponent. In this case, we don't add the exponents, we multiply them.

- If you raise a term with an exponent to an exponent, multiply the exponents

For example:

$$(g^3)^4 = g^{12}$$

Note that this only works with terms where there is only multiplication. If two or more terms with exponents are added or subtracted and the entire quantity is raised to an exponent, we can NOT just distribute the exponent.

Here are a couple of examples for you to try:

3. Which expression is equivalent to $r(r^2)(r^4)$?

   (A) r^6
   (B) r^7
   (C) r^8
   (D) $3r^6$
   (E) $3r^8$

In this case, we have three terms that all have the same variable being multiplied. We need to add the exponents. The trick is that we have to remember that r is really r^1. Now our expression is $r^1 \times r^2 \times r^4$. If we add the exponents, the result is r^7. Choice B is correct.

4. Which expression is equivalent to $[3x^2(2x^4)]^3$?

   (A) $6x^8$
   (B) $6x^{24}$
   (C) $18x^8$
   (D) $18x^{24}$
   (E) $216x^{18}$

According to the order of operations, we need to perform operations in parentheses first. This means we first need to multiply $3x^2$ and $2x^4$. We can break the terms apart, rearrange, and then combine like terms:

$3x^2 \times 2x^4$
$3 \times x^2 \times 2 \times x^4$
$3 \times 2 \times x^2 \times x^4$
$6x^6$

Now we need to perform $[6x^6]^3$. We distribute the exponent to each term and the expression becomes $6^3 \times x^{18}$. If we simplify that becomes $216x^{18}$. Answer choice E is correct.

Now we will work on multiplying with polynomials. The key to remember is that you have to multiply each term in each set of parentheses by each term in the other set of parentheses.

- When we multiply polynomials, we have to multiply every term in one set of parentheses by every term in the other set of parentheses

One way to do this is to make a table to stay organized.

For example, let's say the problem is $(x + 2)(x - 4)$.

We can make the table and multiply the rows by the columns:

	x	$+2$
x	x^2	$+2x$
-4	$-4x$	-8

Now we add up each product: $x^2 + 2x - 4x - 8$. When we combine like terms, the result is $x^2 - 2x - 8$.

Here are a couple of questions for you to try:

5. Which expression is equivalent to $(4x - 1)(2x + 3)$?

   (A) $8x^2 - 3$
   (B) $8x^2 - 4$
   (C) $8x^2 + 10x - 3$
   (D) $4x^2 + 10x - 3$
   (E) $4x^2 - 3$

We can make a table to answer this question:

	$4x$	-1
$2x$	$8x^2$	$-2x$
$+3$	$+12x$	-3

Now we sum the products: $8x^2 + 12x - 2x - 3$. If we combine like terms, the result is $8x^2 + 10x - 3$. Answer choice C is correct.

6. Which expression is equivalent to $(x^2 - 3x - 2)(x^2 + 4x - 5)$?

    (A) $x^4 - 12x^2 + 10$
    (B) $x^4 + x^3 - 12x^2 + 7x + 10$
    (C) $x^4 + x^3 - 19x^2 + 5x + 10$
    (D) $x^4 + x^3 - 19x^2 + 7x + 10$
    (E) $x^4 + 2x^3 - 15x^2 + 3x - 10$

We can still make a table, it will just have more rows and columns since there are more terms in each polynomial:

	x^2	$-3x$	-2
x^2	x^4	$-3x^3$	$-2x^2$
$+4x$	$+4x^3$	$-12x^2$	$-8x$
-5	$-5x^2$	$+15x$	$+10$

Now we sum the products: $x^4 - 3x^3 + 4x^3 - 2x^2 - 12x^2 - 5x^2 - 8x + 15x + 10$. If we combine like terms the result is $x^4 + x^3 - 19x^2 + 7x + 10$. Answer choice D is correct.

Now we will work on division. To answer these questions, remember that if all the terms are being multiplied, then we can break them apart and reduce.

- Break apart terms and then reduce when dividing one monomial by another

For example, let's say we need to simplify the following expression:

$$\frac{10r^3s^4t}{15r^2s^2t}$$

Our first step is to break apart the fraction, lining up like terms:

$$\frac{10}{15} \times \frac{r^3}{r^2} \times \frac{s^4}{s^2} \times \frac{t}{t}$$

Now we can write out each term as factors:

$$\frac{2 \times 5}{3 \times 5} \times \frac{r \times r \times r}{r \times r} \times \frac{s \times s \times s \times s}{s \times s} \times \frac{t}{t}$$

Now we cancel out the factors that appear on both the top and the bottom. We are left with:

$$\frac{2}{3} \times r \times s \times s \times 1$$

If we simplify this, we get:

$$\frac{2rs^2}{3}$$

Here is an example that is similar to some questions you may see on the SSAT:

7. Simplify:

$$\frac{4cd^3f^5}{6cdf^3}$$

(A) $\dfrac{d^2f^2}{3}$

(B) $\dfrac{2d^2f^2}{3}$

(C) $\dfrac{2cd^2f^2}{3}$

(D) $\dfrac{cd^2f^2}{2}$

(E) $\dfrac{d^2f^2}{2}$

In order to answer this question, it is easiest if we break apart the fraction:

$$\frac{4}{6} \times \frac{c}{c} \times \frac{d^3}{d} \times \frac{f^5}{f^3}$$

Now we just cancel and get:

$$\frac{2}{3} \times 1 \times d^2 \times f^2$$

We can rewrite this as:

$$\frac{2d^2 f^2}{3}$$

Answer choice B is correct.

Simplifying Expressions with Negative Exponents

You may see a question on the SSAT that requires you to know how to deal with negative exponents.

The rules for negative exponents are simple:

1. If the variable with a negative exponent is in the numerator, move it to the denominator and make the exponent positive.
2. If the variable with a negative exponent is in the denominator, move it to the numerator and make the exponent positive.

Let's look at the following examples:

$$x^{-2} = \frac{1}{x^2}$$

$$\frac{1}{x^{-2}} = x^2$$

$$\frac{3x^{-2}y^3 z}{2^{-3}x^4 y^{-2}z^{-1}} = \frac{3 \times 2^3 \times y^3 \times y^2 \times z \times z}{x^4 \times x^2} = \frac{24y^5 z^2}{x^6}$$

Here are a couple of example problems for you to try:

1. $\dfrac{4b^{-3}d}{8b^2c^{-2}d} =$

   (A) $\dfrac{2b^5d}{4c^2}$

   (B) $\dfrac{c^2d}{2b^5}$

   (C) $\dfrac{2c^2}{b^5}$

   (D) $\dfrac{c^2}{2b^5}$

   (E) $\dfrac{c^2}{2b^5d}$

For our first step, we will rewrite the expression, breaking apart the like terms.

$$\frac{4b^{-3}d}{8b^2c^{-2}d} = \frac{4}{8} \times \frac{b^{-3}}{b^2} \times \frac{1}{c^{-2}} \times \frac{d}{d}$$

Notice that there was no "c" in the numerator so we had to put 1 over c^{-2}. Now we can simplify and reduce.

$$\frac{4}{8} \times \frac{b^{-3}}{b^2} \times \frac{1}{c^{-2}} \times \frac{d}{d} = \frac{1}{2} \times \frac{1}{b^5} \times \frac{c^2}{1} \times 1 = \frac{c^2}{2b^5}$$

Answer choice D is correct.

2. $\dfrac{6h^{-2}j}{3^{-1}k^2m^{-3}} =$

(A) $\dfrac{2h^2j}{k^2m^3}$

(B) $\dfrac{2jm^2}{h^2k^2}$

(C) $\dfrac{3h^2j}{k^2m^3}$

(D) $\dfrac{18h^2j}{k^2m^3}$

(E) $\dfrac{18jm^3}{h^2k^2}$

We will use the same method for answering this question.

$$\frac{6h^{-2}j}{3^{-1}k^2m^{-3}} = \frac{6}{3^{-1}} \times \frac{h^{-2}}{1} \times \frac{j}{1} \times \frac{1}{k^2} \times \frac{1}{m^{-3}} =$$

Now we can reduce and simplify:

$$6 \times 3 \times \frac{1}{h^2} \times \frac{j}{1} \times \frac{1}{k^2} \times \frac{m^3}{1} = \frac{18jm^3}{h^2k^2}$$

Answer choice E is correct.

Simplifying Expressions that have Negative Numbers and Exponents

There are three important rules you need to know when dealing with negative numbers and exponents:

1. If the negative sign is not in parentheses, then the answer will be negative no matter what.
2. If the negative sign is in parentheses and the exponent is even, then the answer will be positive.
3. If the negative sign is in parentheses and the exponent is odd, then the answer will be negative.

Examples:

$$-3^2 = -(3 \times 3) = -9$$
$$-(3^2) = -(3 \times 3) = -9$$
$$(-3)^2 = -3 \times -3 = 9$$
$$(-3)^3 = -3 \times -3 \times -3 = -27$$

Here are some examples for you to try – just remember to follow PEMDAS!

1. Evaluate the expression -2^4.
   (A) -16
   (B) -8
   (C) -4
   (D) 4
   (E) 16

To answer this question, keep in mind that the whole thing should be negative. If we expand the expression, we get:

$$-2^4 = -(2 \times 2 \times 2 \times 2) = -16$$

Answer choice A is correct.

2. Evaluate: $-3(-2)^3$
   (A) -24
   (B) -16
   (C) 6
   (D) 24
   (E) 216

The important thing to remember for this question is that we have to use PEMDAS. This means that we handle what is in parentheses first. Since $(-2)^3 = -8$, then our problem becomes $-3 \times -8 = 24$. Answer choice D is correct.

You may also see questions that have fractions within parentheses. The important rule to know for these types of questions is that we can distribute an exponent to both the numerator and denominator, as long as we remember to apply it to every term.

Examples:

$$\left(\frac{2}{3}\right)^2 = \frac{2^2}{3^2} = \frac{4}{9}$$

$$\left(\frac{2x}{3y}\right)^2 = \frac{2^2 x^2}{3^2 y^2} = \frac{4x^2}{9y^2}$$

Here are a couple of examples for you to try:

3. $-\left(\frac{3}{4}\right)^3 =$

   (A) $-\dfrac{9}{16}$

   (B) $-\dfrac{27}{64}$

   (C) $\dfrac{9}{16}$

   (D) $\dfrac{9}{25}$

   (E) $\dfrac{27}{64}$

We have to remember that if the negative sign is in front of the parentheses, the answer will be negative. We also have to remember that we can distribute an exponent to a fraction. If we do this, we get:

$$\left(\frac{3^3}{}\right) = -\frac{27}{64}$$

correct.

4. $\left(-\dfrac{2}{5}\right)^2 =$

    (A) $-\dfrac{2}{5}$

    (B) $-\dfrac{4}{25}$

    (C) $\dfrac{4}{5}$

    (D) $\dfrac{2}{25}$

    (E) $\dfrac{4}{25}$

In this case, the negative sign was in the parentheses and the exponent is even, so we know the answer must be positive.

$$\left(-\dfrac{2}{5}\right)^2 = -\dfrac{2}{5} \times -\dfrac{2}{5} = \dfrac{4}{25}$$

Answer choice E is correct.

Radicals

You may have seen questions that use a square root sign, or radical ($\sqrt{}$). A square root symbol asks us to find the number when squared that would give us the number under the radical.

For example:

$\sqrt{4} = 2$
$\sqrt{9} = 3$
$\sqrt{25} = 5$

We can simplify radicals by breaking them into their component parts, factoring them using numbers that are perfect squares.

✓ When we simplify radicals, we write them numbers under them as the product of as many perfect squares as possible

For example:

$$\sqrt{8} = \sqrt{4} \times \sqrt{2} = 2\sqrt{2}$$

We can do this as long as there is not addition or subtraction. For example, we can NOT break apart $\sqrt{9 + 16}$ and get $\sqrt{9} + \sqrt{16}$, which would give us 3 +4 or 7. Rather, we have to follow order of operations and do the operation under the radical first, which results in $\sqrt{25}$ or 5.

- We can NOT break apart a radical if there is an addition/subtraction sign under the radical

We can also combine radicals as long as they have the same number under the radical. For example, $2\sqrt{3} + 7\sqrt{3}$ becomes $9\sqrt{3}$. We would not be able to combine $2\sqrt{3} + 7\sqrt{2}$, however, because $\sqrt{2}$ and $\sqrt{3}$ are not like terms.

- We can combine radicals as long as they have the same number under the radical

Just as we can break apart radicals that are being multiplied, we can also break apart radicals that are being divided. For example:

$$\sqrt{\frac{16}{9}} = \frac{\sqrt{16}}{\sqrt{9}} = \frac{4}{3}$$

Here are some questions for you to try:

1. What is the value of $\sqrt{32}$?
    - (A) $4\sqrt{2}$
    - (B) $4\sqrt{3}$
    - (C) $8\sqrt{2}$
    - (D) $8\sqrt{3}$
    - (E) $16\sqrt{2}$

This question is asking us to simplify a radical expression. To do that, we break apart the number under the radical: $\sqrt{32} = \sqrt{16} \times \sqrt{2} = 4\sqrt{2}$. Answer choice A is correct.

2. Which of the following is equivalent to $\sqrt{18} + \sqrt{54}$?

   (A) $3\sqrt{2}$
   (B) $3\sqrt{3}$
   (C) $6\sqrt{2}$
   (D) $6\sqrt{6}$
   (E) $3\sqrt{2} + 3\sqrt{6}$

To answer this question, we need to simplify each radical to lowest terms. We can break $\sqrt{18}$ into $\sqrt{9} \times \sqrt{2}$, which is equal to $3\sqrt{2}$. We can break $\sqrt{54}$ into $\sqrt{9} \times \sqrt{6}$, which is equal to $3\sqrt{6}$. Now we put those together: $3\sqrt{2} + 3\sqrt{6}$. Since $\sqrt{2}$ and $\sqrt{6}$ are not like terms, we cannot further combine them, and answer choice E is correct.

We can also have roots that are not square roots. For example, if we take the cube root of a number, we are determining what number cubed would give us that number. We write a small number within the radical to indicate a different root.

For example, $\sqrt[3]{64} = 4$ because $4^3 = 64$.

Here is a question for you to try:

3. Which is equivalent to $\sqrt[3]{\dfrac{8}{125}}$?

   (A) $\dfrac{4}{25}$

   (B) $\dfrac{1}{5}$

   (C) $\dfrac{2}{5}$

   (D) $\dfrac{3}{5}$

   (E) $\dfrac{4}{5}$

Our first step is to break apart the radical so that it becomes $\frac{\sqrt[3]{8}}{\sqrt[3]{125}}$. Now we need to find $\sqrt[3]{8}$ and $\sqrt[3]{125}$. Since 2^3 is equal to 8, $\sqrt[3]{8} = 2$, and since 5^3 is equal to 125, $\sqrt[3]{125} = 5$. Therefore, $\frac{\sqrt[3]{8}}{\sqrt[3]{125}} = \frac{2}{5}$, and choice C is correct.

Another important rule to know about radicals is that if they are on denominator of a fraction, we have to "rationalize the denominator," or get rid of the radical on the bottom of the fraction. We do this by multiplying the denominator and numerator by the radical.

- We can't have a radical on the bottom of a fraction
- We have to multiply the top and the bottom of the fraction by that radical

For example:

$$\frac{2}{\sqrt{3}} \times \frac{\sqrt{3}}{\sqrt{3}} = \frac{2\sqrt{3}}{3}$$

We created an equivalent fraction that does not have a radical in the denominator.

Here are a couple of questions for you to try:

4. Which expression is equivalent to $\frac{4}{\sqrt{5}}$?

   (A) $2\sqrt{5}$

   (B) 2

   (C) $4\sqrt{5}$

   (D) 4

   (E) $\frac{4\sqrt{5}}{5}$

In the original expression, there was a radical in the denominator, so we needed to multiply both the numerator and the denominator by that radical:

$$\frac{4}{\sqrt{5}} \times \frac{\sqrt{5}}{\sqrt{5}} = \frac{4\sqrt{5}}{5}$$

Answer choice E is correct.

Exponents can also be expressed as fractions. You may have already worked with fractional exponents without realizing it. The square root is another way of saying the one-half power. Similarly, the cube root is another way of saying the one-third power.

Here are a few examples:

$$\sqrt[3]{x} = x^{1/3}$$
$$\sqrt[4]{n} = n^{1/4}$$
$$\sqrt{a^3} = (a^3)^{1/2} = a^{3 \times 1/2} = a^{3/2}$$

Notice in the last example that a is raised to one power and then that result is raised to another power. To determine the final exponent, we multiply those two powers together.

Here are a couple examples for you to try:

1. $(16)^{1/2} =$

    (A) $\dfrac{1}{16}$

    (B) 4

    (C) 8

    (D) 16

    (E) 256

Remember that raising a number to the one-half power means the same thing as taking the square root. The square root of 16 is 4, so answer choice B is correct.

2. $\sqrt[3]{b^7} =$

    (A) 10

    (B) $b^{3/7}$

    (C) b^{21}

    (D) $(b^2)\sqrt[3]{b}$

    (E) $\dfrac{1}{3}b^7$

This problem is asking us to find the cube root of b to the seventh power. This is the same as asking us to take b to the seventh power, and then take that to the one-third power. To get the answer, we multiply those two powers together:

$$\sqrt[3]{b^7} = b^{7 \times 1/3} = b^{7/3}$$

However, that doesn't look like one of our answer choices. Let's try reducing the fractional exponent:

$$b^{7/3} = b^{(2 + 1/3)} = b^2 \times b^{1/3} = b^2 \times \sqrt[3]{b}$$

Now we can see that answer choice D is correct.

Factoring and Quadratic Equations

Factoring polynomials requires breaking a polynomial into its factors. For example, let's say we need to factor $x^2 - x - 6$. Since $(x + 2)(x - 3)$ multiplies to $x^2 - x - 6$, $x + 2$ and $x - 3$ are the factors of $x^2 - x - 6$.

There are different methods for factoring, many of which involve guessing and checking various numbers. However, this is a multiple-choice test. One of the answer choices must work. We can use the FOIL method to check each one and see which one gives the desired quadratic (you can also use the table method that we used to multiply polynomials). FOIL stands for First, Outer, Inner, and Last. This reminds us to multiply the first terms by each other, the outer terms by each other, the inner terms by each other, and the last terms by each other.

- For questions requiring factoring, it is often easier to just multiply out the answer choices to see what works
- We can use FOIL to multiply the factors (or a table like we did in the multiplying polynomials section)

For example, let's say we want to know what the product $(2x + 3)(x - 4)$ is equal to.

First: $2x^2$
Outer: $-8x$
Inner: $+3x$
Last: -12

If we add these terms, the result is $2x^2 - 5x - 12$.

Here are a couple of questions for you to try:

1. Which is equivalent to $x^2 - 3x - 40$?

    (A) $(x - 5)(x - 8)$
    (B) $(x - 5)(x + 8)$
    (C) $(x + 5)(x - 8)$
    (D) $(x - 10)(x + 4)$
    (E) $(x + 10)(x - 4)$

We can multiply out the answer choices using FOIL:

$$(x - 5)(x - 8) = x^2 - 8x - 5x + 40 = x^2 - 13x + 40$$
$$(x - 5)(x + 8) = x^2 + 8x - 5x - 40 = x^2 + 3x - 40$$
$$(x + 5)(x - 8) = x^2 - 8x + 5x - 40 = x^2 - 3x - 40$$
$$(x + 10)(x - 4) = x^2 - 4x + 10x - 40 = x^2 + 6x - 40$$
$$(x - 10)(x + 4) = x^2 + 4x - 10x - 40 = x^2 - 6x - 40$$

Since answer choice C gives us the polynomial in the question, it is the correct answer choice.

2. Which expression is equivalent to $6m^2 + 46m + 28$?

    (A) $(m + 7)(m + 4)$
    (B) $(m + 14)(m + 2)$
    (C) $(3m + 4)(2m + 7)$
    (D) $(6m + 4)(m + 7)$
    (E) $(6m + 14)(m + 2)$

We can solve for each answer choice for this one as well. We can save ourselves a little work, though, because if we look at choices A and B, there is no way for the first term to have a coefficient of 6 with those answer choices. We can eliminate them.

$(m + 7)(m + 4)$- already eliminated
$(m + 14)(m + 2)$- already eliminated
$(3m + 4)(2m + 7) = 6m^2 + 21m + 8m + 28 = 6m^2 + 29m + 28$
$(6m + 4)(m + 7) = 6m^2 + 42m + 4m + 28 = 6m^2 + 46m + 28$
$(6m + 14)(m + 2) = 6m^2 + 12m + 14m + 28 = 6m^2 + 26m + 28$

Answer choice D results in the quadratic given in the question so choice D is correct.

You may also see questions that ask you for the solution to quadratic equations. We can handle these questions in a similar fashion: plugging in answer choices to see what works. Keep in mind that quadratic equations often have more than one solution.

- If a question asks for the solution to a quadratic equation, plug in answer choices and see which one works

Here are a couple of questions for you to try:

3. Which are the solutions to $-x^2 + 3x + 10 = 0$?
   (A) $-2, 5$
   (B) $-5, 2$
   (C) $-5, -2$
   (D) $-1, 10$
   (E) $1, -10$

We can plug in answer choices and see what works. Remember that both numbers need to work so if one number in the answer choice doesn't work, we can eliminate the answer choice without checking the second number.

$$-2: \; -x^2 + 3x + 10 = -(-2)^2 + 3(-2) + 10 = -4 - 6 + 10 = 0$$

Since -2 does make the expression equal to 0, -2 is a solution, and answer choice A or C must be correct. Now we need to figure out whether the other solution is 5 or -5.

$$5: \; -x^2 + 3x + 10 = -(5)^2 + 3(5) + 10 = -25 + 15 + 10 = 0$$

Substituting in 5 for x also gave the expression a value of 0, so the solutions are -2 and 5. Answer choice A is correct.

4. Which of the following is one possible solution for $3x^2(x + 5) = 0$?

   (A) −5
   (B) −3
   (C) 3
   (D) 5
   (E) 15

We can plug in the answer choices and see which results in a value of 0 for the left side of the equation.

$$-5\text{:}\, 3(-5)^2(-5 + 5) = 75(0) = 0$$

Since substituting in −5 for x made the left side of the equation equal to 0, −5 is a possible solution and answer choice A is correct. We don't need to try the other answer choices since there can only be one correct answer.

Those are the basics that you need to know about advanced algebra. Be sure to complete the practice set!

Advanced Algebra Practice Set

1. If $m = 6$ and $n = 3$, then what is $m^2 - n^3$ equal to?

    (A) -1
    (B) 3
    (C) 9
    (D) 27
    (E) 36

2. What is $4a^2 + (2b)^3$ equal to if $a = 5$ and $b = 1$?

    (A) 6
    (B) 22
    (C) 46
    (D) 102
    (E) 108

3. What is $-(3)^2 + (-3)^2$ equal to?

    (A) -18
    (B) -6
    (C) 0
    (D) 6
    (E) 18

4. Simplify the expression $(x^3 - 2x^2 + 6x - 4) - (2x^3 - 3x^2 + 4x - 5)$

    (A) $-x^3 + x^2 + 2x + 1$
    (B) $3x^3 - 5x^2 + 10x - 9$
    (C) $-x^3 - 5x^2 + 10x - 9$
    (D) $x + 1$
    (E) $3x^6$

5. Evaluate $(c^3 + 4cd^2 - 2d^3 + 5) + (-c^2d + 3d^3 - 6)$

   (A) $cd + 5d^2 - 1$
   (B) $3c + 4d + 11$
   (C) $3c + 4d - 1$
   (D) $c^3 - c^2d + 4cd^2 + d^3 - 1$
   (E) $c^3 + c^2d + 4cd^2 - 5d^3 + 11$

6. Simplify $\dfrac{6r^2s^4t}{2s^2t^4} \times \dfrac{rst^4}{3r^3s^3}$

   (A) t

   (B) 3t

   (C) 6rst

   (D) $9r^4s^4t^7$

   (E) $\dfrac{9r^4s^4}{t^7}$

7. $\dfrac{4a^2b^{-1}c^{-3}}{6b^2c^{-2}} =$

   (A) $-\dfrac{4}{3}a$

   (B) $\dfrac{2}{3}a^2$

   (C) $\dfrac{2a^2c}{3b}$

   (D) $\dfrac{2a^2}{3b^3c}$

   (E) $\dfrac{4a}{3bc}$

8. Evaluate $-4^3 + (-3)^2 + (-2)^3 - (1)^4$

    (A) -82

    (B) -64

    (C) -48

    (D) -46

    (E) 72

9. $\sqrt[4]{n^{11}} =$

    (A) n^{-7}

    (B) n^7

    (C) $n^{11} - n^4$

    (D) $n^2 \times n^{3/4}$

    (E) $n^2 \times \sqrt[4]{n}$

10. What is the greatest common factor of $15m^6, 27m^4, 36m^{10}$?

    (A) $3m^4$

    (B) $6m^4$

    (C) $3m^{10}$

    (D) $6m^{10}$

    (E) $72m^{10}$

11. What is the greatest common factor of $18xy^4, 45x^3y^2$, and $54xy^5z$?

    (A) $3xy^2$

    (B) $3xy^4z$

    (C) $9xy^2$

    (D) $9xy^4z$

    (E) $18xy^2$

12. What is the least common multiple of $5b^2c^3d, 6b^4c^2, 12b^6c$?

    (A) $5b^2c$

    (B) $5b^2cd$

    (C) $30b^2c$

    (D) $30b^6c^3d$

    (E) $60b^6c^3d$

13. Which is equivalent to the expression $m(m^3)(m^4)$?

  (A) m^7
  (B) m^8
  (C) m^{10}
  (D) m^{12}
  (E) m^{16}

14. Which expression is equivalent to $[4r(3r)^3]^2$?

  (A) $12r^6$
  (B) $12r^8$
  (C) $432r^6$
  (D) $432r^8$
  (E) $11{,}664r^8$

15. Which expression is equivalent to $(5x + 1)(3x - 3)$?

  (A) $15x^2 - 9x + 3$
  (B) $15x^2 + 9x - 3$
  (C) $15x^2 - 12x + 3$
  (D) $15x^2 + 12x - 3$
  (E) $15x^2 - 12x - 3$

16. Which expression is $(v^2 - 3v + 5)(v^2 + 7v - 2)$?

  (A) $v^4 + 4v - 10$
  (B) $v^4 + 4v^3 - 18v^2 + 41v - 10$
  (C) $v^4 + 11v^3 - 18v^2 + 41v - 10$
  (D) $v^4 + 11v^3 - 14v^2 + 41v - 10$
  (E) $v^4 + 11v^3 - 14v^2 + 29v - 10$

17. Which is equivalent to $\sqrt{72} - \sqrt{32}$?

  (A) $2\sqrt{2}$
  (B) $4\sqrt{2}$
  (C) $\sqrt{40}$
  (D) 4
  (E) 8

18. Which expression is equivalent to $\frac{3}{\sqrt{8}}$?

    (A) $3\sqrt{8}$

    (B) $\frac{3\sqrt{2}}{4}$

    (C) $\frac{3\sqrt{2}}{8}$

    (D) $3\sqrt{2}$

    (E) $6\sqrt{2}$

19. Which expression is equivalent to $(m + 7)^2$?

    (A) $m^2 + 49$

    (B) $m^2 + 7m + 49$

    (C) $m^2 + 14m + 49$

    (D) $m^2 - 49$

    (E) $m^2 - 14m - 49$

20. Which are the solutions to $-x^2 + x + 20 = 0$?

    (A) $2, -10$

    (B) $-2, 10$

    (C) $4, -5$

    (D) $-4, 5$

    (E) $-4, -5$

21. Which of the following is one possible solution for $2x^2(x - 3) = 0$?

    (A) -3

    (B) -1

    (C) 1

    (D) 2

    (E) 3

Answers to Advanced Algebra Practice Set

1. C
2. E
3. C
4. A
5. D
6. A
7. D
8. B
9. D
10. A
11. C
12. E
13. B
14. E
15. E
16. B
17. A
18. B
19. C
20. D
21. E

Word Problems

The phrase "word problems" strikes fear into the heart of many students. On the SSAT, it doesn't have to!

Word problems on the SSAT tend to be very predictable. Identify the type of problem and you are halfway there.

The types of word problems that you are most likely to see on the SSAT are:

1. Plugging in answer choices to see what works
2. Figuring out the overlap in two groups
3. Dividing items into different groups
4. Distance problems
5. Manipulating equations without solving
6. Price reduction questions

Some of these question types are really very easy, some of them are harder. As you work through these different problem types, think about how you can identify them on the actual test.

- Think about what makes each problem type unique

Plugging In Answer Choices to See What Works

We covered this problem type in the math strategies section, so we will just jump to a sample problem.

Let's see if you can remember what strategy to use on the following example:

1. Gus has 17 roses and Hannah has 13 roses. How many roses must Gus give to Hannah if they are going to have the same number of roses?

   (A) 1
   (B) 2
   (C) 3
   (D) 4
   (E) 5

Did you remember that in order to solve this problem we should plug in answer choices, starting with choice C? Let's try choice C. If Gus gave Hannah 3 roses, then he would have 14 and Hannah would have 16. This doesn't work and we can see that Gus needs to give Hannah fewer roses. Let's try choice B. If Gus gives Hannah 2 roses, then Gus would have 15 and Hannah would have 15. Since they now have the same number of roses, choice B is correct.

Another type of question where you can plug in answer choices is the "wheels" questions. These questions give you a total number of wheels and then ask you to determine how many you have of different types of vehicles, such as unicycles, bicycles, and automobiles.

Here is what they look like:

2. In front of a school, there are an equal number of bicycles and automobiles. If the number of bicycle wheels plus the number of automobile wheels is equal to 12, how many bicycles are in front of the school?

   (A) 2
   (B) 3
   (C) 4
   (D) 5
   (E) 6

Let's plug in our answer choices and see what works. We will start with choice C. If we had 4 bicycles, that would be 8 wheels. The problem tells us that we have an equal number of bicycles and automobiles. That means we would have 4 automobiles, which would have 16 wheels. This adds up to 24 wheels, which is way too many. Let's try choice A and see if that works. If we had 2 bicycles, that would give us 4 wheels. We would also have 2 automobiles, which would give us 8 more wheels. This is a total of 12 wheels, so choice A is correct.

Here is another one for you to try:

3. At a street festival, there are an equal number of unicycles and bicycles.
    The number of bicycle wheels plus the number of unicycle wheels is 9.
    How many unicycles are there at the street festival?

    (A) 2
    (B) 3
    (C) 4
    (D) 5
    (E) 6

If we start with choice C, we have 4 unicycles (4 wheels) and 4 bicycles (8 wheels).
This adds up to 12 wheels, which is too many. If we try choice B, we get that there
are 3 unicycles (3 wheels) and 3 bicycles (6 wheels). This gives us a total of 9
wheels, so choice B is correct.

Another problem type where you can plug in answer choices is where they give you a fixed cost
plus a variable cost. For example, if the problem says that a telephone call costs $1 for the first
minute and 50 cents for each minute after the first minute, then our fixed cost would be $1 and
the variable cost would be 50 cents per minute after the first minute.

For these questions, just start with the middle answer choice and see what works.

Here is an example:

4. To ride in a taxicab costs $2.50 for the first mile and $0.60 cents for each
    half mile after that. For how many miles could a passenger ride for $4.90?

    (A) 1.5
    (B) 2.0
    (C) 2.5
    (D) 3.0
    (E) 5.0

Let's start with choice C. If a passenger rode for 2.5 miles, it would cost $2.50 for the first mile and then $1.80 for the three half-miles after that (did you notice that the rate was per half mile and not per mile?). This adds up to $4.30, which is less than the $4.90 that the passenger paid. We will try the next biggest answer choice, or choice D. If a passenger rode for three miles, it would cost $2.50 for the first mile and the $2.40 for the four half-miles after that. That adds up to $4.90, so choice D is correct.

Figuring Out the Overlap in Two Groups

These questions tell us how many people belong to two different groups and then tell us how many total people there are. If we add the two groups together, it is greater than the total number of people, so there must be some overlap in the two groups.

To solve these problems:

1. Add the two groups together
2. From this number subtract the total number of people
3. This gives us the correct answer choice, or how many people belong to both groups.

Here is how the question can look on the SSAT:

1. In an elementary school, 400 students own a bike and 350 students own a scooter. If a total of 700 students own either a bike or a scooter or both, how many students must own both a bike and a scooter?
   (A) 0
   (B) 50
   (C) 75
   (D) 100
   (E) 300

To solve this problem, first we add the two groups together. That gives us 750 students. However, there are only 700 students who own either a bike or a scooter. If we subtract 700 from 750, we get that 50 students must own both a bike and a scooter, so answer choice B is correct.

Here is another one for you to try:

2. In a recent poll, 500 people were found to have either a brother or a sister or both. If 300 of these people had a brother and 350 of these people had a sister, then how many people have both a brother and a sister?

   (A) 50
   (B) 100
   (C) 150
   (D) 200
   (E) 300

If we add 300 and 350, we get 650. We then subtract 500 from this number and get 150. This means that 150 people must have both a brother and a sister, so choice C is correct.

Dividing Items into Different Groups

These problems require us to divide items into different groups. The question will give us different conditions that need to be met and then ask a question about how many groups there could be.

To answer these questions:

1. Draw out the items.
2. Try out your answer choices to see what you can make work with the rules given – if you are trying to get the smallest number of groups remember that you need as many in each group as possible and if you are trying to get the largest number of groups, you want each group to have less members.
3. If the question asks for the smallest number, start with the smallest answer choice. If that doesn't work, try the next biggest answer choice, and so on. If it asks for the largest number of groups, start with the largest answer choice.
4. Be aware that the answer choices might not be in order!

Here is an example:

1. There are 15 people waiting in line at a restaurant. If there can be no more than 5 people at a table and no two tables can have the same number of people seated at them, what is the smallest number of tables needed to seat all 15 people?

   (A) 8
   (B) 10
   (C) 3
   (D) 2
   (E) 5

Let's start with plugging in answer choice D since it is the smallest. If we had two tables, one could have 5 people and one could have 4 people since no two tables can have the same number of people. This adds up to 9 people, so choice D does not work. Now let's try choice C since it is the next smallest answer choice. If we had 5 people at one table, 4 people at the next table, and 3 people at the last table, that would only add up to 12 people, which is not enough. Now we try choice E. The first table would have 5 people, the next table would have 4 people, the next table would have 3 people, the next table would have two people, and the last table would have 1 person. This adds up to 15, so choice E is correct.

Here is another one for you to try:

2. There are twenty students on a fieldtrip. They need to divide into groups. If each group must have at least 3 students but no more than six, what is the largest number of groups that the students can form?

   (A) 4
   (B) 3
   (C) 7
   (D) 6
   (E) 8

Since we are looking for the largest number, we want to make each group as small as possible. However, the problem tells us that we can't have less than three students in each group. Let's start with choice E since it is the largest. If we had 8 groups, then we wouldn't have enough students for each group to have at least

3 students, so choice E is out. Now we try choice C and run into the same problem. We don't have enough students so that each group would have at least 3 people. If we try choice D, we would have enough students for each group to have at least 3 people, so choice D is correct.

Distance Problems

Distance problems are quite sneaky – but not if you know what to look for!

These problems give you the distance that two people are from the same point and then ask you how far apart those two people are.

The trick to these questions is that unless they tell us the direction of each person from the fixed point, we can't figure out how far apart they are!

- Unless a direction is given, we CANNOT figure out how far apart the two people are

Here is what this question looks like on the SSAT:

1. Frannie lives 8 blocks from the library. Kelly lives 4 blocks from the library. What is the distance, in blocks, between Kelly's house and Frannie's house?
    - (A) 4
    - (B) 8
    - (C) 12
    - (D) 16
    - (E) Cannot be determined with the information given

This problem does not tell us what direction each girl lives from the library. They could live in the same direction or the opposite direction or somewhere in between. Therefore, choice E is correct.

Manipulating Equations Without Solving

Some questions on the SSAT will ask you how numbers will change without requiring you to perform calculations.

Here is an example of one of these questions:

1. If a cake is cut into 10 pieces instead of 8 pieces, which statement must be
    true?
    (A) Each piece of cake will be smaller
    (B) Each piece of cake will be larger
    (C) There will be two more pieces of cake than there were before
    (D) There will be two fewer pieces of cake than there were before
    (E) The pieces will be of all different shapes

The key to this question is that the answer MUST be true. The only thing that we
can know for sure is that there will be two more pieces of cake, so choice C is
correct.

Other questions will ask you to set up an equation and then you have to use the associative
property to figure out how to answer the question without actually solving.

The associative property is simply:

$$(A \times B) \times C = A \times (B \times C)$$

Here is an example of how this question looks on the actual SSAT:

2. If one third the weight of a hippopotamus is 620 pounds, then the weight of
    4 hippopotamuses of the exact same weight as the given hippopotamus can
    be found by multiplying 620 by
    (A) one-fourth
    (B) one-third
    (C) three
    (D) four
    (E) twelve

To solve, let's set up some equations. One third the weight of the hippopotamus
is 620, so to find the weight of the whole hippopotamus, we would multiply 620
by 3.

weight of one hippo $= 620 \times 3$

Now the problem tells us that we are trying to find the weight of 4 hippos, so we multiply the weight of one hippo by 4.

$$weight\ of\ 4\ hippos = (620 \times 3) \times 4$$

Now we can use the associative property.

$$weight\ of\ 4\ hippos = 620 \times (3 \times 4) = 620 \times 12$$

The correct answer is choice E.

Here is another one for you to try:

3. If one-half the weight of a car is 1,450 pounds, then the total weight of five cars of the exact same weight as the first car can be found by multiplying 1,450 by

    (A)   one-fourth
    (B)   one-half
    (C)   five
    (D)   ten
    (E)   twenty

First let's set up an equation that represents the weight of one car:

$$weight\ of\ 1\ car = 1,450 \times 2$$

Now, let's set up an equation that would work for five cars:

$$weight\ of\ 5\ cars = weight\ of\ 1\ car \times 5 = (1,450 \times 2) \times 5$$

Let's use that associative property:

$$weight\ of\ 5\ cars = 1,450 \times (2 \times 5) = 1,450 \times 10$$

Answer choice D is correct.

Price Reduction Questions

Price reduction questions are a doozy. They require many steps, but if you follow each sentence closely, then you can figure them out. Also remember that you have to use all the information given!

- Follow each sentence closely so that you don't lose track of where you are
- Remember to use all the information given

Here is what these questions look like:

1. A buffet restaurant has an average of 300 diners each day. Currently, the restaurant charges the same price for adults and children. In order to bring in more business, the owner plans to reduce the price of a child's meal from $7.00 to $5.00 but leave the price of the adult meal at $7.00. If the restaurant has 200 adult diners, how many child diners must they have in order for daily sales to remain the same as before the reduction for a child's meal?

   (A) 120
   (B) 130
   (C) 140
   (D) 145
   (E) 150

Let's start by figuring out the daily sales. If we multiply the price ($7) by the number of diners (300), we get daily sales of $2,100. Under the new plan, if there were 200 adult diners, the restaurant would bring in $1,400 for the adult diners. If we subtract $1,400 from $2,100, we get that the restaurant must make $700 off of the child diners. If we divide $700 by the cost of each meal ($5), we get that the restaurant must bring in 140 child diners. Answer choice C is correct.

Here is one for you to try:

2. An amusement park averages 500 visitors per day. In order to increase business, the amusement park owner is going to reduce the admission price from $20 to $12 after 2 PM. If 350 people pay $20, how many people have to pay $12 in order keep daily sales the same as they were before the $12 price reduction plan?

(A) 200
(B) 250
(C) 325
(D) 375
(E) 400

First, we figure out how much daily sales were at the beginning of the problem. We multiply $20 by 500 visitors to get that the park was bringing in $10,000. After the price reduction plan, there were still 350 people paying $20. That means that daily sales from this group were $7,000. This tells us that the park must make $3,000 off of the people paying $12. If we divide $3,000 by $12, we find that 250 people must be paying $12 in order to keep daily sales the same. Answer choice B is correct.

Now you know some of the problem types for word problems – and how to solve them!

Word Problems Practice Set

1. If a pie is cut into 7 pieces instead of 6, which statement must be true?

    (A) There will be more pieces of pie
    (B) There will be fewer pieces of pie
    (C) Each piece will be the same size
    (D) Each piece will be larger
    (E) Each piece will be smaller

2. If George lives five blocks from the park and Mildred lives three blocks from the same park, how many blocks apart do George and Mildred live?

    (A) 2 blocks
    (B) 3 blocks
    (C) 5 blocks
    (D) 8 blocks
    (E) Cannot be determined

3. There are 10 people waiting in line for a taxi at the airport. If each taxi must take at least one person but can take no more than 5 people, and no two taxis have the same number of people, what is the smallest number of taxis that is needed to accommodate all 10 people?

    (A) 5
    (B) 4
    (C) 3
    (D) 6
    (E) 7

4. An ice cream stand averages 200 customers per day. In an effort to increase business, the manager plans to reduce the price of a cone from $3 to $2 before 3 PM each day. If 150 people pay $3, then how many customers have to pay $2 in order for daily sales to be the same as they were before the $2 pricing plan was put in effect?

    (A) 25
    (B) 50
    (C) 75
    (D) 100
    (E) 125

5. Caitlin has 22 cookies and Harry has 16 cookies. How many cookies does Caitlin have to give to Harry in order for them to have an equal number of cookies?

 (A) 19
 (B) 8
 (C) 6
 (D) 4
 (E) 3

6. 300 people surveyed regularly walk to work and 250 people surveyed regularly bike to work. If a total of 500 people surveyed either walk to work, bike to work, or both, what is the number of people who regularly walk and regularly bike to work?

 (A) 50
 (B) 100
 (C) 150
 (D) 200
 (E) 250

7. If one quarter of the weight of a bus is 1.2 tons, the weight of four buses of the exact same weight can be found by multiplying 1.2 by

 (A) one-fourth
 (B) one-half
 (C) two
 (D) sixteen
 (E) thirty-two

8. If a phone call costs $1.30 for the first minute and $0.40 for each minute after the first minute, how long a phone call can a person make for $3.70?

 (A) 6 minutes
 (B) 6.5 minutes
 (C) 7 minutes
 (D) 7.5 minutes
 (E) 8 minutes

9. On a playground, the number of tricycles and the number of bicycles is the same. If the number of bicycle wheels plus the number of tricycle wheels equals 25, how many tricycles are on the playground?

    (A) 4
    (B) 5
    (C) 6
    (D) 7
    (E) 8

Answers to Word Problems Practice Set

1. A
2. E
3. C
4. C
5. E
6. A
7. D
8. C
9. B

Geometry

On the SSAT, the geometry section deals mostly with angles and shapes and their measurements. You may also need to deal with a number line or a graph.

In this section, we will cover:

- Polygons
- Perimeters
- Area of a rectangle
- Volume
- Area of a circle
- Angles
- Parallel lines rules
- Angles in a quadrilateral
- Triangles
- Area of a triangle
- The Pythagorean Theorem
- Coordinate geometry

Polygons

The root "poly" means many, so a polygon is a many-sided shape. Remember that a circle is not considered a polygon.

- Triangles, rectangles, pentagons and hexagons are examples of polygons

You won't need to define a polygon on the test, but you will need to be able to recognize one.

Perimeters

The perimeter is the measurement of the outside of a polygon.

- The formula for the perimeter is $P = s + s + s + s$ depending on how many sides the polygon has.

For example, if the lengths of the sides of a rectangle are 4, 6, 4, and 6, the perimeter is $P = 4 + 6 + 4 + 6 = 20$.

- If you are given just the length and the width of a rectangle, multiply each by 2 and then add those numbers together to find the perimeter

On the test, you may be given all the measurements needed to calculate the perimeter, or just some of the measurements, and you will have to determine the others before you can calculate the perimeter.

Here is an example of how these concepts may be tested:

1. If the length of a rectangular room is 6m, and the width is half the length, what is the perimeter of the room?

    (A) 3m
    (B) 6m
    (C) 9m
    (D) 12m
    (E) 18m

Since the length of the room is 6, we can eliminate choices A and B. The width of the room is half the length, or 3m. Adding the length and width is 9m, but in a room there are two lengths and two widths, so we need to double the length and width. We add $P = 6 + 3 + 6 + 3 = 18$m, which is answer choice E.

Here is another problem to do:

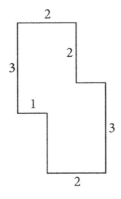

2. All angles in the figure above are right angles. What is the perimeter of the figure?

    (A) 11
    (B) 12
    (C) 13
    (D) 14
    (E) 16

To find the perimeter of the figure, we first have to figure out some of the side lengths. From the bottom horizontal pieces, we can see that the width of the figure is 3 (1+2). That means that the unlabeled segment on the right has to be 1. From the right side of the figure, we can figure out that the height of the figure is 5 (3+2), so we can see that the unlabeled segment on the left must be 2. Now we just add all of our segment lengths together to get 16, or choice E.

Now we are going to try a few harder perimeter problems. These are multi-step problems so it is important that you use all the information given and answer the correct question.

- Use all information given
- Make sure you are answering the correct question

3. Hexagon A has sides with equal lengths and a perimeter of 36 cm. Hexagon B has sides that are each 1 cm shorter than the sides of Hexagon A. What is the perimeter of Hexagon B?

    (A) 6 cm
    (B) 28 cm
    (C) 30 cm
    (D) 31 cm
    (E) 35 cm

Our first step is to figure out the side length of Hexagon A. Since a hexagon has 6 sides, we divide 36 by 6 and get that each side has a length of 6. Now we know that the side lengths of Hexagon B must be 5, since they are 1 shorter than the side lengths of Hexagon A. We multiply the side length by the number of sides (5×6) and get that the perimeter is 30. Answer choice C is correct.

4. Sal planted grass seed in a rectangular field that is 40 meters wide and 200 meters long. If he wants to put rope around the field to keep people from running across the new grass, how much rope will he need to use?

    (A)   240 meters
    (B)   480 meters
    (C)   800 meters
    (D)   960 meters
    (E)   8,000 meters

This question does not use the word perimeter at all. It is describing a situation and then you have to figure out that perimeter is the concept to be applied. Once we figure that out, it is easy to add the side lengths ($40 + 200 + 40 + 200$) and get that the perimeter is 480 meters, or answer choice B.

5. If a rectangle has a length of n yards and a width that is 6 yards more than its length, then what is the perimeter of that rectangle?

    (A) $4n + 12$ yards
    (B) $4n + 6$ yards
    (C) $4n - 24$ yards
    (D) $2n + 12$ yards
    (E) $2n + 6$ yards

Since we have variables in the answer choices for this question, we can plug in our own numbers. Let's make $n = 4$. This means that the length of the rectangle is 4 yards and the width is $4 + 6$, or 10 yards. If we add up two lengths and two widths, we can see that the perimeter is 28 yards. That is our target. Now we plug in 4 for n in the answer choices. Answer choice A gives us 28 when we plug in 4 for n, so it is the correct answer choice.

Area of a Rectangle

The area of a rectangle is the amount of space taken up by the inside of the shape.

- The formula for the area of a rectangle is $A = l \times w$, where l is the length and w is the width

If you have a rectangle that is 4 inches by 6 inches, we can calculate the area to be $A = 4 \times 6 = 24$ inches.

Remember that a square is a special rectangle.

- The formula for the area of a square is $A = s \times s = s^2$, where s is the length of one side

You may be asked to find the area directly, or you may need to know the area of an object to determine how many smaller objects fit inside. To do this, you need to figure out the area of the smaller object, and divide it into the area of the larger object.

Here is an example of how these concepts may be tested:

1. How many square pieces of paper that are 4 inches on a side can be placed on a rectangular piece of paper that is 48 inches long and 40 inches wide if the squares are to completely cover the rectangle and no two squares overlap?
   (A) 40
   (B) 48
   (C) 120
   (D) 192
   (E) 480

To solve this problem, we need to calculate the area of the small square and the rectangle.

Area of the square: $A = s \times s = 4 \times 4 = 16$ square inches

Area of the rectangle: $A = l \times w = 48 \times 40 = 1,920$ square inches

Next, we divide the area of the rectangle by the area of the square. To get an estimate of the result, we can use 20 square inches as the area of the square, and

2,000 square inches as the area of the rectangle. When we divide 2,000 by 20, the result is 100. Using this as an estimate, choices A, B, D, and E can be eliminated and we are left with choice C. When we use the actual numbers, we get $1{,}920 \div 16 = 120$ times. The correct answer is choice C.

Here is another one for you to try:

2. A contractor built a one-story house for the Mendez family that was 50 feet long and 40 feet wide. He charged them $120,000 for the house. What was their cost per square foot?

   (A) $.017
   (B) $6.00
   (C) $17.00
   (D) $60.00
   (E) $600.00

To answer this question, first we must figure out the area of the house. If we do $l \times w = 50 \times 40 = 2{,}000$, we get that the house is 2,000 square feet. Now we divide the price by the number of square feet to get that each square foot cost $60. Answer choice D is correct.

Volume

On the SSAT, you will need to know how to find the volume of a cube, a rectangular prism, and a cylinder.

A cube is a special type of rectangular prism where all the sides are the same length. The volume of a cube is always calculated as

$$V = s^3$$

where s is the length of one of the sides.

A classic problem involves fitting small cubes into a larger cube. Here is an example:

1. The small cube below is 1 inch on all sides. How many cubes of this size would be required to fill a larger cube that is 2 inches on all sides?

    (A) 2
    (B) 4
    (C) 8
    (D) 16
    (E) 32

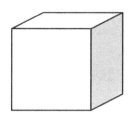

Technique 1: Think of the cube having to be doubled in all 3 dimensions. It must be twice as wide, twice as long, and twice as high. Therefore, the 2-inch cube will be $2 \times 2 \times 2 = 8$ times as big, and thus would need 8 smaller cubes. Answer choice C is correct.

Technique 2: Another way to think of the problem is to compare the volumes of the two cubes. The volume of the small cube is $1 \times 1 \times 1 = 1\ in^3$. The 2-inch cube is $2 \times 2 \times 2 = 8\ in^3$. The larger cube has 8 times the volume of the smaller cube. Again, answer choice C is correct.

Use whichever technique feels easier for you to use.

Here's another problem for you to try:

2. How many 2-inch cubes are needed to create a larger cube that has a base perimeter of 24 inches?

    (A) 12
    (B) 27
    (C) 36
    (D) 72
    (E) 81

Technique 1: If the base perimeter is 24 inches, the length of the side is $24 \div 4$, or 6 inches. The large cube is 6 inches long, 6 inches wide, and 6 inches high. This means that, starting with the 2-inch cube, the small cube must be tripled in length, width, and height in order to create the larger cube, and this would be $3 \times 3 \times 3 = 27$ times as big, which is answer choice B.

Technique 2: The volume of the small cube is $2 \times 2 \times 2 = 8\ in^3$. The volume of the larger cube is $6 \times 6 \times 6 = 216\ in^3$. Divide the larger volume by the smaller volume to get $216 \div 8 = 27$, which is answer choice B.

The volume formulas that you need to know for a rectangular prism and a cylinder are:

$$volume\ of\ a\ rectangular\ prism = length \times width \times depth$$
$$volume\ of\ a\ cylinder = \pi \times radius^2 \times height$$

Here are a couple questions like those you might see on the SSAT:

3. A large box has a volume of 180 ft³. If the box is a rectangular prism, then which of the following could be the dimensions of the box?

    (A) 1 ft × 9 ft × 0.5 ft
    (B) 2 ft × 9 ft × 10 ft
    (C) 6 ft × 6 ft × 6 ft
    (D) 6 ft × 10 ft × 30 ft
    (E) 60 ft × 60 ft × 60 ft

To answer this question, we need to multiply the dimensions together. We can see that the dimensions of choice A would not multiply to a number as large as 180 so we can rule out choice A. Let's move on to choice B. If we multiply $2 \times 9 \times 10$ then we get 180. Choice B is correct.

The next problem is challenging. We would only expect the very top scorers to get this problem so do your best to understand it but don't worry if you find it too hard.

4. Kate's chocolate syrup is sold in small cans that are cylinders with a height of 3 inches and a base diameter of 1 inch and in large cans that are cylinders with a base diameter of 3 inches. If the large cans hold 9 times as much syrup as the small cans, then what is the height of the large cans?

    (A) 1 inch
    (B) $\sqrt[3]{3}$ inches
    (C) $\sqrt{3}$ inches
    (D) 3 inches
    (E) 9 inches

First, we need to find the volume of the small cans. We will use our formula for area of a cylinder since a can is in the shape of the cylinder. Remember that the problem gives us diameter, so we must divide that by 2 to get the radius.

$$volume\ of\ a\ cylinder = \pi \times radius^2 \times height$$

$$volume\ of\ small\ can = \pi \times \left(\frac{1}{2}\right)^2 \times 3 = \frac{3}{4}\pi$$

Now we know that the volume of the large can is 9 times the volume of the small can, so we can calculate that volume to be $9 \times \frac{3}{4}\pi = \frac{27}{4}\pi$. Using our formula again:

$$volume\ of\ a\ cylinder = \pi \times radius^2 \times height$$

$$volume\ of\ large\ can = \frac{27}{4}\pi = \pi \times \left(\frac{3}{2}\right)^2 \times height$$

$$\frac{27}{4}\pi = \frac{9}{4}\pi \times height$$

$$height = 3$$

Answer choice D is correct.

Area of a Circle

To find the area of a circle, we use the basic formula:

$$Area = \pi r^2$$

In this formula, r stands for the length of the radius. For example, if we had a circle with a radius of 4, its area would be equal to 16π.

On the SSAT, they are more likely to ask you a question that asks you to use the formula for the area of circle as one step in a longer problem. Usually they test the area of the circle within a "shaded region" problem. In these questions, we often have to find the area of a larger area and then subtract the area of a smaller region to find the shaded area.

There are a couple of things that you need to remember with these "shaded region" questions:

1. If a circle is inscribed within a square, then the diameter of the circle is equal to the side length of the square. (Be sure to keep diameter and radius straight – remember that the diameter is twice the radius!)
2. We may need to find a sector of a circle and we just use a proportion to do that.

For example, let's say that the area of our circle is 12π. Now we need to find the area of a quarter of that circle. We can just set up a proportion and solve:

$$\frac{1}{4} = \frac{x}{12\pi}$$
$$x = 3\pi$$

Here are a couple of problems for you to try:

1. A circle with a radius of 6 is inscribed within a square.

What is the area of the shaded region?
(A) $144 - 36\pi$
(B) $144 - 144\pi$
(C) 144
(D) 36
(E) 36π

To answer this question, we first need to find the area of the square. If we keep in mind that the diameter of the circle is equal to the side length of the square, then we know that the side length of the square is 12 (diameter is equal to 2 × radius). If the side length is 12, we know that the area is 12 × 12, or 144. Now we have to find the area of the circle since we have to subtract off the area of the circle in order to find the area of the shaded region. Since $area = \pi r^2$ for circles, we know that the area of the circle is 36π. Since answer choice A correctly shows the area of the square minus the area of the circle it is the correct answer.

2. In the following figure, point M is the center of the circle, points N and O are vertices of the triangle and are on the circle, and angle NMO is a right angle.

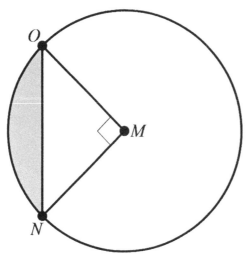

If the length of $\overline{MO}$ is 6, then what is the area of the shaded region?

(A) 6π

(B) $9\pi - 6$

(C) $9\pi - 18$

(D) $36\pi - 18$

(E) $36\pi - 72$

This problem is a little more involved. We have to use the fact that the measure of angle NMO is 90 degrees. That means that the area of the sector of the circle we need to find is $\frac{1}{4}$ the area of the total circle. Since the radius is 6, we know that the area of the entire circle is $\pi \times (6)^2$, or 36π. Since $\frac{1}{4} \times 36\pi = 9\pi$, the area of the sector that we need is 9π. Now we need to subtract the area of triangle MNO in order to find the shaded region. Since it is a right triangle, we know that the length of $\overline{MN}$ equals the base and the length of $\overline{MO}$ equals the height. Since $\overline{MO}$ and $\overline{MN}$ are both radii of the same circle they are both equal to 6. Using $area = \frac{1}{2}bh$, we can find that the area of triangle MNO is $\frac{1}{2}(6)(6)$, or 18. Since answer choice C correctly shows the area of the sector (9π) minus the area of the triangle (18) it is the correct answer choice.

Angles

The foundation of all of geometry is angles. An angle is where 2 lines or line segments meet.

<u>Angle:</u>

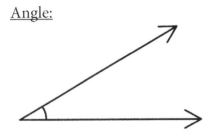

Here are some important facts about angles:

- A right angle has 90°
- A straight angle has 180°
- Opposite (or vertical) angles are equal

A right angle looks like this:

We designate a right angle like this:

The little box is the symbol to tell you that the angle measure is 90°, which is a right angle.

A straight angle is just a straight line. So why does it have an angle measure of 180°? Well, here is the straight line:

Now, put a line down the middle:

Now you see that it is made up of 2 right angles, each measuring 90°, so the total is 180°. Remember, a straight angle has 180°.

Here is an example of how this could be tested on the SSAT:

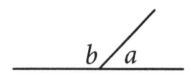

1. In the figure above, angle *a* measures 50°. What is the measure of angle *b*?
    (A) 40°
    (B) 50°
    (C) 100°
    (D) 130°
    (E) Cannot be determined

A straight line has 180°, so $a + b = 180°$

If we plug in what is given and solve, we get:

$$50° + b = 180°$$
$$b = 130°$$

Answer choice D is correct.

Now let's look at opposite angles (they are also sometimes called vertical angles):

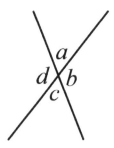

Angles *a* and *c* are equal to each other. Angles *b* and *d* are also equal to one another.

Here is how this concept could be tested on the SSAT:

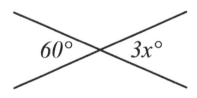

Figure not drawn to scale

2. In the figure above, what is the value of *x*?

    (A) 15
    (B) 20
    (C) 50
    (D) 60
    (E) 180

We know that opposite angles are equal, so we know that $3x = 60$. If we solve for *x*, we get that it is equal to 20, or answer choice B.

Parallel Lines Rules

When you are dealing with parallel lines, there are a lot of fancy names for different angle relationships. For the SSAT, you will probably not need to know these names.

Rather than memorize a lot of rules, just know that pairs of angles in parallel lines questions will either add to 180° or have the same measure. Essentially, if they are both acute (less than

90 degrees) or both obtuse (greater than 90 degrees), then the angles have the same measure. If one angle is acute and the other angle is obtuse, then their measures add to 180°.

- With parallel line questions, the angles are either equal in measure or the measures add to 180°

These questions do not show up very often, so we will just do one example:

1. In the following figure, lines A and C are parallel to each other.

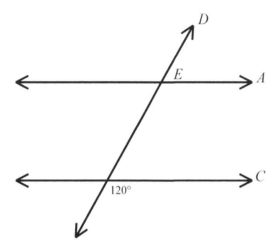

What is the measure of angle *E*?

(A) 240°
(B) 180°
(C) 120°
(D) 90°
(E) 60°

From the picture, we can see that angle *E* is less than 90 degrees. If we look at our answer choices, only answer choice E is less than 90 degrees, so it must be the correct answer. If you did not see that, then you could just subtract the obtuse angle given (120°) from 180° and get that the measure of the obviously acute angle *E* must be 60°.

Angles in a Quadrilateral

Questions that test the angles in a quadrilateral test one simple fact: the angles in a quadrilateral add to 360°. We just need to keep in mind that sometimes triangles are put together to create a quadrilateral and we need to look for that quadrilateral.

- Angles in quadrilateral add to 360°
- Look out for triangles that are put together to create a quadrilateral

Here are a couple of questions that test these concepts:

1. What is the sum of the measures of all of the angles of a parallelogram?

  (A) 180°
  (B) 240°
  (C) 270°
  (D) 360°
  (E) 400°

Since a parallelogram is a type of quadrilateral, its angles add to 360°. Answer choice D is correct.

2. What is the measure of angle *ADC*?

  (A) 25°
  (B) 30°
  (C) 35°
  (D) 60°
  (E) 90°

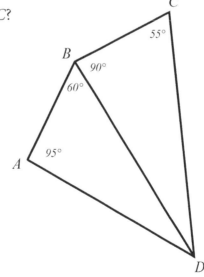

The key to answering this question is recognizing that angle *ADC* is part of a quadrilateral. We have to add together the other angles of the triangles and subtract from 360°. Since the other angles add up to 300°, we know that angle *ADC* is equal to 60°. Answer choice D is correct.

Triangles

Some of the facts that you need to know about triangles include:

1. All angles in a triangle add to 180°.
2. An isosceles triangle is a triangle with two angles with equal measures (the sides opposite those angles are also equal in length).
3. An equilateral triangle is a triangle where all three sides are the same length (and all the angle measures are 60°).
4. The length of one side of a triangle must be greater than the difference between the other two sides, and less than the sum of the other two sides.
5. An interior angle of a triangle plus the adjacent exterior angle add to 180° (this is true of all polygons – not just triangles)

Here is how these concepts could be tested on the SSAT:

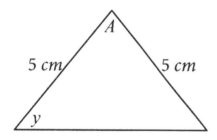

1. In the triangle in the figure above, the measure of angle A is 80 degrees. What is the angle measure of y in degrees?

    (A) 40
    (B) 45
    (C) 50
    (D) 80
    (E) It cannot be determined from the information given

We can identify this triangle as an isosceles triangle because we are given two sides of the same length. The angles opposite these sides are equal. Since we know that the sum of the angles in a triangle equals 180 degrees, we can determine the value of y, eliminating answer choice E. The sum of the two unknown angles is $180° - 80° = 100°$. Divide this by 2 (since there are 2 remaining angles that are equal) and $100° \div 2 = 50°$. The correct answer is choice C.

2. What are the exterior angles of an isosceles right triangle?

   (A) 45°, 45°, 90°
   (B) 90°, 135°, 135°
   (C) 60°, 60°, 60°
   (D) 60°, 120°, 120°
   (E) 270°, 315°, 315°

To answer this question, first we need to figure out the measures of the interior angles. We know that one angle must be 90° since it is a right triangle. It is also isosceles, so the other two angles must be the same. Since they also have to add to 90°, we know that each angle is 45°. So we know that our three angles are 90°, 45°, and 45°. Now we need to find the supplements of these angles since an interior angle and its adjacent exterior angle must add to 180°. The supplements of these angles are 90°, 135°, and 135°, so answer choice B is correct.

3. In the figure below, if $x = 3z$, what is the value of y in terms of z?

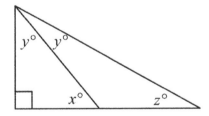

   (A) $\dfrac{3}{z}$

   (B) $\dfrac{z}{3}$

   (C) $\dfrac{z}{4}$

   (D) $90 - 3z$

   (E) $90 + \dfrac{z}{3}$

It may make it easier to either redraw the triangle, replacing x with $3z$, or drawing a new triangle. Once you do this, you will realize that you only need to work with one triangle, the smaller one with a right angle.

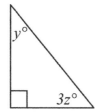

Using the knowledge that the sum of the angles is 180°, we can write the equation $90 + y + 3z = 180$ and solve for y. Subtract 90 from both sides and $y + 3z = 90$. Now subtract $3z$ from both sides, and $y = 90 - 3z$. The correct answer is choice (D).

4. An equilateral triangle has a perimeter of 60. What is the length of each side?

    (A) 10
    (B) 12
    (C) 15
    (D) 20
    (E) 30

In an equilateral triangle, all three sides are the same length. This means that we need to divide 60 by 3 in order to find the side length. Since $60 \div 3 = 20$, answer choice D is correct.

5. The length of side AB of Triangle ABC is 10, while the length of side BC is 8. Which of the following is a possible value for the length of side AC?

    (A) 14
    (B) 18
    (C) 22
    (D) 26
    (E) 30

For this question, we have to remember that the length of the third side of a triangle must be smaller than the sum of the other two sides. Since the other two sides add to 18, the length of AC must be less than 18. Answer choice A is correct.

You may also see a triangle question that you can reason through.

Here is an example:

6. Refer to the following figure to answer the question:

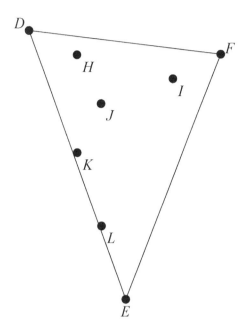

If a segment was drawn from point D to the midpoint of side EF, which would be the midpoint of that newly-drawn segment?

(A) Point H
(B) Point I
(C) Point J
(D) Point K
(E) Point L

For this question, just remember that a midpoint is exactly in the middle of a side. If we draw in the midpoint of EF and then connect it to point D we can see that point J is the only point even on that line. Choice C is correct.

Area of a Triangle

The area of a triangle is the space inside a triangle. The formula is $A = \frac{1}{2}bh$. In a right triangle, like the one below, this formula is easy to use.

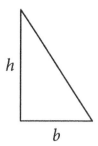

When the triangle is not a right triangle, you have to draw in the height as shown in the triangles below.

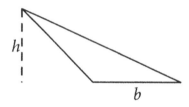 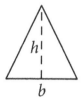

The same formula is used here, although you may need to determine the height from other information given about the triangle.

- The formula for area of a triangle is $A = \dfrac{1}{2}bh$

Here is an example of how these concepts may be tested:

1. What is the area of the shaded region if $ABCD$ is a square?

   (A) 7
   (B) 14
   (C) 42
   (D) 49
   (E) It cannot be determined from the information given

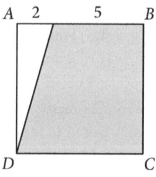

Although all the dimensions of the shaded region are not given, we can use the information about the square and the triangle to solve this problem, so choice (E) can be eliminated. First, find the area of the square. The length of AB is $2 + 5 = 7$. The area of a square is $A = s^2$, so the area of square $ABCD$ is $A = s^2 = 7^2 = 49$. Next, calculate the area of the triangle. Side $AD = AB$, so the area of the triangle is $A = \dfrac{1}{2}bh = \dfrac{1}{2}(2)(7) = 7$. Now, subtract the area of the triangle from

the area of the square to find the area of the shaded region, $A = 49 - 7 = 42$.
The correct answer is choice C.

The Pythagorean Theorem

One geometry concept that sometimes shows up on the SSAT is the Pythagorean Theorem, which deals with the lengths of the sides of a right triangle.

Pythagorean Theorem: $c^2 = a^2 + b^2$

The value c in the formula is the longest side's length. The longest side is called the hypotenuse, and it is always the side that is opposite the right angle in the triangle.

Use this formula only for <u>right</u> triangles!

Let's do a quick example:

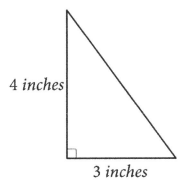

4 inches

3 inches

Use the Pythagorean Theorem to find the length of the hypotenuse of this right triangle.

We recognize this as a right triangle, because the little square box is at the bottom left of the triangle. The hypotenuse is the longest side, and it is the length that is opposite the right angle.

$$c^2 = a^2 + b^2$$
$$c^2 = 3^2 + 4^2$$
$$c^2 = 9 + 16$$
$$c^2 = 25$$
$$c = 5$$

The length of the hypotenuse is 5 inches.

On the SSAT, you may see what are called 3-4-5 triangles that don't require you to calculate square roots.

Here is an example:

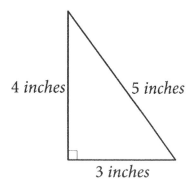

4 inches

5 inches

3 inches

If we see a right triangle and the legs (not the hypotenuse) are each 3 and 4, then we can know that the hypotenuse is 5 without doing any math.

You may also see a related triangle – one where the sides are 6, 8, and 10.

For a sample problem using the Pythagorean Theorem, check out the first problem in the coordinate geometry section. The Pythagorean Theorem is generally not directly tested, rather you have to apply it to solve other problems.

Coordinate Geometry

For coordinate geometry problems, just remember that the coordinates are (x, y). If you forget whether to go over or up first, just remember: first you run and then you jump.

Here is a sample coordinate geometry problem:

1. The coordinates of triangle ABC are A (1, 2), B (5, 2), and C (1, 7). What is the length of $\overline{BC}$?

    (A) 3
    (B) $\sqrt{41}$
    (C) $\sqrt{50}$
    (D) $\sqrt{74}$
    (E) None of these

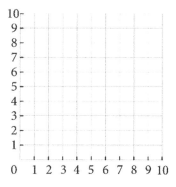

Here is what the triangle looks like:

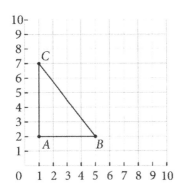

The length of AB is $5 - 1 = 4$. The length of AC is $7 - 2 = 5$. The length of BC, the hypotenuse, is found by using the Pythagorean Theorem:

$$c^2 = a^2 + b^2$$
$$c^2 = 4^2 + 5^2$$
$$c^2 = 16 + 25$$
$$c^2 = 41$$
$$c = \sqrt{41}$$

The correct answer is B.

Some problems on the SSAT require you to reflect a line over an axis. What happens if we reflect the line shown below in the y-axis? This just means to flip the line about the y-axis.

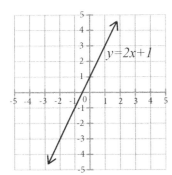

Notice that the point $(0, 1)$ would not move at all, but the point at $(1, 3)$ would reflect into Quadrant II and would become $(-1, 3)$. The point at $(-1, -1)$ would flip to become $(1, -1)$. (Another way to think of this reflection is to see that the reflected line would now have equation $y = -2x + 1$.)

Here is a problem that deals with reflecting a line:

2. The line $y = 2x + 1$ is reflected in the y axis. The line $y = 3$ is drawn on the axes. What is the area of the shape enclosed by the 3 lines?

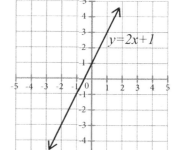

(A) 0.5 square units
(B) 1 square unit
(C) 1.5 square units
(D) 2 square units
(E) 4 square units

If we draw out the reflection and add the line $y = 3$, we would get:

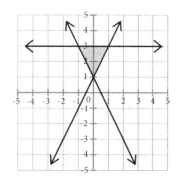

The shape is an upside-down triangle, which has a base of 2 and a height of 2. We use the formula for the area of a triangle and substitute.

$$A = \frac{1}{2}bh$$
$$= \frac{1}{2}(2)(2)$$
$$= 2$$

The correct answer is 2 square units, or answer choice D.

You now know the basics of geometry on the SSAT!

Geometry Practice Set

1. Consider a cube that is 2 inches on all sides. How many cubes of this size would be required to fit into a larger cube that is 8 inches on all sides?

   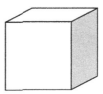

   (A) 4
   (B) 16
   (C) 32
   (D) 64
   (E) 128

2. In the following figure, lines G and H are parallel to each other.

   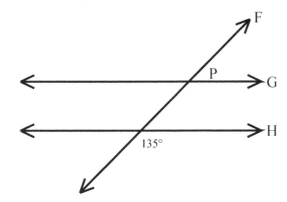

   What is the measure of angle P?

   (A) 180°
   (B) 135°
   (C) 90°
   (D) 65°
   (E) 45°

3. In triangle ABC, side AB has a length of 6 and side BC has a length of 15. Which of the following could be the length of side AC?

   (A) 9
   (B) 15
   (C) 21
   (D) 22
   (E) 24

4. In the triangle to the right, what is the value of x?

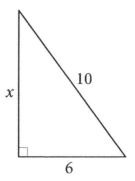

(A) 4

(B) 6

(C) 8

(D) 10

(E) Cannot be determined

5. A circle is inscribed within a square.

If the square has an area of 100, then what is the area of the shaded region?

(A) $10 - 5\pi$

(B) $25 - 10\pi$

(C) $100 - 25\pi$

(D) $100 - 50\pi$

(E) $100 - 100\pi$

6. In the following figure, triangle QRS is a right triangle with angle RQS as the right angle. Points R and S are on the circle, and point Q is the center of the circle.

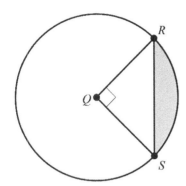

If the area of triangle RQS is 8, then what is the area of the shaded region?

(A) 4π – 8
(B) 8 – 4π
(C) 8 – 8π
(D) 8π – 8
(E) 16π – 8

7. What is the area of the quadrilateral?

(A) 11
(B) 12
(C) 15
(D) 27
(E) Cannot be determined

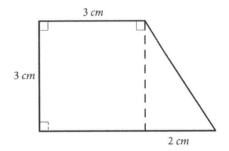

8. A solid cylinder with a base diameter of 2 and a height of 5 is placed within a box. The box is a rectangular prism with a height of 5 and a square base with a side length of 2. What is the volume of the empty space in the box surrounding the cylinder?

(A) 10 – 2π
(B) 10 – 5π
(C) 20 – 5π
(D) 20 – 10π
(E) 20π – 20

9. Nadia needs to run communication wire around the entire perimeter of a football field. If the field is 120.0 yards long by 53.3 yards wide, then how much wire does she need?

    (A) 106.6 yards
    (B) 173.3 yards
    (C) 240.0 yards
    (D) 280.6 yards
    (E) 346.6 yards

10. Which of the following could be the measures of the angles of a rhombus?

    (A) 80°, 80°, 100°, and 100°
    (B) 30°, 30°, 60°, and 60°
    (C) 75°, 85°, 95°, and 105°
    (D) 120°, 120°, 150°, and 150°
    (E) 80°, 80°, 80°, and 120°

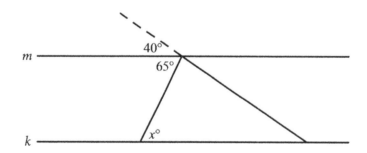

11. In the figure above, lines m and k are parallel. What is the value of x?

    (A) 40
    (B) 65
    (C) 75
    (D) 105
    (E) Cannot be determined

12. All of the sides of a pentagon have an equal length of L units. What is the perimeter of a hexagon with each of its sides 2 units shorter then each side of the pentagon?

   (A) $L - 2$
   (B) $5L - 10$
   (C) $6L - 2$
   (D) $6L - 10$
   (E) $6L - 12$

Answers to Geometry Practice Set

   1. D
   2. E
   3. B
   4. C
   5. C
   6. A
   7. B
   8. C
   9. E
   10. A
   11. B
   12. E

Visualization Problems

Sometimes you have to see beyond what is on the paper, and you have to think and visualize, and sometimes use your pencil, in order to get the problem right.

- Use your pencil – draw it out

The key to these problems is to not just jump on the first answer that looks right! These problems stretch your thinking, and often the quick answer that you jump on is not the right one.

- Don't jump on the first answer that looks right

For these problems, you need to ALWAYS look at all 5 answer choices before you answer the question.

The first type of problem that you should be familiar with is the "3-D" to "2-D" type. You are given a 3-D object and you have to decide what a part of it looks like in 2-D.

Here is an example:

Figure 1:

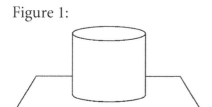

1. A cylindrical container of oatmeal with a flat bottom rests on a piece of paper, as shown in Figure 1. Which of the following best represents the set of points where the container touches the paper?

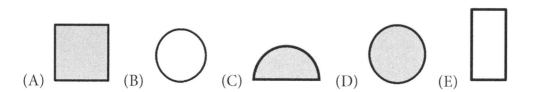

(A)   (B)   (C)   (D)   (E)

Think about the bottom of a flat cylindrical container such as an oatmeal box or a container of salt. Imagine setting it on a piece of paper. First, you know that where it touches the paper it will be a circle. This eliminates choices A and E. You can eliminate choice C because it is only half a circle. So now look at B and D. Answer B might be your first quick choice, and it is wrong! The bottom of the container is perfectly flat, so it touches the paper at the circle, PLUS all the points inside the circle, too. Therefore, the correct answer is D.

The next type of problem deals with visualizing limits and considering ALL of the possibilities of what can happen. Sometimes it is a word problem and sometimes it is a picture problem. The rules for this type of problem are:

1. Use your pencil AND your brain! Draw the problem out.
2. Read every word of the problem. There are hints about how to answer it.
3. Consider EVERY answer choice and think before you mark your answer.

Let's try an example.

2. A cow is tied to a fencepost in the middle of a 60-foot fence. The rope is 20 feet long. What are the size and shape of his grazing area?

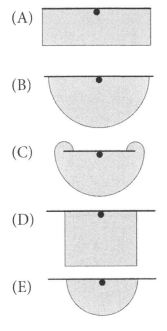

(A)

(B)

(C)

(D)

(E)

Get your pencil out for this one! Draw the post and the fence, and then draw the rope.

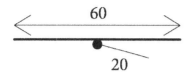

Now, act like a hungry cow. You are at the end of the rope. If you keep the rope tight, the pattern will be circular, so choices A and D are eliminated. Notice that the rope is shorter than the length of half the fence, so the cow can't get around the fence to graze on the other side, so choice C is out. This leaves choices B and E. If you quickly chose choice B, then you made the fatal decision for this type of problem! Notice that choice B allows the cow to eat almost to the very end of the 60-foot fence, whereas choice E restricts her from being too close to the end of the fence. The rope is 20 feet long and the end of the fence is 30 feet away (60 feet ÷ 2), so the cow can't get very close to the end of the fence. Choice E is correct.

The third type of problem that requires visualization is about patterns. A simple example is to see what happens if you turn a shape upside down. See what happens when you turn this triangle upside down:

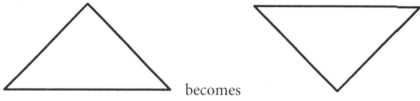

becomes

That was easy. Now see what happens when you turn a shape upside down and then flip it sideways:

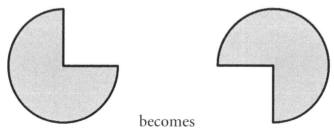

becomes

It's a little bit harder now!

The key to this type of problem is to do some self-talk. Ask yourself: "How does the first item become the second item, and what steps were taken to get there?" Then talk to yourself about it! For the pie shape above, there are TWO things that were done to it. First, it was turned upside down, so that the empty part was on the bottom right. Then it was flipped sideways, so then the empty part was flipped from the bottom right to the bottom left, which is the final answer.

Here is an example of what a pattern question may look like on the SSAT:

3.

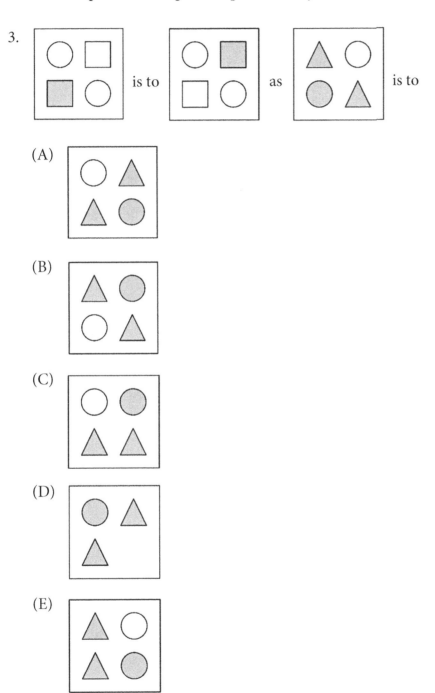

(A)

(B)

(C)

(D)

(E)

This problem checks to see that your brain can see the pattern when something is changed. In the pattern introduced in the question, the circles didn't change shape, position, or shading. The only thing that changed was that the squares switched positions. So do the same thing to the new figure. Keep the shaded triangles where they are, and then switch the 2 circles so that the shaded circle is now on the upper right. Answer choice B is the correct one.

Now you know the basics for visualizations problems. The best way to get good at these problems is just to practice them, so be sure to complete the visualization practice set.

Visualization Practice Set

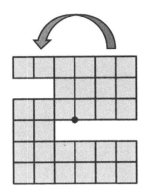

1. Given the figure above, if it rotates a quarter turn in the counterclockwise direction, which of the following would be the result?

(A)
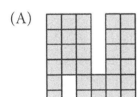

(B)
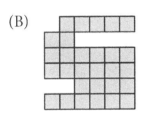

(C)
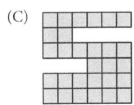

(D)
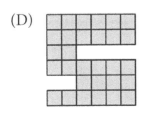

(E)
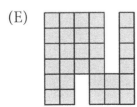

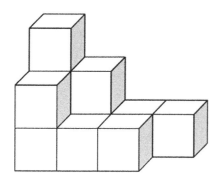

2. Given the figure above, how many small cubes were used to create this figure?

    (A) 7
    (B) 8
    (C) 9
    (D) 10
    (E) 11

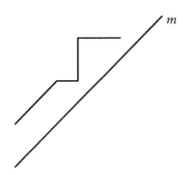

3. If the figure above is reflected over line m, what will the resulting figure look like?

(A)

(B)

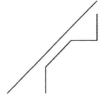

(C)

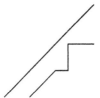

(D)

(E)

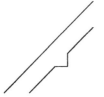

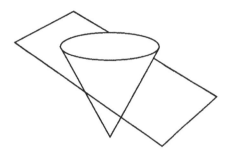

4. A plane slices through the cone-shaped object as shown above. What is the shape of the figure where the cone and the plane intersect?

(A)

(B)

(C)

(D)

(E)

Answers to Visualization Practice Set

1. A
2. E
3. D
4. E

Graphs

On the SSAT you will encounter several types of graphs that you will have to answer questions about. You will see a line graph, a bar graph, or a circle graph.

The good news is that you will not have complicated math to do. The bad news is that you will have to read each question very carefully. That is the key to succeeding with these problems.

Common phrases and what they mean:

- "How many more…" means subtract
- "What percent of…" means find a percent
- "What is the difference…" means subtract
- "What fraction of…" means find a fraction
- "The greatest increase is…" means subtract
- "The combined total of…" means add

Here is a sample of a circle graph and a question.

1. A coach has kept track of the number and type of broken bones of his college rugby teams for the last 10 years. His results are presented in the circle graph. What percent of broken bones were broken collarbones?

    (A) 6
    (B) 12
    (C) 18
    (D) 24
    (E) 40

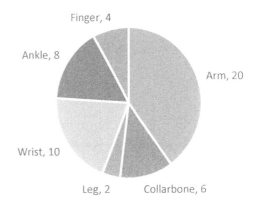

Broken Bones in College Rugby

Read the question carefully. We want to find a percent. To find a percent, we first need the total. Add up all the broken bones, and the total is 50. Now we use our formula for percent:

$$\frac{part}{whole} = \frac{percent}{100}$$

$$\frac{6 \ broken \ collarbones}{50 \ broken \ bones} = \frac{percent}{100}$$

$$6 \times 100 = 50 \times percent$$
$$600 = 50 \times percent$$
$$12 = percent$$

The correct answer is B.

The next type of graph is a line graph. This type of graph often displays data over time, such as month to month or day to day.

Here is an example:

2. Elena is studying vocabulary wordlists. Each day she studies a new wordlist, and each night she takes a test to see how many words she has learned that day. Her results for last week are given in the graph below.

During what 2-day period did the largest change in number of correct words occur?

(A) Monday to Tuesday
(B) Tuesday to Wednesday
(C) Wednesday to Thursday
(D) Thursday to Friday
(E) None of these

Notice that the question is about change. It doesn't ask about improvement, so even a 'negative' answer will be possible. Let's look at each period:

Monday to Tuesday: 10 to 14, so the change is 4
Tuesday to Wednesday: 14 to 6, so the change is 8
Wednesday to Thursday: 6 to 11, so the change is 5
Thursday to Friday: 11 to 18, so the change is 7

The greatest change is from Tuesday to Wednesday, so answer choice B is correct.

The next type of graph you will see is a bar chart, where the height of the bar shows how many times something happened or how many there are of some category.

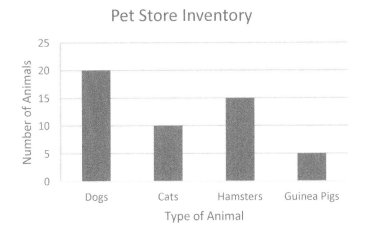

The owner of a small pet store performs an inventory of the animals in his store. The results are summarized in the bar graph above.

3. The number of guinea pigs is what percent of the number of dogs?

   (A) 5%
   (B) 10%
   (C) 25%
   (D) 50%
   (E) Cannot be determined

You must read this question carefully! The number of guinea pigs is 5 and the number of dogs is 20. What are you to do with these two numbers??

To figure this out, go back to the question and substitute the numbers instead of the words. The question now becomes: "5 is what percent of 20?" And now it is easy to do the math.

$$\frac{5}{20} = \frac{x}{100}$$
$$5 \times 100 = 20x$$
$$500 = 20x$$
$$x = 25$$

The correct answer is C.

The best way to ace the graph questions is through practice. Be sure to complete the graphs practice set.

Graphs Practice Set

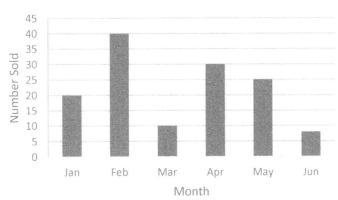

Matt's Bicycle Shop

1. During which of the following two-month periods did Matt's Shop sell the most bicycles?

   (A) January and February
   (B) February and March
   (C) March and April
   (D) April and May
   (E) May and June

2. In August, ten fewer than twice the number of bikes sold in April were sold. How many bikes were sold in August?

   (A) 15
   (B) 25
   (C) 40
   (D) 50
   (E) 60

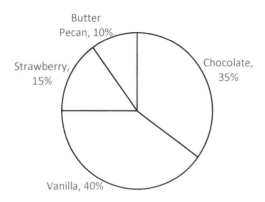

Ice Cream Preferences

Butter Pecan, 10%

Strawberry, 15%

Chocolate, 35%

Vanilla, 40%

A total of 300 people were asked their favorite ice cream. The results are summarized in the circle graph.

3. How many people preferred chocolate ice cream?

   (A) 35
   (B) 45
   (C) 105
   (D) 120
   (E) Cannot be determined

4. How many more people preferred vanilla than butter pecan?

   (A) 30
   (B) 60
   (C) 90
   (D) 120
   (E) 150

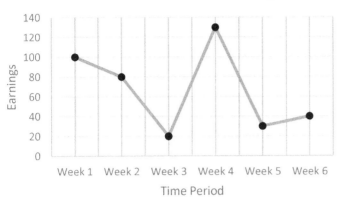

Rachel's Part-time Job Earnings

5. Rachel has a part-time job helping her elderly neighbor with chores and errands. Each week she keeps track of her earnings, and the chart for her first 6 weeks of work are displayed in the line graph. What percent of her total earnings for this period was earned in Week 2?

(A) 10
(B) 20
(C) 40
(D) 50
(E) 80

6. Comparing Rachel's Week 3 earnings to her week 2 earnings, we would say that

(A) They are $\frac{1}{4}$ as much
(B) They are $\frac{1}{3}$ as much
(C) They are half as much
(D) They are twice as much
(E) They are four times as much

Answers to Graphs Practice Set

1. A
2. D
3. C
4. C
5. B
6. A

Tips for the Writing Sample

Please Note: The writing sample on the Upper Level SSAT was updated for the 2012-2013 testing season. The advice and information in this book is up to date, but books from other publishers may not have been updated yet, so do not be alarmed if the information in this book and others does not match. You can always check www.ssat.org if you have any questions since that is the official website of the SSATB.

When you take the SSAT, you will be asked to complete a writing sample. You will be given 25 minutes and two pages to write your response. Your writing sample will NOT be scored. Rather, a copy of it will be sent to the schools that you apply to.

With the recently redesigned writing sample, you will be given a choice between an essay topic and a creative topic.

The questions are relatively open-ended. The old topics were simply statements that you had to agree or disagree with – quite snooze-worthy. The new prompts give you much more room to show your creativity, even if you choose the essay prompt.

So what kind of questions can you expect to see?

For the essay prompt, you might see questions like:

- What would you change about your school and why?
- If you could relive one day, what day would it be and why would you want to do it over?

For the creative prompts, they might look like "story starters" that a teacher may have used in your school. The test writers will give you a starting sentence and you take it from there.

Here are some examples of what these questions could look like:

- A strange wind blew through town on that Thursday night.
- He thought long and hard before slowly opening the door.
- She had never been in an experience quite like this before.

To approach the writing sample, follow this four-step plan:

Step 1: Choose Topic

- There is no "right" choice when deciding between an essay and fiction prompt.

- If you are extremely creative and love playing with language, the fiction prompt is a great way to showcase this talent. This talent may not appear elsewhere on your application, so here is your chance.

- If you are great at organizing ideas and developing examples, the essay prompt may be for you.

- If you do decide ahead of time whether to write about the creative or essay prompt, be flexible. You may get to the test, read the creative prompt and just take off with it. Alternatively, you may read the creative prompt and have nothing, but the essay prompt looks intriguing.

Step 2: Plan

- Take just a couple of minutes and plan, it will be time well spent.

- If you are writing an essay, plan what your main point (thesis) will be and what examples you are going to use.

- If you are writing from the creative prompt, decide where your story is going. You want to build to a climax, so decide ahead of time what that will be. You don't want lots of descriptive language that goes nowhere. Decide what your problem will be and how you intend to resolve it.

Step 3: Write

- Break your writing into paragraphs – don't do a two-page blob.

- If you are writing an essay topic, aim for 4-5 paragraphs (introduction, 2-3 body paragraphs, and a conclusion.)

- If you choose a creative topic, remember to start new paragraphs for dialogue and to break up long descriptions.

- Write legibly. It does not have to be perfect and schools know that you have a time limit. But if the admissions officers can't read what you wrote, they can't judge it.

Step 4: Edit / Proofread

- Save a couple of minutes for the end to look over your work.

- You won't be able to do a major editing job where you move around sentences and rewrite portions.

- Look for where you may have left out a word or misspelled something. If a word is not legible, fix that.

- Make your marks simple and clear. If you need to take something out, just put a single line through it. Use a carat to insert words that you forgot.

The writing sample is not graded, but the schools that you apply to do receive a copy.

So What are Schools Looking For?

Organization

Schools want to see that you can organize your thoughts before writing.

If you choose the essay topic, shoot for a 4-5 paragraph essay. There should be an introductory paragraph with a clear thesis, or main point. There should then be 2-3 body, or example, paragraphs. Each of these paragraphs should have their own, distinct theme. There should then be a concluding paragraph that ties up your ideas and then suggests what comes next. For example, if you wrote about how to improve your school, maybe you could finish up by describing how these changes could help other schools as well.

If you chose the creative topic, there should still be structure to your story. There needs to be a problem, which builds to a climax, and then a resolution. Since you only have two pages and 25 minutes to get this done, you should know your problem before you begin to write.

Word choice

Use descriptive language. Don't describe anything as "nice" or "good". Tell us specifically why something is nice or good. Better yet, show us and don't tell us. For example, don't say that you would make the cafeteria nicer in your school, tell us how you would rearrange the tables to create greater class unity and improve nutritious selections in order to improve students' academic achievement.

Use transitions. When you switch ideas, use words such as "however", "but", "although", and "in contrast to". When you are continuing with an idea, use words such as "furthermore" or "in addition". Students who do not use transition words is one of the biggest complaints of English teachers, so show the reader that you know how to use them.

Creativity and development of ideas

It is not enough just to be able to fit your writing into the form that you were taught in school. These prompts are designed to show how you think. This is your chance to shine! For the creative prompts, this is your chance to come up with unique ideas. If you choose the essay topic, the readers will be looking more at how well you develop your ideas. Can you see the outcome of actions? Can you provide details that are both relevant to the essay and supportive of your thesis or main idea?

The writing sample is a place for you to showcase your writing skills. It is just one more piece of information that the admissions committee will use in making their decisions.

Practice Test

Answer Sheets

The following two pages contain answer sheets for the practice test. These pages can be removed from this book.

Additional copies of the answer sheets can be downloaded at:

www.testprepworks.com/student/download

If possible, complete this test in one sitting. Very rough scoring guidelines are provided only to illustrate how the scoring works. For a more accurate score, purchase the official practice book at *www.ssat.org*.

This page intentionally left blank

Section 1: Quantitative

1 (A) (B) (C) (D) (E)	10 (A) (B) (C) (D) (E)	18 (A) (B) (C) (D) (E)
2 (A) (B) (C) (D) (E)	11 (A) (B) (C) (D) (E)	19 (A) (B) (C) (D) (E)
3 (A) (B) (C) (D) (E)	12 (A) (B) (C) (D) (E)	20 (A) (B) (C) (D) (E)
4 (A) (B) (C) (D) (E)	13 (A) (B) (C) (D) (E)	21 (A) (B) (C) (D) (E)
5 (A) (B) (C) (D) (E)	14 (A) (B) (C) (D) (E)	22 (A) (B) (C) (D) (E)
6 (A) (B) (C) (D) (E)	15 (A) (B) (C) (D) (E)	23 (A) (B) (C) (D) (E)
7 (A) (B) (C) (D) (E)	16 (A) (B) (C) (D) (E)	24 (A) (B) (C) (D) (E)
8 (A) (B) (C) (D) (E)	17 (A) (B) (C) (D) (E)	25 (A) (B) (C) (D) (E)
9 (A) (B) (C) (D) (E)		

Section 2: Reading Comprehension

1 (A) (B) (C) (D) (E)	15 (A) (B) (C) (D) (E)	29 (A) (B) (C) (D) (E)
2 (A) (B) (C) (D) (E)	16 (A) (B) (C) (D) (E)	30 (A) (B) (C) (D) (E)
3 (A) (B) (C) (D) (E)	17 (A) (B) (C) (D) (E)	31 (A) (B) (C) (D) (E)
4 (A) (B) (C) (D) (E)	18 (A) (B) (C) (D) (E)	32 (A) (B) (C) (D) (E)
5 (A) (B) (C) (D) (E)	19 (A) (B) (C) (D) (E)	33 (A) (B) (C) (D) (E)
6 (A) (B) (C) (D) (E)	20 (A) (B) (C) (D) (E)	34 (A) (B) (C) (D) (E)
7 (A) (B) (C) (D) (E)	21 (A) (B) (C) (D) (E)	35 (A) (B) (C) (D) (E)
8 (A) (B) (C) (D) (E)	22 (A) (B) (C) (D) (E)	36 (A) (B) (C) (D) (E)
9 (A) (B) (C) (D) (E)	23 (A) (B) (C) (D) (E)	37 (A) (B) (C) (D) (E)
10 (A) (B) (C) (D) (E)	24 (A) (B) (C) (D) (E)	38 (A) (B) (C) (D) (E)
11 (A) (B) (C) (D) (E)	25 (A) (B) (C) (D) (E)	39 (A) (B) (C) (D) (E)
12 (A) (B) (C) (D) (E)	26 (A) (B) (C) (D) (E)	40 (A) (B) (C) (D) (E)
13 (A) (B) (C) (D) (E)	27 (A) (B) (C) (D) (E)	
14 (A) (B) (C) (D) (E)	28 (A) (B) (C) (D) (E)	

Section 3: Verbal

1 (A) (B) (C) (D) (E)	21 (A) (B) (C) (D) (E)	41 (A) (B) (C) (D) (E)
2 (A) (B) (C) (D) (E)	22 (A) (B) (C) (D) (E)	42 (A) (B) (C) (D) (E)
3 (A) (B) (C) (D) (E)	23 (A) (B) (C) (D) (E)	43 (A) (B) (C) (D) (E)
4 (A) (B) (C) (D) (E)	24 (A) (B) (C) (D) (E)	44 (A) (B) (C) (D) (E)
5 (A) (B) (C) (D) (E)	25 (A) (B) (C) (D) (E)	45 (A) (B) (C) (D) (E)
6 (A) (B) (C) (D) (E)	26 (A) (B) (C) (D) (E)	46 (A) (B) (C) (D) (E)
7 (A) (B) (C) (D) (E)	27 (A) (B) (C) (D) (E)	47 (A) (B) (C) (D) (E)
8 (A) (B) (C) (D) (E)	28 (A) (B) (C) (D) (E)	48 (A) (B) (C) (D) (E)
9 (A) (B) (C) (D) (E)	29 (A) (B) (C) (D) (E)	49 (A) (B) (C) (D) (E)
10 (A) (B) (C) (D) (E)	30 (A) (B) (C) (D) (E)	50 (A) (B) (C) (D) (E)
11 (A) (B) (C) (D) (E)	31 (A) (B) (C) (D) (E)	51 (A) (B) (C) (D) (E)
12 (A) (B) (C) (D) (E)	32 (A) (B) (C) (D) (E)	52 (A) (B) (C) (D) (E)
13 (A) (B) (C) (D) (E)	33 (A) (B) (C) (D) (E)	53 (A) (B) (C) (D) (E)
14 (A) (B) (C) (D) (E)	34 (A) (B) (C) (D) (E)	54 (A) (B) (C) (D) (E)
15 (A) (B) (C) (D) (E)	35 (A) (B) (C) (D) (E)	55 (A) (B) (C) (D) (E)
16 (A) (B) (C) (D) (E)	36 (A) (B) (C) (D) (E)	56 (A) (B) (C) (D) (E)
17 (A) (B) (C) (D) (E)	37 (A) (B) (C) (D) (E)	57 (A) (B) (C) (D) (E)
18 (A) (B) (C) (D) (E)	38 (A) (B) (C) (D) (E)	58 (A) (B) (C) (D) (E)
19 (A) (B) (C) (D) (E)	39 (A) (B) (C) (D) (E)	59 (A) (B) (C) (D) (E)
20 (A) (B) (C) (D) (E)	40 (A) (B) (C) (D) (E)	60 (A) (B) (C) (D) (E)

Section 4: Quantitative

1 (A) (B) (C) (D) (E)	10 (A) (B) (C) (D) (E)	18 (A) (B) (C) (D) (E)
2 (A) (B) (C) (D) (E)	11 (A) (B) (C) (D) (E)	19 (A) (B) (C) (D) (E)
3 (A) (B) (C) (D) (E)	12 (A) (B) (C) (D) (E)	20 (A) (B) (C) (D) (E)
4 (A) (B) (C) (D) (E)	13 (A) (B) (C) (D) (E)	21 (A) (B) (C) (D) (E)
5 (A) (B) (C) (D) (E)	14 (A) (B) (C) (D) (E)	22 (A) (B) (C) (D) (E)
6 (A) (B) (C) (D) (E)	15 (A) (B) (C) (D) (E)	23 (A) (B) (C) (D) (E)
7 (A) (B) (C) (D) (E)	16 (A) (B) (C) (D) (E)	24 (A) (B) (C) (D) (E)
8 (A) (B) (C) (D) (E)	17 (A) (B) (C) (D) (E)	25 (A) (B) (C) (D) (E)
9 (A) (B) (C) (D) (E)		

Writing Sample

The writing sample is a way for schools to learn a little more about you. Below are two possible writing topics. Please choose the topic that you find most interesting. Fill in the circle next to the topic you chose and then use this page and the next to write your essay.

    (A)   What makes a person a hero? Give three examples of people you think are heroes.

    (B)   The door opened with a slow creak and…

Complete your writing sample on this page and the next. You have 25 minutes to complete this section.

CONTINUE TO THE NEXT PAGE

STOP

Section 1: Quantitative

25 questions

30 minutes

Directions: Each problem is followed by five answer choices. Figure out each problem and then decide which answer choice is best.

---

1. Which of the following is a possible solution for $4b(b + 6) = 0$?

   (A) $b = -12$
   (B) $b = -10$
   (C) $b = -6$
   (D) $b = 4$
   (E) $b = 6$

---

2. In order to solve the equation $-\dfrac{n}{3} = 5$, what number would you need to multiply both sides by?

   (A) -3
   (B) 0
   (C) $\dfrac{1}{3}$
   (D) 3
   (E) 5

---

3. $100 - 6\dfrac{11}{12} =$

   (A) $92\dfrac{11}{12}$

   (B) $93\dfrac{1}{12}$

   (C) $93\dfrac{5}{12}$

   (D) $93\dfrac{11}{12}$

   (E) $94\dfrac{11}{12}$

CONTINUE TO THE NEXT PAGE

4. If a taxi arrives at the taxi stand with a frequency of one taxi every six minutes, then how many taxis would arrive at the taxi stand in one hour?

(A) 6
(B) 10
(C) 15
(D) 60
(E) 360

5. Find the product of 0.032 and 10.0.

(A) 0.00032
(B) 0.0032
(C) 0.032
(D) 0.32
(E) 3.2

6. Points A, B, C, and D are all on the same line. If point B is the midpoint of segment AD, point C is the midpoint of segment BD, and the length of segment AD is 12 cm, what is the length of segment CD?

(A) 10 cm
(B) 8 cm
(C) 6 cm
(D) 4 cm
(E) 3 cm

7. Write the fractions below in order from least to greatest:

$$\frac{7}{12}, \frac{3}{4}, \frac{5}{8}$$

(A) $\frac{3}{4}, \frac{5}{8}, \frac{7}{12}$

(B) $\frac{3}{4}, \frac{7}{12}, \frac{5}{8}$

(C) $\frac{7}{12}, \frac{5}{8}, \frac{3}{4}$

(D) $\frac{7}{12}, \frac{3}{4}, \frac{5}{8}$

(E) $\frac{5}{8}, \frac{3}{4}, \frac{7}{12}$

CONTINUE TO THE NEXT PAGE

8. The mean test score for four students was 84. The mean test score for a different two students was 90. What is the mean test score for all six students?

   (A) 86
   (B) 87
   (C) 88
   (D) 89
   (E) 90

9. Carol polled 60 of her classmates, asking them whether they owned a bike or a scooter. If 42 students said that they owned a bike, 39 students said they owned a scooter, and every student said that he or she owned at least a bike or a scooter, then how many students own both a bike and scooter?

   (A) 18
   (B) 21
   (C) 42
   (D) 60
   (E) 81

10. Which could be the value of the least of three consecutive odd integers if the product of the least and the greatest is -3?

   (A) -5
   (B) -3
   (C) 1
   (D) 3
   (E) 5

11. Jill paid $4.20 for a board of wood that was $3\frac{1}{2}$ yards long. What was her cost per board foot?

   (A) 0.04 ¢
   (B) 0.40 ¢
   (C) $0.04
   (D) $0.40
   (E) $4.00

CONTINUE TO THE NEXT PAGE

Refer to the following graph for questions 12-13:

How Brady spends his monthly allowance

12. The amount of money that Brady spends on clothing is what percent of the amount he spends on savings and music?

(A) 50%

(B) 60%

(C) 70%

(D) 72%

(E) 80%

13. What fraction of Brady's monthly allowance is spent on movies?

(A) $\dfrac{3}{10}$

(B) $\dfrac{1}{5}$

(C) $\dfrac{3}{5}$

(D) $\dfrac{2}{15}$

(E) $\dfrac{4}{15}$

CONTINUE TO THE NEXT PAGE

14. Evaluate: $250 - 4(30) + 35 \div 7$

    (A) 24

    (B) 105

    (C) 135

    (D) 270

    (E) 1060

---

15. A bus took between $2\frac{1}{2}$ and 3 hours to make a 140-mile trip. The bus' average speed must have been between (answers given in miles per hour)

    (A) 35 and 39

    (B) 39 and 46

    (C) 46 and 56

    (D) 56 and 62

    (E) 62 and 66

---

16. $\dfrac{9a^{-2}c^3}{3b^4c^{-2}} =$

    (A) $\dfrac{3c^5}{a^2b^4}$

    (B) $\dfrac{3c^3}{a^2b^4}$

    (C) $\dfrac{6c^5}{a^2b^4}$

    (D) $\dfrac{6c^3}{a^2b^4}$

    (E) $\dfrac{9c^5}{a^2b^4}$

---

17. If $4w - 5w + 6 = 12 - 3w$, then what is w equal to?

    (A) -3

    (B) 3

    (C) 4

    (D) 6

    (E) 8

CONTINUE TO THE NEXT PAGE

18. The length of a rectangle is three times its width. If the perimeter of the rectangle is 32, then what is the area of the rectangle?

   (A) 4
   (B) 12
   (C) 32
   (D) 36
   (E) 48

19. $862 \div 7 =$

   (A) $\dfrac{8}{7} + \dfrac{6}{7} + \dfrac{2}{7}$

   (B) $\dfrac{8}{7} \times \dfrac{6}{7} \times \dfrac{2}{7}$

   (C) $\dfrac{800}{7} \times \dfrac{60}{7} \times \dfrac{2}{7}$

   (D) $\dfrac{800}{7} + \dfrac{60}{7} + \dfrac{2}{7}$

   (E) $\dfrac{80}{6} + \dfrac{62}{6}$

20. Simplify: $(6x^3 + 4x^2 - 2) - (x^2 + 3x - 6)$

   (A) $6x^3 + 3x^2 - 3x + 4$
   (B) $6x^3 + 3x^2 + 3x + 4$
   (C) $6x^3 + 3x^2 + 3x - 8$
   (D) $5x^3 + 4x^2 - 3x + 4$
   (E) $5x^2 + 3x^2 - 3x + 4$

21. What is the slope of a line that is perpendicular to the line $3x + 4y = 5$?

   (A) $-\dfrac{4}{3}$

   (B) $-\dfrac{3}{4}$

   (C) $\dfrac{3}{4}$

   (D) $\dfrac{4}{3}$

   (E) 3

CONTINUE TO THE NEXT PAGE

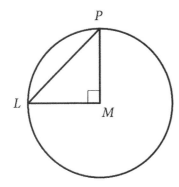

22. In the figure, M is the center of a circle. Vertices L and P of triangle LMP are on the circle and $\angle LMP$ measures 90 degrees. If the area of triangle LMP is 18, then what is the area of circle M?

(A) 9π
(B) 18π
(C) 24π
(D) 30π
(E) 36π

---

23. Evaluate: $-2(-4)^2$

(A) -48
(B) -36
(C) -32
(D) 16
(E) 32

---

24. Cubes that are 2 cm on each side are stacked to create a larger cube with a volume of 64 cm^3. How many smaller cubes were used to create the larger cube?

(A) 4
(B) 8
(C) 16
(D) 32
(E) 64

CONTINUE TO THE NEXT PAGE

25. If $m > 1$, then which of the following is least?

    (A) $m + 2$

    (B) $3m - 2$

    (C) $2 - \dfrac{m}{m}$

    (D) $4m - 3m$

    (E) $\dfrac{m}{m} + 1$

STOP

IF YOU HAVE TIME LEFT YOU MAY CHECK YOUR ANSWERS IN THIS SECTION ONLY

Section 2: Reading Comprehension

40 questions

40 minutes

Directions: Read each passage in this section carefully and answer the questions that follow. Choose the best answer based on the passage.

Great part of that order which reigns among mankind is not the effect of government. It has its origin in the principles of society and the natural constitution of man. It existed prior to government, and would exist if the formality of government was abolished. The mutual dependence and reciprocal *Line 5* interest which man has upon man, and all the parts of civilized community upon each other, create that great chain of connection which holds it together. The landholder, the farmer, the manufacturer, the merchant, the tradesman, and every occupation, prospers by the aid which each receives from the other, and from the whole. Common interest regulates their concerns, and forms their law; *10* and the laws which common usage ordains, have a greater influence than the laws of government. In fine, society performs for itself almost everything which is ascribed to government.

To understand the nature and quantity of government proper for man, it is necessary to attend to his character. As Nature created him for social life, she *15* fitted him for the station she intended. In all cases she made his natural wants greater than his individual powers. No one man is capable, without the aid of society, of supplying his own wants, and those wants, acting upon every individual, impel the whole of them into society, as naturally as gravitation acts to a centre.

20 But she has gone further. She has not only forced man into society by a diversity of wants which the reciprocal aid of each other can supply, but she has implanted in him a system of social affections, which, though not necessary to his existence, are essential to his happiness. There is no period in life when this love for society ceases to act.

CONTINUE TO THE NEXT PAGE

1. In lines 4-5 the author refers to "reciprocal interest". Which answer choice best describes what the author means by this term?

    (A) People naturally have many interests.
    (B) People are not inherently interested in being part of society.
    (C) Government encourages people to share interests.
    (D) People have a natural interest in each other.
    (E) Mutual dependence among humans diminishes a civilized community.

2. In line 18 the word "impel" most nearly means

    (A) push forward
    (B) hold back
    (C) distract
    (D) want
    (E) limit

3. The author's primary purpose in writing this passage was to

    (A) prove that governments don't work in the interests of the people
    (B) discuss the role of government in financial transactions
    (C) explain why humans naturally live in society
    (D) provide examples of people living in communities
    (E) illustrate the various needs of man

4. Which of the following best describes the author's attitude about government?

    (A) It is crucial to civilization.
    (B) Man created government to gain power over one another.
    (C) It is corrupt.
    (D) It helps to even out the differences between the landholders and the poor farmers.
    (E) It reflects human social tendencies that existed before government.

CONTINUE TO THE NEXT PAGE

One day, while at work in the coalmine, I happened to overhear two miners talking about a great school for coloured people somewhere in Virginia. This was the first time that I had ever heard anything about any kind of school or college that was more pretentious than the little coloured school in our town.

Line 5   In the darkness of the mine I noiselessly crept as close as I could to the two men who were talking. I heard one tell the other that not only was the school established for the members of any race, but the opportunities that it provided by which poor but worthy students could work out all or a part of the cost of a board, and at the same time be taught some trade or industry.

10   As they went on describing the school, it seemed to me that it must be the greatest place on earth, and not even Heaven presented more attractions for me at that time than did the Hampton Normal and Agricultural Institute in Virginia, about which these men were talking. I resolved at once to go to that school, although I had no idea where it was, or how many miles away, or how I was going

15   to reach it; I remembered only that I was on fire constantly with one ambition, and that was to go to Hampton. This thought was with me day and night.

In the fall of 1872 I determined to make an effort to get there, although, as I have stated, I had no definite idea of the direction in which Hampton was, or of what it would cost to go there. I do not think that any one thoroughly

20   sympathized with me in my ambition to go to Hampton unless it was my mother, and she was troubled with a grave fear that I was starting out on a "wild-goose chase."

5. The mood of the third paragraph (lines 10-16) can best be described as

(A) irritation
(B) excitement
(C) discouragement
(D) indifference
(E) exhaustion

6. In line 9, the word "trade" most nearly means

(A) sell
(B) exchange
(C) occupation
(D) education
(E) college

CONTINUE TO THE NEXT PAGE

7. The author of this passage can best be described as

    (A) resolute
    (B) ironic
    (C) unmotivated
    (D) pleasant
    (E) mysterious

8. The phrase "wild-goose chase" in lines 21-22 refers to

    (A) a hunting ritual
    (B) a mother's overprotectiveness
    (C) a successful quest for an education
    (D) a journey that leads nowhere
    (E) a job opportunity

9. When the author states that the Hampton Normal School "must be the greatest place on earth, and not even Heaven presented more attractions", this is an example of

    (A) personification
    (B) alliteration
    (C) imagery
    (D) parody
    (E) hyperbole

10. It can be inferred from the passage that

    (A) the town in which the author lived offered no school that coloured students could attend
    (B) the school in town which the author could attend was not as prestigious as the Hampton Normal School
    (C) the author did not wish to continue his schooling
    (D) the author's mother did not approve of education
    (E) the coalmine was well lit

CONTINUE TO THE NEXT PAGE

What we commonly refer to as "salt" or "table salt" is actually sodium chloride. Sodium chloride is perhaps the salt that has had the greatest effect on humankind. For one, the discovery of sodium chloride as a food preservative allowed humans to store meat and other protein for several days. There is

Line 5 evidence that humans figured out how to extract salt from sea and spring water about 6,000 years ago. Salts acts as a dehydrator, pulling water out of cells by osmosis. Sodium chloride pulls the water out of bacterial cells, effectively killing the microorganisms that cause food to spoil. Sodium chloride has also made it possible for people to live and work in snowy climates. Salt lowers the freezing

10 point of water so it is applied to roads to prevent them from icing over and becoming impassable.

Sodium chloride is also necessary for biological functions. The body uses it to communicate with muscles and nerves and regulate the fluid balance in cells. In third world countries where citizens subsist on a grain-based diet, a lack of

15 sodium in the diet is a widespread health concern. However, too much salt can have negative health effects. It can lead to increased blood pressure and hypertension, both conditions that are correlated with a higher risk of stroke and heart attack. In wealthier countries, too much sodium in the diet has created a health crisis.

11. According to the passage, sodium chloride is

(A) responsible for malnutrition in poorer countries
(B) governed by many laws
(C) present in seawater
(D) the only safe food preservative
(E) rare

12. Which title best summarizes the main idea of this passage?

(A) How to Preserve Food
(B) Where Salt Was Discovered
(C) The Limits of Sodium
(D) Sodium: Good in Moderation
(E) Salt: A Health Disaster

CONTINUE TO THE NEXT PAGE

13. The author uses quotation marks around the words "salt" and "table salt" in line 1 in order to

   (A) differentiate between common terms and a scientific term
   (B) let the reader know that it is a direct quote
   (C) show an ironic use of the words
   (D) emphasize the importance of those terms
   (E) show the relationship between those two terms

14. The author implies that sodium

   (A) is hard to extract
   (B) raises the risk of icy roads
   (C) was recently discovered
   (D) causes water to rush into cells
   (E) is not found in large quantities in grains

15. What is the author most likely to discuss next?

   (A) how salt was discovered
   (B) the health benefits of limiting sodium intake
   (C) health challenges faced by citizens of third world countries
   (D) the process of osmosis
   (E) other food preservatives

16. The author's tone can best be described as

   (A) impassioned
   (B) indifferent
   (C) humorous
   (D) informative
   (E) enthusiastic

CONTINUE TO THE NEXT PAGE

American politics are often marked by contentious fighting and strong adherence to party platforms. There are two main parties – the Democrats and the Republicans. Increasingly, elected officials vote strictly along party lines leaving our legislature in gridlock.

Line 5

Some of the most famous partisans of all time have actually been party switchers, however. Ronald Reagan, one of the most widely recognized Republican presidents of all time, was actually registered as a Democrat until 1962. He once commented that he did not feel that he had left the Democratic Party, but rather that the Democratic Party had changed so that he no longer

10

shared its views. On the other side, one of the standard bearers of the Democratic Party is Hilary Clinton. She has served as a Democratic senator, Secretary of State in a Democratic administration, and is the wife of Bill Clinton, one of the most famous Democratic presidents of all time. As a teenager, however, she had campaigned for Republican candidates and was even elected president of

15

Wellesley College's Young Republicans Club. However, policy issues such as the Vietnam War caused her to become a Democrat. While they eventually came to represent two very different political parties, Ronald Reagan and Hilary Clinton had one thing in common – the ability to adapt to changing political views.

17. The primary purpose of this passage is to

   (A) give the history of American political parties
   (B) argue that more politicians should switch parties
   (C) describe how two people changed their party loyalty
   (D) explain the popularity of Ronald Reagan
   (E) provide the reason why the two parties are contentious

18. What does the author mean by the phrase "vote strictly along party lines" in line 3?

   (A) Politicians only support laws brought forward by someone in their own party.
   (B) Before big votes, there is a party.
   (C) Politicians don't consider which party has proposed a law.
   (D) Political parties have become less important.
   (E) Political parties are often divided on which laws to support.

CONTINUE TO THE NEXT PAGE

19. The author's attitude toward Ronald Reagan and Hilary Clinton can best be described as one of

(A) contempt
(B) frustration
(C) amazement
(D) indifference
(E) respect

20. Which statement would the author most likely agree with about current elected officials?

(A) They often switch parties.
(B) Their disagreements prevent laws from being passed.
(C) They are productive.
(D) They belong to many political parties.
(E) They are likely to be reelected.

21. The author suggests that Ronald Reagan left the Democratic Party for what reason?

(A) His own political views changed.
(B) He was asked to leave.
(C) The Democratic Party changed and he no longer agreed with its views.
(D) A new party was formed.
(E) He was running against Hilary Clinton.

CONTINUE TO THE NEXT PAGE

During his brief interview with Mr. Fogg, Passepartout had been carefully observing him. He appeared to be a man about forty years of age, with fine, handsome features, and a tall, well-shaped figure; his hair and whiskers were light, his forehead compact and unwrinkled, his face rather pale, his teeth magnificent. His countenance possessed in the highest degree what physiognomists call "repose in action," a quality of those who act rather than talk. Calm and phlegmatic, with a clear eye, Mr. Fogg seemed a perfect type of that English composure which Angelica Kauffmann has so skillfully represented on canvas. Seen in the various phases of his daily life, he gave the idea of being perfectly well balanced, as exactly regulated as a Leroy chronometer. Phileas Fogg was, indeed, exactitude personified, and this was betrayed even in the expression of his very hands and feet; for in men, as well as in animals, the limbs themselves are expressive of the passions.

He was so exact that he was never in a hurry, was always ready, and was economical alike of his steps and his motions. He never took one step too many, and always went to his destination by the shortest cut; he made no superfluous gestures, and was never seen to be moved or agitated. He was the most deliberate person in the world, yet always reached his destination at the exact moment.

He lived alone, and, so to speak, outside of every social relation; and as he knew that in this world account must be taken of friction, and that friction retards, he never rubbed against anybody.

As for Passepartout, he was a true Parisian of Paris. Since he had abandoned his own country for England, taking service as a valet, he had in vain searched for a master after his own heart. Passepartout was by no means one of those pert dunces depicted by Moliere with a bold gaze and a nose held high in the air; he was an honest fellow, with a pleasant face, lips a trifle protruding, soft-mannered and serviceable, with a good round head, such as one likes to see on the shoulders of a friend. His eyes were blue, his complexion rubicund, his figure almost portly and well built, his body muscular, and his physical powers fully developed by the exercises of his younger days. His brown hair was somewhat tumbled; for, while the ancient sculptors are said to have known eighteen methods of arranging Minerva's tresses, Passepartout was familiar with but one of dressing his own: three strokes of a large-tooth comb completed his toilet.

CONTINUE TO THE NEXT PAGE

22. Which word best describes Mr. Fogg as he is portrayed in the passage?

   (A) decisive

   (B) portly

   (C) unsuccessful

   (D) bored

   (E) unpredictable

23. The word "superfluous" in line 16 could best be replaced with which of the following words without changing the meaning?

   (A) extraordinary

   (B) irritated

   (C) minor

   (D) unnecessary

   (E) dramatic

24. It can be inferred from the passage that Angelica Kauffman was a

   (A) novelist

   (B) painter

   (C) valet

   (D) chef

   (E) journalist

25. According to the passage, how does Mr. Fogg know Passepartout?

   (A) They are longtime friends.

   (B) They went to college together.

   (C) Mr. Fogg works for Passepartout.

   (D) They live in the same place.

   (E) Mr. Fogg was interviewing Passepartout.

26. The primary purpose of this passage is to

   (A) explain why Mr. Fogg needs a valet

   (B) create a sense of suspense

   (C) provide descriptions of two characters

   (D) educate the reader on the duties of a valet

   (E) present two conflicting viewpoints

CONTINUE TO THE NEXT PAGE

Julian Percy is perhaps one of the greatest scientists who ever lived and yet he is hardly a household name. He invented a foam from soybeans that was used to extinguish gas and oil fires that saved the lives of countless soldiers during World War II. He also created cortisone, a widely used treatment for rheumatoid

Line 5 arthritis. One of his earliest accomplishments was to use compounds found in the Calabar bean to produce a remedy for glaucoma, a disease that is one of the leading causes of blindness in America. Despite his obvious brilliance, however, roadblocks were constantly thrown in his path due to his race.

Julian was born in Alabama in 1899 to an African-American family. At

10 that time in Alabama, African-American children were not expected to advance past the eighth grade, but his parents had greater expectations for young Julian. He graduated from DePauw University in Indiana and then received a scholarship to obtain his master's degree from Harvard University. They would not allow him to pursue a doctorate because of the color of his skin, though. He

15 went to University in Vienna in Austria to earn his doctorate and then returned to the United States. Upon his return he found that hiring managers lost interest when they discovered his race.

Julian didn't let the prejudices of others prevent him from bringing important products to market, however. In 1954 he founded Julian Laboratories

20 for this purpose. When he sold this company in 1961, he became one of the first African-American millionaires in America.

Julian's story is important to the history of scientific advancement. It is also one of the greatest stories of resilience. It deserves a spot in the canon of literature about the indomitable spirit of American inventors.

27. The author's primary purpose in writing this passage is to

    (A) provide a description of life as an African-American
    (B) encourage the reader to share one man's story
    (C) discuss the challenges of bringing a new treatment to the market
    (D) discuss the role of race in America
    (E) compare and contrast different inventors

CONTINUE TO THE NEXT PAGE

28. The author's attitude towards Julian Percy can best be described as

   (A) deep respect
   (B) undeserved admiration
   (C) qualified appreciation
   (D) harsh disapproval
   (E) casual indifference

29. In line 8 the word "roadblocks" most nearly means

   (A) gates
   (B) words of encouragement
   (C) successes
   (D) obstructions
   (E) costs

30. The author implies which of the following?

   (A) Other scientists are just as important as Julian Percy.
   (B) Julian Percy should be better known than he is.
   (C) The process of developing a new medical treatment is long.
   (D) Glaucoma is untreatable.
   (E) DePauw University did not accept Julian Percy.

CONTINUE TO THE NEXT PAGE

On December 22, 1938, Marjorie Courtenay-Larimer received a very unusual phone call. It was from a fisherman who had just brought in an unusual load. Marjorie was the curator of a local natural history museum in a small South African town and the fisherman thought she should come take a look. She promptly made her way to the wharf and climbed aboard the trawler *Nerine*. As she picked her way through a slimy pile of mostly sharks, she noticed a blue fin belonging to a fish that even she had not seen.

Line 5

After taking the fish to a taxidermist, Marjorie attempted to contact a local expert, J.L.B. Smith, to help her identify the fish. She drew a crude sketch and mailed it to him. When he received the sketch, his imagination was piqued and he sent her a telegram instructing her "MOST IMPORTANT PRESERVE SKELETON AND GILLS [OF] FISH DESCRIBED." For many years, Smith had desperately wanted to make an important zoological discovery and he sensed that this fish might be a find that would rock the scientific world.

10

It turned out his instincts were correct. The fish was a coelacanth, a species that was believed to have gone extinct 65 million years ago. In describing his first sight of the fish, Smith wrote, "Although I had come prepared, that first sight [of the fish] hit me like a white-hot blast and made me feel shaky and queer, my body tingled." He could not contain his excitement at the thought that this creature had emerged from the depths of the sea – and that his name would be attached to a discovery of enormous importance in the world of ichthyology.

15

20

After the identity of the coelacanth was confirmed, J.L.B. Smith and Marjorie Courtenay-Larimer set out to let the world know of this "Lazurus species". Just as Lazarus had risen from the dead in the bible, this fish had emerged from the annals of extinct species very much alive.

25

31. It can be inferred from the passage that ichthyology (line 21) is the study of

(A) boats
(B) scientists
(C) skeletons
(D) land mammals
(E) fish

CONTINUE TO THE NEXT PAGE

32. As portrayed in the passage, J.L.B Smith can best be described as a

    (A) bored professional
    (B) frequent visitor to museums
    (C) passionate scientist
    (D) person known for many important discoveries
    (E) curator

33. The word "annals" in line 25 could be replaced with which of the following without changing the meaning of the sentence?

    (A) record
    (B) scientists
    (C) fish
    (D) zoological discovery
    (E) museum

34. It can be inferred from the passage that

    (A) Marjorie Courtenay-Larimer received no credit for the discovery.
    (B) J.L.B. Smith had a preference for dramatic language.
    (C) Coelacanths are the only known "Lazurus species".
    (D) The captain of the *Nerine* knew nothing about fish.
    (E) The coelacanth was a previously undiscovered species.

35. It can be inferred from the passage that which of the following was very important to J.L.B Smith?

    (A) his travels
    (B) his professorship
    (C) his working relationship with Marjorie Courtenay-Larimer
    (D) widespread recognition of his work
    (E) academic publishing

CONTINUE TO THE NEXT PAGE

Master William Horner came to our village to school when he was about eighteen years old: tall, lank, straight-sided, and straight-haired, with a mouth of the most puckered and solemn kind. His figure and movements were those of a puppet cut out of shingle and jerked by a string; and his address corresponded

Line 5   very well with his appearance. Never did that prim mouth give way before a laugh. A faint and misty smile was the widest departure from its propriety, and this unaccustomed disturbance made wrinkles in the flat, skinny cheeks like those in the surface of a lake, after the intrusion of a stone. Master Horner knew well what belonged to the pedagogical character, and that facial solemnity stood high on the

10   list of indispensable qualifications. He had made up his mind before he left his father's house how he would look during the term. He had not planned any smiles (knowing that he must "board round"), and it was not for ordinary occurrences to alter his arrangements; so that when he was betrayed into a relaxation of the muscles, it was "in such a sort" as if he was putting his bread and butter in

15   jeopardy.

Truly he had a grave time that first winter. The rod of power was new to him, and he felt it his "duty" to use it more frequently than might have been thought necessary by those upon whose sense the privilege had palled. Tears and sulky faces, and impotent fists doubled fiercely when his back was turned, were

20   the rewards of his conscientiousness; and the boys—and girls too—were glad when working time came round again, and the master went home to help his father on the farm.

36. It can be inferred from that passage that

   (A)   Master Horner was an accomplished teacher
   (B)   the students respected Master Horner
   (C)   teaching was not a full-time job for Master Horner
   (D)   Master Horner laughed frequently
   (E)   school was in session through the summer when this passage was written

37. In this passage, Master Horner is compared to

   (A)   a stone
   (B)   a rod
   (C)   tears
   (D)   farming
   (E)   a puppet

CONTINUE TO THE NEXT PAGE

38. It can be inferred that Master Horner thought teachers

   (A) should not smile or laugh
   (B) needed to be well-trained
   (C) were supposed to set the example in a classroom
   (D) should be entertaining
   (E) have many qualifications

39. How did the narrator feel when the farming season came?

   (A) perplexed
   (B) happy
   (C) indifferent
   (D) angry
   (E) tranquil

40. The primary purpose of this passage is to

   (A) present two conflicting viewpoints
   (B) present a thesis and examples
   (C) introduce a character
   (D) build suspense
   (E) provoke anger from the reader

STOP

IF YOU HAVE TIME LEFT YOU MAY CHECK YOUR ANSWERS IN THIS SECTION ONLY

Section 3: Verbal

60 questions
30 minutes

This section has two types of questions – synonyms and analogies.

Synonyms

Directions: Each question has a word in all capital letters and then five answer choices that are in lower case letters. You need to choose the answer choice that has the word (or phrase) that is closest in meaning to the word that is in capital letters.

1. ADVISABLE:

    (A) triumphant
    (B) suitable
    (C) flagrant
    (D) perplexing
    (E) timid

2. DISGRACE:

    (A) shame
    (B) ease
    (C) disturb
    (D) fool
    (E) grieve

3. FLOURISH:

    (A) discount
    (B) educate
    (C) realize
    (D) crumple
    (E) thrive

4. ACCENTUATE:

    (A) reap
    (B) emphasize
    (C) distort
    (D) shield
    (E) commiserate

5. GLARE:

    (A) soft noise
    (B) limited time
    (C) icy surface
    (D) harsh light
    (E) ragged edge

6. ROUTE:

    (A) switch
    (B) comment
    (C) path
    (D) trench
    (E) boom

CONTINUE TO THE NEXT PAGE

7. PORTION:

   (A) section
   (B) equipment
   (C) dread
   (D) effect
   (E) invention

8. COMPILE:

   (A) remind
   (B) deviate
   (C) gather
   (D) object
   (E) wail

9. TRIVIAL:

   (A) definite
   (B) quaint
   (C) subsequent
   (D) favorable
   (E) unimportant

10. MUNDANE:

   (A) explicit
   (B) banal
   (C) atrocious
   (D) serious
   (E) ineffectual

11. DEPRESSION:

   (A) interest
   (B) rock
   (C) progress
   (D) hollow
   (E) possession

12. PRESTIGE:

   (A) standing
   (B) movement
   (C) tower
   (D) disappointment
   (E) mystery

13. CUMBERSOME:

   (A) united
   (B) concerned
   (C) inconvenient
   (D) successful
   (E) stalled

14. ROVE:

   (A) wander about
   (B) feel bad
   (C) round up
   (D) arrive late
   (E) plan ahead

15. UNFOUNDED:

   (A) disgraced
   (B) groundless
   (C) steadfast
   (D) previous
   (E) subservient

16. MATTER:

   (A) team
   (B) resolution
   (C) pact
   (D) concession
   (E) substance

CONTINUE TO THE NEXT PAGE

17. CORPULENT:

    (A) emotionless

    (B) powerful

    (C) stolen

    (D) overweight

    (E) moral

18. PRIME:

    (A) not ideal

    (B) bottomless

    (C) most important

    (D) rounded

    (E) certainly wrong

19. BOGUS:

    (A) fake

    (B) grinning

    (C) elegant

    (D) prompt

    (E) unusual

20. TANTALIZING:

    (A) bewildering

    (B) withering

    (C) blossoming

    (D) mounting

    (E) alluring

21. INCOGNITO:

    (A) familiar

    (B) disguised

    (C) scowling

    (D) interesting

    (E) earnest

22. DUBIOUS:

    (A) sly

    (B) dainty

    (C) experimental

    (D) doubtful

    (E) tangled

23. DIMINISH:

    (A) gamble

    (B) pronounce

    (C) reduce

    (D) imagine

    (E) baffle

24. ARTLESS:

    (A) unsophisticated

    (B) popular

    (C) safe

    (D) contrary

    (E) gleaming

25. DIN:

    (A) characteristic

    (B) shield

    (C) inflection

    (D) promotion

    (E) noise

26. UNIFORM:

    (A) abandoned

    (B) consistent

    (C) soaked

    (D) illustrious

    (E) cautious

CONTINUE TO THE NEXT PAGE

27. COURTEOUS:

    (A) knowledgeable

    (B) absolute

    (C) polite

    (D) tarnished

    (E) permanent

28. FLAUNT:

    (A) lean back

    (B) settle in

    (C) go forward

    (D) show off

    (E) move aside

29. MAINSTAY:

    (A) exclamation

    (B) supporter

    (C) tendency

    (D) investigation

    (E) boycott

30. QUANDARY:

    (A) dilemma

    (B) section

    (C) champion

    (D) sleeve

    (E) collaboration

CONTINUE TO THE NEXT PAGE

Analogies

Directions: Analogies questions ask you to identify the relationship between words. Choose the answer choice that best finishes the sentence.

31. Disheveled is to appearance as

    (A) messy is to room
    (B) illegible is to painting
    (C) controlled is to environment
    (D) exterior is to door
    (E) temperate is to building

32. Pond is to lake as hill is to

    (A) stream
    (B) river
    (C) plain
    (D) mountain
    (E) desert

33. Hammer is to pounding as

    (A) screwdriver is to drilling
    (B) saw is to cutting
    (C) flute is to strumming
    (D) sneakers is to competing
    (E) button is to warming

34. Tedious is to wearing as unruly is to

    (A) dreadful
    (B) responsible
    (C) disobedient
    (D) continual
    (E) sincere

CONTINUE TO THE NEXT PAGE

35. Thatch is to roof as

    (A) top is to box

    (B) flue is to chimney

    (C) door is to wall

    (D) cushion is to padding

    (E) mud is to walls

36. Betray is to support as

    (A) invite is to dismiss

    (B) save is to rescue

    (C) deny is to succeed

    (D) crank is to limit

    (E) condemn is to observe

37. Pilothouse is to ship as

    (A) land is to water

    (B) cockpit is to plane

    (C) canoe is to barge

    (D) kitchen is to house

    (E) basement is to bedroom

38. Discourage is to obstruct as

    (A) straighten is to tangle

    (B) laugh is to sigh

    (C) ask is to obey

    (D) limit is to abolish

    (E) imitate is to silence

39. Recipe is to ingredients as

    (A) mixer is to spoon

    (B) vegetable is to broccoli

    (C) menu is to entrees

    (D) breakfast is to brunch

    (E) ham is to lettuce

CONTINUE TO THE NEXT PAGE

40. Notoriety is to gangster as pretension is to

   (A) snob
   (B) waiter
   (C) teacher
   (D) laborer
   (E) electrician

41. Enthusiastic is to wary as vague is to

   (A) unclear
   (B) stunning
   (C) attractive
   (D) decent
   (E) specific

42. Accomplice is to criminal as sidekick is to

   (A) lawyer
   (B) judge
   (C) friend
   (D) hero
   (E) alibi

43. Spark is to fire as

   (A) needle is to stitching
   (B) raindrops is to deluge
   (C) ripe is to raw
   (D) steel is to metal
   (E) street is to bike

44. Cold is to frigid as

   (A) dry is to raining
   (B) drenching is to drizzling
   (C) hot is to torrid
   (D) snowy is to damp
   (E) mountainous is to exotic

CONTINUE TO THE NEXT PAGE

45. Pennant is to award as

    (A) thrill is to shudder
    (B) bicycle is to automobile
    (C) coat is to pants
    (D) felony is to crime
    (E) chapter is to book

46. Clay is to pottery as

    (A) marble is to sculpture
    (B) paint is to frame
    (C) rug is to wool
    (D) sentences is to paragraph
    (E) stone is to wood

47. Moral is to self-righteous as

    (A) impeccable is to dirty
    (B) exciting is to straight
    (C) impossible is to difficult
    (D) creative is to artistic
    (E) pious is to sanctimonious

48. Instructions is to manual as

    (A) banner is to sign
    (B) story is to anthology
    (C) bracelet is to necklace
    (D) magazine is to subscription
    (E) acceptance is to rejection

49. Car is to garage as

    (A) motorcycle is to rider
    (B) limousine is to stretch
    (C) tractor is to barn
    (D) skateboard is to flip
    (E) truck is to cab

CONTINUE TO THE NEXT PAGE

50. Cinder is to burning as

    (A)   match is to flame

    (B)   log is to tree

    (C)   spark is to lightning

    (D)   soreness is to running

    (E)   reputation is to respect

51. Gaggle is to geese as

    (A)   pack is to wolves

    (B)   kitten is to cat

    (C)   cattle is to herd

    (D)   corral is to horse

    (E)   cow is to bull

52. Unusual is to customary as dishonest is to

    (A)   cruel

    (B)   sincere

    (C)   crafty

    (D)   absolute

    (E)   playful

53. Consider is to decide as

    (A)   yell is to shout

    (B)   explain is to scold

    (C)   ponder is to determine

    (D)   growl is to groan

    (E)   trade is to exchange

54. Procure is to obtain as

    (A)   broadcast is to receive

    (B)   cherish is to reject

    (C)   travel is to dwell

    (D)   ask is to require

    (E)   burnish is to polish

CONTINUE TO THE NEXT PAGE

55. Shrewd is to ruthless as

   (A) familiar is to regular
   (B) rare is to uncommon
   (C) clean is to immaculate
   (D) brave is to courageous
   (E) abundant is to plentiful

56. Dove is to peace as

   (A) treaty is to war
   (B) cardinal is to nest
   (C) peacock is to feathers
   (D) stork is to baby
   (E) sign is to symbol

57. Interest is to fascinate as

   (A) dislike is to loathe
   (B) witness is to observe
   (C) cease is to pause
   (D) copy is to imitate
   (E) avoid is to express

58. Creep is to run as

   (A) jog is to walk
   (B) dance is to swing
   (C) skip is to hop
   (D) stumble is to fall
   (E) ski is to skate

59. Distort is to truth as

   (A) corrode is to rust
   (B) deflect is to light
   (C) assemble is to directions
   (D) revolve is to spinner
   (E) abandon is to plan

CONTINUE TO THE NEXT PAGE

60. Cranky is to joyful as

    (A)   brisk is to quick

    (B)   persuasive is to uninterested

    (C)   conscious is to loud

    (D)   absurd is to profitable

    (E)   dainty is to oafish

STOP

IF YOU HAVE TIME LEFT YOU MAY CHECK YOUR ANSWERS IN THIS SECTION ONLY

Section 4: Quantitative

25 questions

30 minutes

Directions: Each problem is followed by five answer choices. Figure out each problem and then decide which answer choice is best.

---

1. Which of the following is less than 3.047?

   (A) 3.204

   (B) 3.0407

   (C) 3.048

   (D) 3.37

   (E) 3.050

---

2. Solve for x: $14 + x - 6 = 5x$

   (A) 2

   (B) 4

   (C) 5

   (D) 6

   (E) 8

---

3. Which fraction is $\dfrac{2}{5}$ of $\dfrac{1}{4}$?

   (A) $\dfrac{1}{20}$

   (B) $\dfrac{1}{15}$

   (C) $\dfrac{1}{10}$

   (D) $\dfrac{1}{5}$

   (E) $\dfrac{2}{9}$

CONTINUE TO THE NEXT PAGE

4. Emeline has m more stamps than Heike. If Emeline has 16 stamps, then how many stamps does Heike have?

(A) $\frac{16}{m}$

(B) $m + 16$

(C) $16m$

(D) $16 - m$

(E) $m - 16$

---

5. $0.0025 \times 30.00 =$

(A) 0.0075

(B) 0.075

(C) 0.75

(D) 7.5

(E) 75

---

6. What is the value of $4x - y^3$ when $x = 3$ and $y = 2$?

(A) 0

(B) 1

(C) 2

(D) 3

(E) 4

---

7. There are 600 students in a school. Two-fifths of the students walked to school today. Thirty percent of the students rode a bus. How many more students walked to school than rode the bus today?

(A) 10

(B) 30

(C) 40

(D) 45

(E) 60

CONTINUE TO THE NEXT PAGE

8. Use the following number line to answer the question:

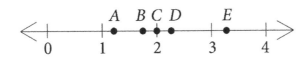

Which point represents the fraction $\dfrac{9}{4}$?

(A) A
(B) B
(C) C
(D) D
(E) E

---

9. Which is equivalent to $(3x + 2)(x - 7)$?

(A) $3x^2 - 19x - 14$
(B) $3x^2 + 19x - 14$
(C) $3x^2 - 19x + 14$
(D) $3x^2 - 5x - 14$
(E) $3x^2 + 5x - 14$

---

10. 30 is 12 percent of

(A) 45
(B) 170
(C) 210
(D) 250
(E) 320

---

11. The perimeter of a pentagon is $10s$. If each side is increased by $2s$, then what is the perimeter of the new pentagon?

(A) 10
(B) $10 + 10s$
(C) 20
(D) $20s$
(E) $20 + 20s$

CONTINUE TO THE NEXT PAGE

12. The length of a rectangle is three times its width. If the area of the rectangle is 27 cm^2, then what is its perimeter?

    (A) 6
    (B) 9
    (C) 18
    (D) 24
    (E) 27

13. The statement "the quotient of five times a number and three times another number is less than or equal to 24" is best represented by

    (A) $5x + 3y \leq 24$

    (B) $\dfrac{5x}{3y} \leq 24$

    (C) $5x \times 3y \leq 24$

    (D) $5x + 3y \geq 24$

    (E) $\dfrac{5x}{3y} \geq 24$

14. Which is equivalent to $\dfrac{5}{\sqrt{5}}$?

    (A) $\sqrt{5}$
    (B) $5\sqrt{5}$
    (C) $\dfrac{\sqrt{5}}{5}$
    (D) 1
    (E) 5

15. What is the ratio of 2 ft. 4 in. to 2 yards?

    (A) 2.4:2
    (B) 1:1
    (C) 7:18
    (D) 1:2
    (E) 2:9

CONTINUE TO THE NEXT PAGE

16. Four students in a class averaged 82 on a test. When a fifth student's score was added, the average increased to 84. What did the fifth student score on the test?

    (A) 84
    (B) 86
    (C) 88
    (D) 90
    (E) 92

---

17. Which could be the side lengths of a triangle?

    (A) 2, 2, 4
    (B) 3, 4, 7
    (C) 4, 5, 8
    (D) 5, 5, 10
    (E) 7, 3, 10

---

18. If the measures of the angles in a parallelogram were added together, then the result would be

    (A) 90°
    (B) 180°
    (C) 270°
    (D) 360°
    (E) 420°

---

19. If 80 percent of b is 20, then what is 10 percent of $8b$?

    (A) 10
    (B) 20
    (C) 24
    (D) 40
    (E) 80

CONTINUE TO THE NEXT PAGE

20. The graph below shows the number of skaters who received each score in an ice skating competition

Ice Skating Competition Results

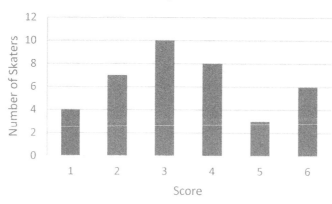

What was the median score?

(A) 3
(B) 6
(C) 7
(D) 8
(E) 10

---

21. A circle is inscribed within a square, as shown.

If the square has an area of 64, what is the area of the shaded region?

(A) $64 - 64\pi$
(B) $64 - 16\pi$
(C) $64 - 8\pi$
(D) $64 - 4\pi$
(E) $32 - 8\pi$

CONTINUE TO THE NEXT PAGE

22. The average of five consecutive even numbers is 24. What is the largest
    number?

    (A) 20
    (B) 22
    (C) 24
    (D) 26
    (E) 28

23. The original price of a sweater is $20. If the price is increased by 20% and
    then this new price is decreased by 20%, what is the final price of the
    sweater?

    (A) $19.20
    (B) $20.00
    (C) $20.80
    (D) $21.00
    (E) $22.00

24. The numbers M and Q have an average of 50. If M is greater than Q than
    which of the following must be true?

    (A) $M + Q = 50$
    (B) $M - Q = 50$
    (C) $M - 50 = 50 - Q$
    (D) $Q - 50 = M - 50$
    (E) $50 - M = 50 - Q$

25. If $b + c = 12$ and $c + d = 8$, then what is value of c?

    (A) 4
    (B) 6
    (C) 8
    (D) 10
    (E) cannot be determined with information given

STOP

IF YOU HAVE TIME LEFT YOU MAY CHECK YOUR ANSWERS IN THIS SECTION ONLY

Answers

Answers to Section 1: Quantitative

Correct Answers	Your Answers	Answered Correctly	Answered Incorrectly	Omitted
1. C				
2. A				
3. B				
4. B				
5. D				
6. E				
7. C				
8. A				
9. B				
10. B				
11. D				
12. D				
13. A				
14. C				
15. C				
16. A				
17. B				
18. E				
19. D				
20. A				
21. D				
22. E				
23. C				
24. B				
25. C				
Total				

Raw score = Total # answered correctly _____ – total # answered incorrectly _____ ÷ 4

Your raw score: _____

Answers to Section 2: Reading Comprehension

Correct Answers	Your Answers	Answered Correctly	Answered Incorrectly	Omitted
1. D				
2. A				
3. C				
4. E				
5. B				
6. C				
7. A				
8. D				
9. E				
10. B				
11. C				
12. D				
13. A				
14. E				
15. B				
16. D				
17. C				
18. A				
19. E				
20. B				
21. C				
22. A				
23. D				
24. B				
25. E				
26. C				
27. B				
28. A				
29. D				
30. B				
31. E				
32. C				

33. A				
34. B				
35. D				
36. C				
37. E				
38. A				
39. B				
40. C				
Total				

Raw score = Total # answered correctly _____ – total # answered incorrectly _____ ÷ 4

Your raw score: _____

Answers to Section 3: Verbal

Correct Answer	Your Answer	Answered Correctly	Answered Incorrectly	Omitted
1. B				
2. A				
3. E				
4. B				
5. D				
6. C				
7. A				
8. C				
9. E				
10. B				
11. D				
12. A				
13. C				
14. A				
15. B				
16. E				
17. D				
18. C				
19. A				
20. E				
21. B				
22. D				
23. C				
24. A				
25. E				
26. B				
27. C				
28. D				
29. B				
30. A				
31. A				
32. D				

33. B				
34. C				
35. E				
36. A				
37. B				
38. D				
39. C				
40. A				
41. E				
42. D				
43. B				
44. C				
45. D				
46. A				
47. E				
48. B				
49. C				
50. D				
51. A				
52. B				
53. C				
54. E				
55. C				
56. D				
57. A				
58. D				
59. B				
60. E				
Total				

Raw score = Total # answered correctly _____ – total # answered incorrectly _____ ÷ 4

Your raw score: _____

Answers to Section 4: Quantitative

Correct Answers	Your Answers	Answered Correctly	Answered Incorrectly	Omitted
1. B				
2. A				
3. C				
4. D				
5. B				
6. E				
7. E				
8. D				
9. A				
10. D				
11. D				
12. D				
13. B				
14. A				
15. C				
16. E				
17. C				
18. D				
19. B				
20. A				
21. B				
22. E				
23. A				
24. C				
25. E				
Total				

Raw score = Total # answered correctly _____ – total # answered incorrectly _____ ÷ 4

Your raw score: _____

Interpreting Your Scores

On the SSAT, your raw score is the number of questions that you answered correctly on each section minus the number of questions you answered incorrectly divided by 4. Nothing is added or subtracted for the questions that you omit.

Your raw score is then converted into a scaled score. This scaled score is then converted into a percentile score. Remember that it is the percentile score that schools are looking at. Your percentile score compares you only to other students in your grade.

Below is a chart that gives a very rough conversion between your raw score on the practice test and a percentile score.

PLEASE NOTE – The purpose of this chart is to let you see how the scoring works, not to give you an accurate percentile score. You will need to complete the practice test in *The Official Guide to the Upper Level SSAT* in order to get a more accurate percentile score.

Approximate raw score needed for 50th percentile		
Section 1 + Section 4: Quantitative	Section 2: Reading comprehension	Section 3: Verbal
28-32	20-24	24-28

Looking for more practice?

Check out these other titles for the Upper Level SSAT:

30 Days to Acing the Upper Level SSAT

- ✓ 15 "workouts" – each a 30-minute exercise with vocabulary and practice questions for every multiple-choice section of the test

- ✓ Test-taking strategies for each section

The Best Unofficial Practice Tests for the Upper Level SSAT

- ✓ 2 full-length practice tests (different from the practice test in *Success on the Upper Level SSAT)*

Books by Test Prep Works

	Content instruction	Test-taking strategies	Practice problems	Full-length practice tests
ISEE				
Lower Level (for students applying for admission to grades 5-6)				
Success on the Lower Level ISEE	✓	✓	✓	✓ (1)
30 Days to Acing the Lower Level ISEE		✓	✓	
The Best Unofficial Practice Tests for the Lower Level ISEE				✓ (2)
Middle Level (for students applying for admission to grades 7-8)				
Success on the Middle Level ISEE	✓	✓	✓	✓ (1)
The Best Unofficial Practice Tests for the Middle Level ISEE				✓ (2)
Upper Level (for students applying for admission to grades 9-12)				
Success on the Upper Level ISEE	✓	✓	✓	✓ (1)
The Best Unofficial Practice Tests for the Upper Level ISEE				✓ (2)
SSAT				
Middle Level (for students applying for admission to grades 6-8)				
Success on the Middle Level SSAT	✓	✓	✓	✓ (1)
The Best Unofficial Practice Tests for the Middle Level SSAT				✓ (2)
Upper Level (for students applying for admission to grades 9-12)				
Success on the Upper Level SSAT	✓	✓	✓	✓ (1)
30 Days to Acing the Upper Level SSAT		✓	✓	
The Best Unofficial Practice Tests for the Upper Level SSAT				✓ (2)

TEST PREP WORKS, LLC.

Made in the USA
Monee, IL
27 December 2022

23802435R00289